SERVICES PLUS

Effective Service Management

John Haywood-Farmer, associate professor

School of Business Administration,
The University of Western Ontario

Jean Nollet, professor

École des Hautes Études Commerciales,
the business school affiliated with Université de Montréal

SERVICES PLUS

Effective Service Management

G. Morin Publisher Ltd

P.O. BOX 180, BOUCHERVILLE, QUEBEC, CANADA
J4B 5E6   TEL. : (514) 449-2369   FAX: (514) 449-1096

ISBN 2-89105-336-2

Registered Copyright 2nd Quarter 1991
National Library of Canada

SERVICES PLUS — Effective Service Management
© G. Morin Publisher Ltd, 1991
All rights reserved

1 2 3 4 5 6 7 8 9 0   G M E 9 1   0 9 8 7 6 5 4 3 2 1

Copy editing: Katherine Tallman

CONTENTS _____

PREFACE

Although there have been services since the beginning of civilization, the academic study of them is only in its infancy. However, despite the short history of service management as an academic discipline, the service sector is quite well developed. Services now overwhelmingly dominate every developed economy; indeed, the extent of penetration of services is one measure of how well developed an economy is.

Measuring services can be very difficult both at the macro and micro levels. Economists define a service sector for statistical purposes but the statistics can be very misleading. Many organizations classified as manufacturers actually produce huge amounts of uncounted services and many compete on their service outputs rather than their goods. At the micro level, defining a service and measuring its quality and productivity precisely are major challenges. Although examples of relatively poor services abound, many services are excellent and spectacularly successful. Well managed service can be an incredibly powerful competitive weapon. One of our underlying precepts is that managers and scholars can learn by studying both successes and failures.

This book is about managing services, particularly pertaining to establishing a 'service culture.' It is relevant to managers and scholars interested in the traditional 'service industries'; most of the examples are from that group. However, the principles discussed are also applicable to other types of organizations that produce significant services. One feature of service management is that it is increasingly difficult to separate the traditional management fields of operations, marketing and human resources in any meaningful way. This book does not try to do so; it integrates traditional management issues in these three areas in a service setting.

Another feature of service management is that it looks easy. But this is deceptive; the more you look, the tougher it gets. Although this book was written primarily for managers, it will also be of interest to students of service management. It contains a lot of information and we hope it is written in a style that will be easy to read.

The book is divided into two major sections. The first eight chapters deal with management topics; examples are chosen from across the spectrum of service industries. The coverage is fairly traditional — the place of service in developed economies, defining and segmenting services, designing services, managing capacity, managing quality, managing productivity, and managing growth. Unlike many books, this one has an extensive list of references and a bibliography of examples and academic articles.

The last six chapters deal with specific service industries — public services, health, transportation, financial services, professional services and hospitality. The goal is to provide an overview of significant service industries and to demonstrate how the principles developed in the early part of the book have been (and can be) applied in these services.

No book is written and published solely by its authors and this one is no exception. We would like to acknowledge the significant contributions made by Elizabeth Verlaan of Western Business School and Chantal Faulkner of Hautes Études Commerciales for help with references and figures respectively. Denis Fallu, Céline Laprise, Lucie Robidas, Nicole Chicoine, Georges Laporte and Gaëtan Morin of the publisher's staff and Katherine Tallman showed uncalled-for patience and gave invaluable assistance in editing the manuscript. We would also like to thank our respective schools, WBS and HEC for financial assistance, and our department chairmen Michiel R. Leenders and Mattio O. Diorio for their support. We would like to recognize the several generations of students and our academic colleagues in the emerging field of service management who have inspired us to write this book. Their collective efforts have measurably strengthened this book and we thank them. Finally, we would like to thank our families, particularly our wives, Mary Haywood-Farmer and Louise Nollet to whom the book is dedicated, who have made their own sacrifices to this book.

John Haywood-Farmer
Jean Nollet
March, 1991

CHAPTER 1

ON THE ROAD TO SERVICES

An Overview of Services

1.1   The importance of service industries

Life in North America, Europe and Japan is profoundly affected by
service industries, often accompanied by goods. When we get up in the
morning, we use a utility — electricity or gas — to prepare breakfast,
read a newspaper, drive to work (or take public transit) on roads controlled by traffic signals and/or police. Throughout the day, we send and
receive messages by mail, telephone and computer, eat in restaurants
and are entertained by television, videos or movies. These are just a few
of the services that are the hallmarks of 'developed' societies.

Economists often determine how developed an economy is by measuring the relative importance of its service sector. It is well known that
developed countries, such as Canada, the United States and Great Britain,
derive as much as 70% of their employment and gross domestic product
from the service sector, with manufacturing (25%) and resource extraction (mining, forestry, agriculture, etc.) (5%) making up the remainder.
In these countries, the relative size of the service sector has been growing
over the past 40 years, and some observers predict that it will account for
80% by early in the 21st century. In many industrialized nations, the
number of people employed in manufacturing and resource extraction
has remained relatively steady while employment in services has grown.
Countries that are less developed have relatively small service sectors,
particularly for domestic consumption.

The above figures are generalizations and should be treated with caution. Not only do they cut across many, very different economies, but they are also very imprecise even within a single economy. The three major economic sectors are inextricably intertwined; statistical analysis that classifies an organization as resource extraction, manufacturing or service is unrealistic. One study concluded that the service activities of manufacturing companies generate about 75% of their total value added. General Motors is classified as a manufacturer, yet it derives a large portion of its revenue and profit from service activities. Conversely, fast food restaurants are usually considered part of the service sector, but they derive much of their value added from manufacturing food products. As Grönroos noted:

> Now, and even more so in the future, it is difficult to produce better goods than the competitors. Most frequently it is not an exaggeration to say that everyone can make the goods. What counts in more and more industries are the services which the firm can offer in a competitive manner in addition to the mere technical solution embedded in the goods. *Manufacturers will have to realize that they, too, live in the service economy*, and that they will have to learn the rules of service.[100, p.10]

The well-documented growth in services may be somewhat less spectacular than noted. Drucker noted that many manufacturers are buying some of their services instead of producing them themselves.[67] This has had the dual effect of bringing previously hidden services out into the open and reducing the apparent size of the manufacturer.

Creative managers have many opportunities, locally as well as internationally, to create a significant competitive advantage based on service, regardless of the type of organization. For example, railroads have been able to compete more effectively with trucking companies by using the piggyback concept. Many existing concepts are applicable to new services and markets, and, of course, many concepts have yet to be thought of.

A second reason for the unreliability of the figures above is the continuing uncertainty over how "service" should be defined. Regardless of how it is defined, it is clear that the service sector is big and growing.

It should be emphasized that it is difficult to have a strong service sector without a well-developed manufacturing and/or resource extraction base, with the possible exception of economies based on tourism. Similarly, it is becoming increasingly difficult to have a strong manufacturing-based economy without a well-developed service sector. As was noted in *The Economist*, "efficient services help to oil the wheels of the rest of the economy; their absence can make development a painfully slow process."[83] How meaningful can large increases in manufacturing or agriculture be if transportation, for example, does not support the improvement? An inadequate transportation system can add 10-20% to product cost which reduces its international competitiveness. Manufacturers are competing more and more at the level of meeting customer needs and expectations by providing services — financing, delivery, advice, repairs, etc. Increased productivity in manufacturing and resource extraction makes it possible for more people to work in the service sector.

Figure 1-1 shows both the relative size of the various economic sectors in industrialized countries and the necessary support provided to the upper level (services) by the more essential lower levels (manufacturing and resource extraction). This representation is similar to Maslow's needs hierarchy in which satisfying higher needs, such as self-actualization, is only feasible if fundamental needs, such as physical nourishment, are met first.[200] Improvement in productivity in manufacturing and resource extraction are what have made the transition to a service-dominated economy possible. In advanced economies, inefficiency in the service sector is often blamed when overall gains in labor productivity are low. Although this rationale is not universally accepted,

FIGURE 1-1   The relative Importance of the three economic sectors

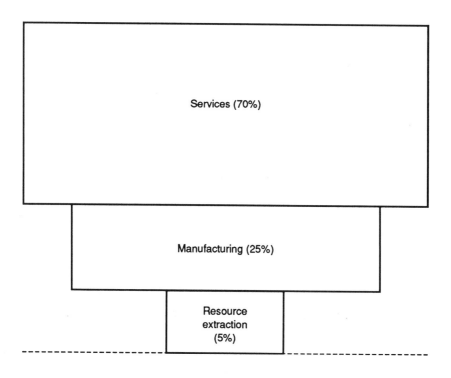

as will be seen later in this chapter, if it is true, it represents a major incentive to improve labor productivity. This justifies a closer look at the service sector.

1.2   The impact of low labor productivity growth on services

During the 19th and early 20th centuries, Britain was the recognized world leader in manufacturing. Even after 1920, when the United States became preeminent in manufacturing, London retained its reputation as *the* international centre for banking and finance, although New York finally emerged as the leader.[15] Now that Japan has surpassed the United States in so many areas of manufacturing, how long will it be before Tokyo dominates in financial services? The trend is already well under way — nine of the world's ten largest banks are Japanese, and the strength of the yen has led to unprecedented accumulations of capital reserves in Japan.

Recognizing that its service sector lags in both productivity and quality, Japan intends to achieve major improvements in both during the 1990s. It appears that Japan is serious. Many Japanese companies want to move into US markets by emphasizing customer service over production skills.[69] However, foreign service firms are succeeding in Japan.[249] Federal Express, for example, is a very successful player in the courier market (which doubled between 1986 and 1988) despite existing Japanese non-tariff trade barriers.

Service industries can be vulnerable to world-wide competition. Companies such as Japan Air Lines, Singapore Airlines, Scandinavian Airlines System, Air Canada and Swissair have done extremely well by making strategic long-term investments in suitable fleets and customer service. Of course, other decisions may make a company more vulnerable. Air Canada, for instance, has rationalized some of its routes following privatization. Accommodation, fast food and financial services are three more industries in which the major players have a global reach with the potential to eliminate small, local enterprises. Globalization will undoubtedly come to other service industries as well.

Many American companies became targets for takeover bids from off-shore investors because of poor manufacturing performance; many lost and are now foreign-owned. One study found that labor productivity improved in the American manufacturing sector at a rate of only 0.5% annually between 1979 and 1983.[15] Although this rate is considered low, the corresponding rate in the service sector was a mere 0.1%. This very low rate may indicate that the service sector will run into the same difficulties the manufacturing sector now faces. One corroborative indicator is the net trade balance, which for the United States fell from US$41 billion in 1981 to US$21.5 billion in 1985.[241]

Eastern European countries also face a major task in achieving their stated goal of improving productivity in services. There is a tremendous need to develop the service sector in these countries, not only in its own right, but also to contribute to the development of the other economic sectors.[83]

1.3   Myths about the service sector

It is widely held that service industries are small, labor intensive, low inventory organizations using unskilled labor with few opportunities for scale economies. Although many of them may have one or more of these characteristics, there are also many exceptions. Retail operations, for example, carry large inventories of goods. Major transportation companies have large inventories of spare parts for fleet maintenance. These are examples of raw materials inventories; unless the concept of inventory is extended to include customers or capacity, service industries do not normally have large work-in-process or finished-goods inventories.

Although the plant and equipment are major assets for most manufacturing organizations, capital stock per worker is reported to be even higher in the service sector.[152] Expensive transportation, medical and research equipment, fixed assets in hotels, resorts and hospitals, and large, sophisticated data banks and communication networks, coupled with high labor productivity in some of these industries, contribute to capital stock per worker. Rapid technological advances, especially in computer technology, and an on-going need for information should lead to continued capital investments in the service sector for some years to come, even during recessions.[241]

Information technology makes significant scale economies possible in organizations such as financial institutions, rental companies, brokerages, reservation systems and health care institutions. This technology also leads to economies of scope by producing and delivering new services through existing systems; for example, financial institutions are now able to offer much broader services. Information technology, through direct links to remote computers, provides much greater flexibility in terms of when and where people work. This technology also makes it possible to manage new levels of complexity more quickly, as is evidenced by extensive data bases in law and medicine, and in airline reservations.[241] These benefits have a price, of course; they require new, more sophisticated management skills.

Growth in white collar services, including professional services, has recently outpaced that in other sectors, and this trend is expected to continue for some years.[152] For example, in the US financial sector the proportion of managerial jobs increased while the proportion of clerical jobs declined between 1978 and 1988. Many service jobs are repetitive and low-paying; they attract an inordinate number of young female or part-time workers, and offer few opportunities for personal growth. White collar service jobs, in contrast, offer significant opportunites for an increasing number of well-educated people to use their knowledge and intellectual skills in jobs suitable to their desires and abilities.

Bednarzik notes a shift in employment patterns for women in US service industries between 1973 and 1985; the proportion of women in the high- and medium-wage categories rose while that in the low-wage category declined.[14] It seems that overall there are good opportunities for higher wages in the service sector because of higher productivity and increased competition for employees. Already many industries find it difficult to hire suitable staff, especially at the extremes of the salary continuum.

One list indicates that 44% of the fastest growing companies (defined by increases in sales over a five-year period) in the US are services.[291] The growth potential is tremendous for companies able to understand this dynamic sector.

An Approach to Service Concepts

1.4   A global perspective

Many service industries tend to hire from within. Although this practice undoubtedly maintains expertise within the industry and serves to motivate both managers and workers, it means that the real benefits of learning from other service or manufacturing industries are lost. A travel agency focusing on business travel can learn at least as much from the fast food industry as it can from travel agencies specializing in customized vacation packages. Service organizations such as public agencies, which tend to encourage lifelong employment, have particular problems in this regard. They are not self-contained and, in a political climate of deregulation and privatization, monopolies and oligopolies are increasingly rare. Both the Canadian and US post offices have found it costly to ignore customer needs. Market share, once it is lost to courier services, FAX machines or computer networks, is very difficult to recover, especially when the alternatives have a better service image. It is unwise to consider an operation to be unique and unassailable. Schmenner notes that "... service managers who continue to claim that their operations are unique may be left in the dust by those who see their operations as more generic."[268, p. 32]

Managers seeking guidance can use various classification schemes to help them find an organization with characteristics similar to their own. Schemes of particular interest to those in marketing have been reviewed.[185] Other schemes of more importance to operations managers are also available, including one that classifies services based on their relative degrees of labor intensity, contact and interaction between system and customer, and service and product customization.[112] The premise is that management tasks are similar in organizations that share these characteristics. There are, of course, important industry-specific features that managers must both know and understand. The difference between an outstanding and an average service manager is probably a combination of field-specific skills and the ability to borrow and apply concepts, knowledge and practices from other fields or types of services. Figure 1-2 illustrates this situation.

FIGURE 1-2   Learning from other industries

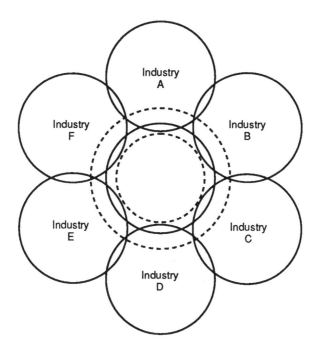

 = zone denoting open mindedness

1.5   Historical developments

Study of a field's development gives both insight into how opportunities for development were perceived and important clues to future development. Figure 1-3 summarizes the evolution of service management since about 1970. This summary is meant to be an overview rather than implying clearly separated, logical steps; indeed, many of the major themes are on-going. At first, manufacturing and marketing concepts developed for the non-service sectors were applied to services. Scholars and practitioners had a natural bias towards known approaches and felt, probably correctly, that services, which were perceived to be backward and less productive, could benefit from traditional management approaches.

FIGURE 1-3   Historical perspective on the evolution of service management

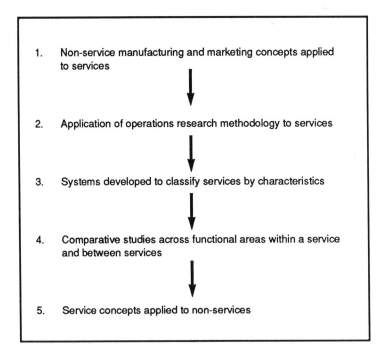

1. Non-service manufacturing and marketing concepts applied to services

2. Application of operations research methodology to services

3. Systems developed to classify services by characteristics

4. Comparative studies across functional areas within a service and between services

5. Service concepts applied to non-services

Later, more effort was devoted to simulation and other operations research techniques because opportunities for improving productivity were apparent. For example, staff scheduling and emergency car location algorithms were developed.

Then, efforts were made to classify services using acknowledged characteristics of services such as labor intensity, intangibility, use of equipment, inventories, etc. This work paved the way for a fourth development, a comparison of the different areas within the service sector. Convergence appeared in the approaches taken by marketing, operations management, human resources management and strategy.

This led to a fifth and last development: the transfer of concepts, such as the role of the customer in an operating system, from services to non-services. So far, this last step has created a much more holistic view of operating systems; they no longer need be approached from a service or non-service point of view, but instead can be seen from some fundamental characteristic such as labor intensity, degree of customization or degree of customer processing. One logical conclusion is that these developments are leading to a new management field. As Hirschhorn argues:

> It is more sensible to argue that we are making the transition to a *post-industrial* rather than a service economy, and we are developing a new *mode of production*, a new combination of labor, capital and organization which restructures work in every sector, while rearranging the relationships between them. Changes *within* sectors, plants and offices are just as important as shifts in the flow of resources *between them*.[124, p. 20]

The Book's Content in a Nutshell

Service organizations often face more complex problems than non-service ones; for example, behavioral characteristics may be particularly important or there may be a strong emphasis on the interface between operations and marketing. In fact, one study concluded that these three aspects are so closely intertwined that many service managers responsible for them could not tell which was more important in their own organization.

Because service concepts cut across traditional lines, this book does not distinguish between ideas oriented to operations, marketing or some other field. Naturally, some aspects, such as customer analysis, are more associated with marketing whereas others, such as scheduling, are more closely related to operations. Above all, this book is about managing services; it deals with ideas believed to be useful regardless of their source.

There are many ways to divide a book into chapters. We have opted for an approach that we have found useful in teaching, researching and observing service management. Chapter 1 is an overview, Chapters 2-8 explain a variety of concepts to do with managing services and Chapters 9-14 deal with specific service industries.

Chapter 1 is an overview outlining the importance of the service sector, some common misconceptions about it, and its historical development.

Chapter 2 defines service, describes ways that services can be classified, states the characteristics of service and elucidates what these characteristics imply for the job of serving customers. Chapter 3 deals with service design issues, emphasizing the customer's role as well as back office operations.

Managing capacity, quality and productivity are often major challenges for service managers. A chapter is devoted to each of these important topics. Chapter 4 discusses ways of managing supply and demand, considering that gearing up to meet peak demand can be very expensive. Chapter 5 describes the characteristics of quality in services and ways to achieve it. Chapter 6, building on material in earlier chapters, examines some of the more promising ways to increase productivity in services.

Chapter 7 covers additional ideas in marketing, operations and human resource management for the service sector that could not be dealt with adequately in earlier chapters. Chapters 2-7 emphasize managing services at the unit level. Chapter 8 represents a more global view of service organizations. It deals with growth options and problems, and with stategic management.

Chapters 9-14 deal with important specific service industries: public services, health services, transportation, financial services, professional services and hospitality. The concepts discussed in earlier chapters are applied to these industries. The reader is also exposed to the major challenges facing these industries.

The emphasis is on introducing a broad scope of ideas and their application rather than on developing any of them in great depth. For further information, we have included an extensive bibliography.

CHAPTER

2

THE SERVICE CONCEPT

What is Service?

The last chapter described how services are inseparable from other economic sectors and how complex services are. This chapter explores that complexity in more detail as well as examining the characteristics of service. We begin with a definition of service, although, as will become obvious, many definitions are acceptable, reflecting the complexity of the service sector.

2.1 A definition of service

Despite more than 25 years of study, scholars in the field of services management do not agree on what service is. Indeed, instead of coming closer to a definition, they seem to be less certain. Figure 2-1 is a generic

FIGURE 2-1 A generic model of a production system

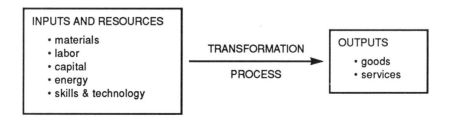

model of a production system. Service has been defined as each one of the components — inputs and resources, transformation process, outputs — as well as other characteristics. These differing views of service are discussed in the sections that follow.

2.2   Services as outputs

One popular and traditional view of services is that they are a type of output of the production system. According to this belief, production systems produce goods or services, or combinations of the two, pointing to their inherent inseparability in many production systems. This view also recognizes that service outputs have special characteristics relative to goods. One output-oriented definition, based on Sasser, et al. is:

> A service is a package of explicit and implicit benefits and facilitating goods produced in a supporting facility.[266, pp. 8-13]

The relative importance of each output depends to a great extent on the type of service and the situation. Individuals and/or equipment satisfy one or more customer needs which could be anything from psychiatry to mail sorting and delivery. The customer may receive not only the generic or core service but also facilitating goods and auxiliary services. The generic service of a football game can be considered to be the game itself. The implicit benefits include associating with a winner (or commiserating with a loser). Beer, hot dogs, popcorn and the ticket are facilitating goods; special bus service to the stadium for increased safety and speed is an auxiliary service. Normally, fans would not attend to obtain only the facilitating goods or auxiliary services. Fans go to be part of the game. The real service (explicit benefit) is entertainment, of which the game is only a part, perhaps even a relatively small part. From such a group of products and services, the customer derives psychological satisfaction, the extent of which often depends on the customer's perception of how completely his or her needs have been met.

This kind of examination can lead to interesting possibilities. Patty Cox Hampton, owner of the Oklahoma City 89ers Triple-A baseball franchise, turned the business around by focusing not on winning games but on making attendance at home games fun — in short, on entertaining customers.[250] Similarly, Arbor Cinema Four of Austin, Texas had success in a declining industry by focusing on providing guests (not patrons) with a total entertainment package.[105] For example, Arbor specially designed their building and they installed a high quality sound system. They have people on site in costume to create the right atmosphere, and they generally have a fetish for small details.

2.3   Characteristics of service outputs

As noted above, service outputs have special characteristics. They have been presented in other works.[52, 89, 266, 277] We will summarize them below. The most widely recognized characteristic of service is *intangibility*. Something intangible cannot be touched or fully grasped mentally, although it may be perceived by another sense and some mental images drawn. Because services are intangible, they can be difficult to describe, buy and sell. They may also be impossible to store. Intangibility can affect the relative importance of the benefits of the service. As Figure 2-2 illustrates, the relative importance of the psychological dimension rises with the level of intangibility.

FIGURE 2-2   Relationship between the components of the service package and tangibility

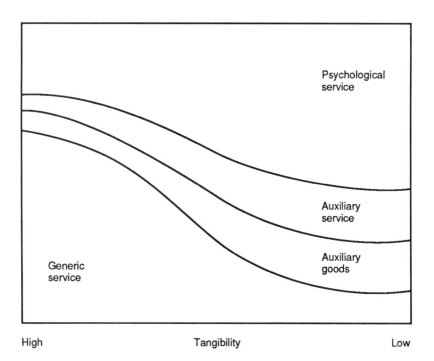

Of course, portions of many sevices are tangible — facilities and facilitating goods. Many authors agree that intangibility is the most distinguishing feature of services. It has been suggested that intangibility is the only characteristic common to all services.[90] One author even proposes that it is more appropriate to speak of tangible and intangible rather than goods and services.[175] Even when there are tangible products, organizations sell surrogates and promises. In Charles Revson's immortal words: "In the factory we make cosmetics, and in the drugstore we sell hope."[156, p. 423] Or, in Levitt's:

> Customers don't buy things; they buy tools to solve problems. Specialists who know the customer's problems are more likely to provide solutions than those who only know the equipment.[174, p. 73]

and:

> A product is more than a tangible thing... From a buyer's viewpoint, the product is a promise, a cluster of value expectations of which its non-tangible qualities are as integral as its tangible parts.[175, p. 98]

Whenever a customer cannot try, inspect or test a product (goods or services) in advance, surrogates — such as pictures or videos — or secondary sources of information — such as experienced customers or current users — are employed to reduce the purchaser's perceived risk. The more intangible and valuable the product, the more important this risk reduction becomes. For example, consulting firms use referrals as their most significant source of new clients.

Figure 2-3 classifies some services according to their relative degrees of tangibility and their scope. Tangibility is not easily quantified; similar

FIGURE 2-3   The varying mix of goods and services

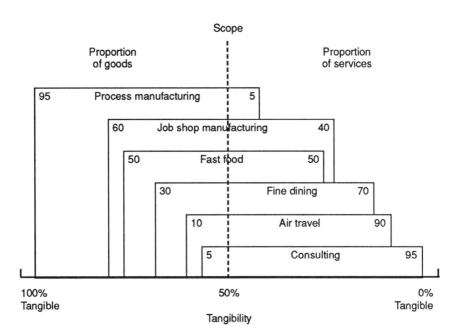

services can be delivered differently by different organizations, making it difficult to locate any service precisely on the tangibility axis. For example, adding facilitating goods or emphasizing the psychological component of the service will affect its degree of tangibility.

The scope dimension is useful in differentiating services with similar levels of tangibility. Five-star hotels and restaurants offer a level of intangible service that is quite different from the similarly intangible level of service offered by less expensive lodging and eating establishments. The scope dimension is also useful for comparing the relative importance of goods and services across industries.

Whenever a customer buys a good or a service, he or she has expectations. A product's real value depends very much on the intangible promise of what the customer perceives he or she will get in return. The entire service package should be directed to fulfill that promise. Any transaction gives rise to mutual expectations of privileges and obligations.[212] An organization's reputation represents a promise and leads to the customer's intangible level of expectation.

Flipo detailed the main intangible factors that affect a customer's perception of service.[90] Customers compare their image of the service supplied with the perceived need the service is to satisfy. Usually they select the supplier with the best perceived ratio. The customer forms his or her image of the supplier by evaluating the service, contact personnel, competitors, clientele, location, facilities, atmosphere, staff, operations, etc. All of these factors, most of which include a significant intangible portion, form a global impression that may be impossible to analyze systematically.

Customers often associate a higher level of risk with intangibility and so use 'risk-reducing reassurances of tangibilized intangibles.'[175, p. 101] For example, when an economics professor built his house, he considered buying a heating system from one of two central heating specialists. Supplier A had his feet up on his desk and his office was messy when he first met the client. His estimate for a single heating system was $4000 installed within 48 hours. Just before the meeting ended, Supplier A's wife asked to see the drawings in case she saw some interesting ideas for her own house. Supplier B, in contrast, had a much cleaner office and a very polite secretary. Supplier B's president made a formal presentation using tables and charts to demonstrate that two small furnaces would give much better temperature control than one large one. This estimated price was $9500. Although the cheaper option would have been quite adequate, the economics professor bought the more expensive system because Supplier B had provided a substantial package of superior intangible services (the presentation, and the professionalism of the office and procedures) to complement the facilitating goods.

A strong brand name is very important in creating a strong brand image — making the intangible somewhat more tangible. Strong brand names are always important, of course, but they take on a special significance in service industries. The intangibility of services leads to widespread use of subjective measures of quality by customers. Because customers' perceptions may well differ significantly from those of management, organizations have to spend a lot of time determining customer perceptions and trying to improve them. A strong brand name is a definite asset. McDonald's Corporation has a very strong and consistent brand name world-wide — an important part of the firm's strategy. VISA implicitly promises cardholders that their cards will be accepted internationally without a problem, providing a welcome sense of security and recognition.[18] A well-chosen brand name has four characteristics: distinctiveness, relevance, memorability and flexibility. It should be unique but easy to remember, ideally evoking images of the type of service offered, but still allowing for geographic, cross-cultural and scope expansion.

The intangibility of services makes it impossible to protect them by patent. Furthermore, many (but definitely not all) services are easy to copy. VISA, for example, can really protect only its name. It cannot protect its concept or operating procedures at all. There are a number of strategies to protect services, including securing resources such as sites, better training and innovation. Innovation may be undertaken for a variety of other reasons, too — to foster an image of being innovative, and to improve service and efficiency.

Intangibility also presents some problems when services are transported internationally. Services, much more than goods, are culturally bound. What works in one country may turn out to be a disaster in another. That is not to say that multinational or global service enterprises are impossible. After all, there are well-known examples in fast food, lodging, transportation, consulting, accounting and brokerage. However, the service may have to be adapted to local conditions, often by hiring local staff. The appropriate degree of adaptation is a crucial managerial decision.

Heterogeneity is a second characteristic of services. Rather than being single, isolated entities, almost all services are parts of clusters of related services, not all of which are necessarily visible. There is also heterogeneity in the service itself, especially in terms of staff. No individual can, or should, be trained to perform like a machine without variation. This complexity suits customers' needs, which are themselves complex and can change dramatically and rapidly. A person on welfare may see the monthly cheque as the main service at the same time as benefiting from less visible counselling, health care and retraining services associated with it. A patron in a restaurant looks for different benefits depending on many factors — the time of day, available time, appetite, companions, location, weather, decor, price, to name just a few. And in the case of an airline, consider how your needs would change, and how quickly, in the event of an in-flight emergency. Variability can be major, as in these examples, or minor. Some supermarket cashiers smile constantly whereas other do so only rarely. Smiling has nothing to do with the ability to process grocery orders quickly and accurately, but for some customers, pleasant cashiers may be an important factor in choosing a supermarket.

Flexibility is a significant feature of services, but it is not always desirable. It is possible to get personalized products from McDonald's; for example, you can order a Big Mac without the sauce, but the price is significantly slower service. Human involvement in service production and delivery influences the perceived value of the service package offered to customers. The impact is negative when a customer experiences different service at two locations of the same organization (or even at different times at the same location), or when he or she perceives that another customer is getting better service. It is more acceptable when services vary as a result of distinctly different service packages, as in the case of different classes of airline tickets.

From a manager's point of view, it is important to understand the heterogeneity of both the components of the service package and of the customers. Flexibility in design and operation are necessary as is a coherent integration of the concept and delivery system. The soundness of the organization's operations and overall strategy makes success possible.

Service packages are characterized by peripheral as well as core services, although the core components are usually more important to customers. No amount of peripheral service can satisfy a busy executive trying to keep to a tight schedule who has just had his or her flight cancelled. However, given a satisfactory core service, the peripheral ones can make all the difference in the world in differentiating the package from the competitor's. In many cases, the core services are virtually identical and priced accordingly; the peripheral ones become crucial and possibly even mandatory.[75] Airlines must operate reservation and check-in services (or contract them out). Passengers choose between competing airlines based on schedules as well as on their perception of such peripheral service features as reliability, comfort, quality of meals, friendliness and location.

Figure 2-4 illustrates the customer's choice between competing services, one that offers a basic, core service and one that has embellished the core service with peripheral services. Some automated teller machines (ATMs), for example, can do only simple transactions — transfer, withdrawal, account balance, whereas others provide many more possibilities — deposit, printed records, bill payments, loans.

FIGURE 2-4   Two offers of services

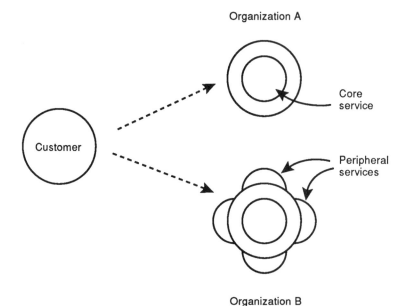

Figure 2-5 illustrates that the relative importance of various components of the service package changes from customer to customer and
from situation to situation. It is reasonable to expect that customers will
be more heterogeneous in their behavior and expectations as the complexity of the service increases. Correspondingly, it should also be more
difficult to deliver good service consistently because of customer heterogeneity. Because most customers have difficulty evaluating the services
individually, it is important to deliver a consistent level of quality. The
customer may well evaluate the overall service as being as poor as its
lowest quality component.

Although it may be tempting to streamline these services by eliminating
some of the peripheral components, most service managers are reluctant
to do so because they are uncertain about the impact on the customers'
perceptions and the remaining aspects of the service. However, most
experts in the procurement field recommend contracting out (buying)
rather than doing it in-house (making). A key reason is that it is difficult
to do well on many fronts at once, which causes a lack of focus. Many
Canadian banks have recently diversified into other financial services,
including brokerage services. Although collected under the heading of
'financial services,' each of these puts such a different demand on management that focus is effectively lost.

FIGURE 2-5 The relative importance of core and peripheral services for a specific customer

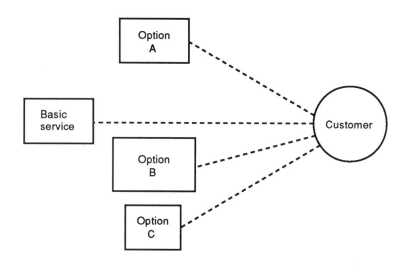

Perishability is a third characteristic of services. Because of the intangibility of the product, most of them cannot be stored in any meaningful way. The service product is therefore very transitory. Once an airplane takes off, the empty seats are opportunities that can never be recovered. Similarly, an idle hour in a doctor's day is time lost forever. This is not to say that there are no inventories in service industries. Inventories can be huge in retail businesses. Facilitating goods and facilities can be stored for later use, but they may have a very limited shelf life (hamburgers).

Although most components of services can't be stored, the capacity to provide the service can be. Excess staff in an emergency ward represents stored capacity. Stored capacity gives management room to move. Pricing is a good example. Stand-by passengers pay lower fares (in exchange for uncertainty over their departure time) so that the airline can get some contribution from otherwise empty seats or transfer demand from other, possibly full, flights. Off-peak prices for amusement parks, theatres, airfare and accommodation, and happy hours in bars and pubs are used to create or shift demand for otherwise unused capacity.

The potential for output corresponds to the available resources which create the service, often at the customer's request. If there is no request, the resources cannot be used productively and no meaningful output can be created, let alone stored. As might be expected, and as

Figure 2-6 illustrates, the transformation and consumption of the service become more simultaneous as intangibility increases.

FIGURE 2-6   Temporal relationship between production and consumption

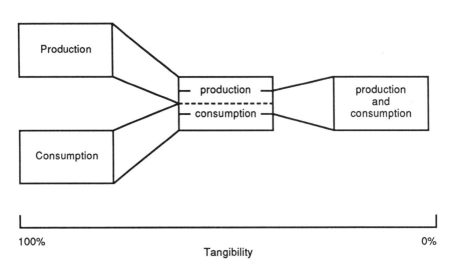

Because service production, delivery and consumption are simultaneous, managers have to build quality into the process. In many services, there is simply no time (nor adequate measures) for inspection after production and before delivery. Besides, the customer plays an integral role in determining quality.

Customer participation in the production process is a fourth characteristic of services that is often present but not necessarily so. In hairdressing salons, restaurants, psychological counselling services or medical treatment centres, there can be no meaningful service without the active participation of the customer. However, dry cleaners, the post office, medical research and transport of goods usually operate in the customer's absence.

Instead of idly watching the service being rendered, customers may be willing, or even prefer, to do part of the service themselves. Increased quality, speed or control, or simply filling idle time, are potential benefits to the customer. For example, many motorists choose self-serve gas stations despite the negligible monetary saving. Motorcyclists prefer to fill their tanks, even when service is otherwise good, because they can control spillage.

Although customer involvement in production can reduce costs and be an effective marketing tool, it also makes special demands on service organizations and managers. Customers are often much harder to control than staff members, and may well be poorly trained for what is required. The result can be reduced throughput, embarrassment, poor service to other customers or, at the extreme, damaged equipment or danger to staff and other customers. A first-time user of an ATM, a shopper with 25 items who insists on using the 8-item-maximum express line, a customer who is slow at bagging his or her groceries and a restaurant patron who is rude or smokes in a non-smoking area are familiar enough. Service managers must anticipate these difficulties and try to avoid them. Having well-maintained equipment that is easy to operate, clear, visible instructions, circulating staff, and service processes and facilities designed to prevent bottlenecks are some ways managers can overcome the problems associated with customer involvement.

The importance of considering both the behavior and role of customers within a system cannot be overemphasized. Consider the following example:

> ... most of the technical literature treats blood banking as a problem in inventory control under uncertain demand and finite life, which it is. But ... certain inefficiencies stem from treating blood purely as an article of commerce and ignoring the fact that it comes from people.[313, p. 33]

This observation does not imply that each service is unique or that providers and customers must always be present during the service process. However, it does emphasize that services contain many subtle attributes resulting in a complex management task. The multi-faceted nature of services also provides many ways to enhance customer service — the ultimate common goal of every service producer.

A second result of customer involvement is that human and physical resources are used as marketing tools as well as for production. Location is a key variable. Units must usually be near customers and in highly visible and easily accessible locations. Parking, specific road access and lines of sight are important considerations. Exceptions are possible for outstanding services. Customers will travel to see the top professionals in any field. Even in more mundane services, location isn't always crucial. Patrons drive across town, past other theatres showing the same movie, to visit Cinema Four in Austin, Texas.[105] Tourists go well out of their way to visit Wall Drug Store in Wall, South Dakota.[286] Both of these establishments have become legends for their entertainment value.

Facilities must also be kept neat and clean. Staff must dress neatly and be adept in interpersonal skills to deal with customers in an appropriate manner. Control of large numbers of geographically dispersed units is also a major challenge. McDonald's, growing at 500 or so units per year, must evaluate about 2,000 sites per year and choose (and develop) 10 per week. This is a major undertaking resulting directly from the growth rate.

Many of the results of customer involvement in service production make the manager's job quite unlike that of managing a factory. Consequently, service organizations must choose their managers carefully using somewhat different criteria than a manufacturing organization would use. Manufacturing facilities may be good sources of service managers, but a good manufacturing manager will not necessarily be a good service manager.

2.4   Services as inputs and resources

Morris and Johnston concluded that outputs do not adequately differentiate between (and thus define) goods producers and service producers.[217] They argued that, based on outputs, the case against any real difference is stronger than that in favor. They proposed instead that organizations be defined in terms of what they process (inputs) instead of the output of the process. They envisaged three pure types of organization — those that process materials, those that process information and those that process customers. Materials processors act on materials to create goods. Information processors act on information and convert it into more usable forms. Customer processors act on customers, who enter the system, receive some sort of treatment during the process (in which they may participate) and are the major outputs of the system.

Clearly most organizations process all conceivable combinations of materials, information and customers. Manufacturing firms process primarily materials and information about materials. In contrast, service firms concentrate on processing customers or information about customers. Figure 2-7 represents this model in which services occupy the right-hand side of the triangle and manufacturers, the left-hand side. There are no precisely defined scales to position an organization in this diagram and, given the variability of services, it would not be a constant position. However, positioning can be thought of in terms of value added. For example, the manufacturer, General Motors, adds value largely by altering materials. In contrast, services, such as beauty salons, add value by processing customers. In the slightly paraphrased words of a Walt Disney Productions trainer: "Everybody knows that General Motors makes cars and McDonald's makes hamburgers. But what does Disney World do? They make people happy."[231]

In Morris and Johnston's view, all types of operations share a wide range of common features but there are significant differences in par-

FIGURE 2-7   Services as inputs

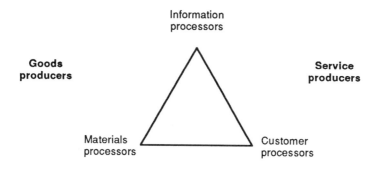

SOURCE: Adapted from Morris and Johnston (reference 217)

ticular between customer processors and materials processors. In the authors' words:

> Each operation, whether it processes customers, information or materials, has facilitating goods, equipment and manpower and each has to deal with issues like capacity planning, operations planning and control, management of inventories or queues, maintenance of equipment, control of quality, etc.[217, p. 14]

The main difference between materials and customer processors lies in the extent to which they have to manage intangibles in the production process. This affects their ability to specify inputs and resources, outputs, and the details of the transformation process itself at the planning stages. Because people are inherently less uniform than materials and react emotively to what is done to them, customer processors need less rigid specifications. Some operations management precepts may not apply. For example, on-going reduction in variability may be seen to decrease quality instead of improving it.

2.5   Services as transformation processes

A third group of scholars considers services to be neither inputs and resources nor outputs, but the transformation process itself. For example, Riddle said: "The distinguishing characteristic of service output is that it is primarily a process or activity."[252, p. 11] Berry contrasted goods and services as follows: "A good is an object, a device, a thing; a service is a deed, a performance, an effort."[17, p. 30] Defining service as a process agrees well with the concepts of intangibility, perishability and direct involvement of customers in the production process discussed earlier in this chapter. Processes are certainly intangible and perishable and, although customer involvement is not necessary, a process-based definition can accommodate it.

2.6   A definitional synthesis

Clearly there are many different ways of looking at services. We have discussed three, but there are others. One author distinguishes between service and manufacturing facilities on the basis of the size of the interface between customers and the production system.[287] And another equates service with not-for-profit activities, even within profit-making organizations.[180] How can there be so much disagreement over definition? How can we resolve it?

We believe that the answer to the first question lies in the fact that services are complex. As we discussed in Chapter 1, the service sector is extremely broad. Not only are individual services heterogeneous in that they have many characteristics and customers with both diverse and changeable needs, but the sector itself is also heterogeneous in its diversity. After all, we are trying in a few words to describe 75% of the economic activity of developed nations. Is it any wonder that there are exceptions for all definitions?

One solution is to simplify the problem by identifying uniform subsets within the service sector. Various taxonomic schemes have been suggested based on different criteria. A three-dimensional one, using degree of labor intensity, degree of service customization, and degree of contact and interaction between the customer and the service system, has certain advantages for operations managers.[112] Another approach is to learn to live with the multiple nature of services in the same way that physicists have come to accept that light is simultaneously particles and waves (not simply particles moving in waves). Or we can combine the various definitions, assuming they are partial and combination will lead to a more complete, albeit awkward, definition.

The Service Concept

2.7   Defining a service concept

'Service concept' is a frequently-used term in service industries, as in: "I really like your concept," or: "He had a sound concept but the market wasn't ready." The term has been described as the answer to the question 'What business are we in?' with a marketing and public relations slant:

'how an organization would like its stakeholders to perceive its service.'[119, p. 16] It is the service sector counterpart to the goods sector's product definition.

To make this definition more operationally useful, we can specify the components of a service. This approach arises from the special characteristics of services noted above. Booms and Bitner extended the traditional marketing mix (the four Ps of marketing: product, place, price, promotion) by adding three more Ps (participants, physical evidence, production process) to make it more suitable to services.[23] Magrath suggests three very similar additions: personnel, physical facilities and process management.[188] These components, which overlap to some extent, are described below.

Product refers to the core service provided. Dry cleaners clean clothes, consultants identify and solve problems, restaurants make and serve meals. The facilitating goods, range of services offered, hours of business, reproducibility and reliability are important components of the product.

Place includes a host of location considerations — the city, the district within the city, the ease of vehicular access, parking, access to the building, etc. Access based on time is included in the product group.

Price refers not only to the price level but also to pricing schemes (discount schedules, combination plans) and value as the customer perceives it.

Promotion, in addition to the standard advertising, selling and publicity activities common to goods producers, includes several important features of other Ps: participants, physical environment, facilitating goods, the service process and tangible clues of physical evidence.

Participants are of two types. One group comprises staff members who participate in the service process — the waiter, the teacher, the automobile service manager, the mechanic. The other group comprises customers involved in creating and delivering the service. Patrons may well choose a bar based on its popularity. Essentially they are looking for a crowd — no crowd, no interest. In such a situation, the customers as a group really create the service. Behavior, appearance and interpersonal skills are important components. Customers often look for excellence, not in service design, but in service delivery. Poor delivery can make a brilliant design worthless. Because members of the service staff are often crucial to delivery, their quality is vital.

Physical evidence is the clue to the service that can be detected by one of the five senses. Location-related features are closely linked to this group. Decor, color, lighting, temperature, layout, noise level, finish, ventilation, odors, signs, etc., are the sorts of things customers use to gauge the level of service.

Production process includes all the steps by which the service is created and delivered to the customer. Naturally, many process characteristics are important — flow, control of flow, customer involvement, flexibility, speed and capacity.

As the above shows, services are complex. What is a good concept? How does a manager go about creating one? We feel that a good concept is one that is internally focused, that is, all the elements from each of the above categories fit into a consistent, coherent whole. Fast food restaurants are a good example. The product is a narrow range of utilitarian food around a theme — hamburgers, fish, chicken, pizza. The prices are modest. The facilities are built in very visible, high-traffic areas with good access and ample parking. Promotion is done through standard media and may include easily identifiable cartoon characters. It uses point-of-sale logos and the site visibility. The serving staff is carefully selected and trained to be not only technically competent but also friendly. The target customers are young lower- to middle-class eaters (not diners), looking for food of acceptable quality that is available quickly in a bright, clean, fun atmosphere. The physical surroundings are well-lit, the chairs neither luxurious nor comfortable and the dishes, disposable. There is no table service beyond cleaning up, except on special occasions, when a staff member might bring a birthday cake. The process is focused on speed, cleanliness and efficiency. No one would mistake a good fast food outlet for any other type of restaurant.

The service process is especially important. It is fundamental both in creating and in delivering the service. In general, a good process is one with logical steps and layout, smooth flow, well-balanced capacities, the right degree and positioning of flexibility, and it separates steps that require customer involvement from the ones that don't. It is clearly important that the customer feel comfortable with the service process and that the process support the other elements of the service concept in all respects.

Creating and maintaining a good concept comes down to meeting the identified needs or desires of a specific target market. It requires good market research to identify the needs and to keep abreast of changes. It also requires painstaking attention to operations detail to create and maintain a focused concept. Walt Disney Productions has a nine-page script for the 'captain' of a jungle boat cruise.[231] The 'captain' has no operating responsibility — the boat is propelled and steered automatically along an underwater track. But he is a cheerleader and coach. Stew Leonard of Stew Leonard's Dairy spends a considerable amount of time listening to customers during weekly focus groups, reading written suggestions and just walking around the store talking to shoppers.[231]

Customer Service: The Name of the Game

2.8   Customer service is important for any organization

"Customer service is too important and costly to be left to chance."[48, p. 209] This statement's truth is obvious to service sector organizations but it is also recognized by many manufacturing firms. Indeed, manufacturing executives in one study of service and manufacturing organizations famous for service claimed that improvements in customer service were nearly as important to them as making better products.[299] Uttal concluded from that study that the masters of customer service:

> ... make outlandish efforts to hire only the right people, to train and motivate them, and to give them the authority necessary to serve customers well. They invest earlier and much more heavily than their competitors in technology to support customer service. They keep an especially sharp eye on the competition. And they constantly ask customers to rate the quality of service they have received.[299, p. 99]

These words deserve to be taken seriously: they herald the growing importance of customer service to all organizations, including manufacturers. Peters and Waterman concluded that:

> ... the excellent companies ... whether their basic business is metal bending, high technology, or hamburgers, ... have all defined themselves as service businesses.[230, p. 168]

The closer a service is to customer expectations, the more likely it is that it will be perceived to be of high quality. Service is associated with solving a problem in a timely and useful fashion. This idea becomes more explicit taking what service industries can do for customers into consideration: meeting personal needs (tourism, retail, personal services), providing technical infrastructural components (transport, communication, business services) and providing social services (health, education, welfare, public administration).[143]

Many customers feel that a personalized service in which they can 'have it their way' is preferable to a standardized one. Personal attention and the impression of control are important even though the service produced may be less predictable in characteristics such as time.[284] But to what extent should an organization be prepared to compromise its service design and delivery to please customers who might be in a different market segment? Which characteristics can be compromised and which are inviolate? When, if ever, does putting the customer first constitute providing a different service?

Customer expectations differ for the various classes of airline ticket because of price and promotion. The price of a first-class ticket is often 50% higher than the regular fare, in exchange for which the customer gets a wider, more comfortable seat, faster, more personal service, and amenities comparable to those in a good restaurant. Business class is aimed at those who want quiet and status, with better service than economy class at a reasonable price. First class and business class represent interesting revenue opportunities for airlines. But how profitable (successful) would a flight with only these two classes of tickets be? Would passengers be as satisfied with the service or do they need economy class for contrast? Comparison also works in reverse. A senior citizen once called economy class 'third class' after observing first-class and business-class service!

2.9   Setting a service level

A service level is a measure of some aspect of importance in a service delivery system. Typically, service levels are expressed as percentages; common examples are: percentage of calls answered within 10 seconds, percentage of times a subway train's doors open and close within a specified acceptable time-frame, percentage of deliveries made within 24 hours, percentage of customer requests that can be met from on-hand inventory.

It is not easy to decide which characteristic(s) to measure nor is it easy to set an appropriate service level. Airlines frequently use a standard for baggage arrival such as 100% available within 15 minutes of landing. Some companies can control baggage by computer from check-in to collection turntable. Some can also check the location on unclaimed or in-transit bags, a most useful feature when there are many flights between two airports or when baggage isn't put on the connecting flight. But is baggage arrival the appropriate measure of service? And is the standard used the right one?

As represented in Figure 2-8, a service level is often based on customer expectations, system capability and the competitors' level of service. The component at the lowest level will tend to set the overall service level. Even an organization with the resources and capability to exceed customer expectations may have little motivation for doing so in a major way. It may provide a competitive edge, but it may also be costly and exceed the customers' willingness to pay (see Figure 2-9). For example, in the mid 1980s, the Voyageur bus company ran a first-class bus service on the 250-kilometre Montreal-Quebec City route. There wasn't much demand for it. Buses are considered poor man's transport. More flights became available and many businesspeople, for whom the service was targeted, prefer to take their own cars. The service was discontinued. Perhaps better market research would have identified in advance the target market's true desires.

FIGURE 2-8   A common way to determine a service level

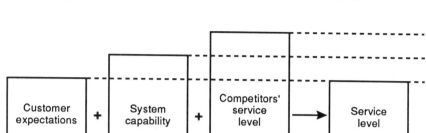

FIGURE 2-9   Matching the expected and perceived service level

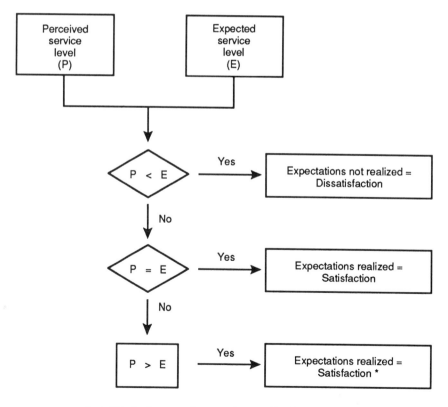

* might indicate excessive costs incurred by the organization

How should an organization decide what level of customer service to offer? The answer is perhaps obvious: research customer needs, decide what is feasible and decide what is justifiable both economically and strategically. These steps might imply installing a very good information system, keeping sufficient inventories where applicable, evaluating each significant performance standard, monitoring departmental and organizational performance with respect to those standards, and making sure that appropriate corrective measures are taken.

Many studies have indicated that most customers are prepared to accept lower service levels in return for more reliability; in other words, they value the service component of reliability more than, say, speed of delivery. The obvious reason for this is that a reliable service allows customers to plan their activities more effectively. A municipal bus system is a good example. The buses on a particular route could average three per hour, with an interval between 15 and 30 minutes — a relatively large deviation. The alternative is that the frequency be reduced to two buses per hour, running within three minutes of the schedule 95% of the time. Most passengers would prefer the latter scenario, especially in inclement weather, because it reduces uncertainty, despite the lower service level (as measured by frequency).

Had Canada Post and the US Postal Service provided an acceptable and consistent service level, it is likely that courier companies would have found entry into the market much more difficult. Once customers lose confidence in an organization's ability to provide the expected service, it is very difficult to win them back, in spite of objective tests to demonstrate that it is achieving its publicized service level. Despite Canada Post's publication of the results of regular performance audits by external consultants, which show that a high proportion of mail is delivered within two working days between city pairs, courier services flourish.

In short, when top managers get serious about customer service and its measure, service level, there is no substitute for an organizational culture focused clearly on satisfying customers and in which people have the tools, knowledge and motivation to follow through.

The Classification of Services

2.10   The usefulness of taxonomies

Service managers have to understand their business well to provide good customer service. Other industries are a useful source of ideas. Too often, service managers think that extensive experience in a given service industry is required to understand it thoroughly, and that their industry is so unique that other industries are irrelevant to them. Seminar leaders often come across the 'what's in it for me?' attitude, the participants' signal that they are interested only in material applicable to their industry.

Service managers must go beyond this myopic attitude if they really want to perform effectively. One of the best ways to do this is to understand thoroughly the strategic importance of taxonomies. According to Snyder, et al.:

> Classifications should provide frameworks that will facilitate the tasks of managers.... From a practical standpoint, the worth of a taxonomy must be measured by its utility in accomplishing these tasks. Thus, ... the classifications are neither right or wrong, but are either useful or useless.[277, p. 455]

The following taxonomies are presented with the intention that they be useful to managers of all service industries. We suggest examining each classification, determining where an organization fits in, understanding the implications of each classification and relating the observations to ideas stemming from the other taxonomies.

Naturally any taxonomy in a field as vast and diverse as the service sector will have exceptions. In fact, the value of taxonomies is in finding generalizations rather than exceptions. They make it possible for managers to learn from examples of excellence in other fields normally outside their realm. They also help managers to position their own businesses more effectively.

The following sections describe a number of classification systems. They have been grouped according to the number of dimensions involved. The list is meant to be illustrative rather than exclusive. Refer to the original publications for more information.

2.11   Some practical unidimensional taxonomies

Killeya and Armistead distinguish between *hard* services, which imply the use of equipment in service delivery, and *soft* services, which involve a service delivery relationship between two individuals without need for equipment.[149] Banking transactions using a human teller are soft; ones using ATMs are hard. Most organizations fall somewhere on the continuum between hard and soft.

Chase divides services into *high contact* and *low contact* on the basis of "the extent of customer contact in the creation of the service," from pure services (health centres, hotels, schools) through mixed services (funeral homes, bank branch offices, retail post offices) and quasi-manufacturing (bank head offices, government administration, postal sorting) to manufacturing (factories producing durable goods).[39] Efficiency is reduced because of the loss of control over service production in high contact services. The underlying philosophy seems to be that systems should be carefully designed to isolate as many operations as possible from the customer, so that known manufacturing techniques can be used. Very little emphasis is placed on the potentially useful role of the customer.

Cross and Walker offer a classification based on retail goods. Their key ideas are summarized in the following:

> Services also can be classified as specialty, shopping, or convenience products, with analogous requirements for distribution intensity. Even a specific service may vary on this dimension. Dental care is a good example. Perhaps basic dental care (cleaning) is a convenience good. Filling of cavities can be a shopping good (riskier for the consumer), however, and orthodontics is a specialty good.[57, p. 53]

2.12   Some two-dimensional taxonomies

Killeya and Armistead's classification (degree of *hardness*) can be combined with *tangibility* to form a two-dimensional categorization. This taxonomy makes it possible to differentiate between services in which facilitating goods dominate and those whose services are almost completely intangible. Even though tangibility is often associated with hardness, forcing the diagram of this model (Figure 2-10) toward the diagonal, there are industries in each quadrant. The circles for each industry in Figure 2-10 illustrate both the uncertainty in locating them precisely on the map and the notion that each industry has a zone it is 'normal' to operate within. An industry might increase or reduce the size of its 'normal' operating zone or move the zone within or outside its quadrant.

Lovelock developed a classification scheme that uses the degree of *tangibility* as one dimension and whether or not a service is rendered to an *individual* or to his or her *possessions* as the other.[185] As Figure 2-11 shows, this taxonomy reveals the impact of so-called tangible actions. Organizations must therefore pay close attention to how customers evaluate intangible action, because effort in service delivery does not guarantee customer satisfaction. Recall that Levitt proposed making intangibles as tangible as possible.[175]

A third two-dimensional classification revolves around the type of relationship between an organization and its customers.[185] Service delivery can be either *continuous* or *discrete*, and service customers may or may not *identify themselves with a specific organization*. Drivers sharing a highway are not normally associated with the highways department; however, members of fraternities, golf clubs or university alumni associations are identified with those organizations. Lovelock relates the continuity of service delivery

FIGURE 2-10   Classification of service organizations by level of technology and mix of goods and services

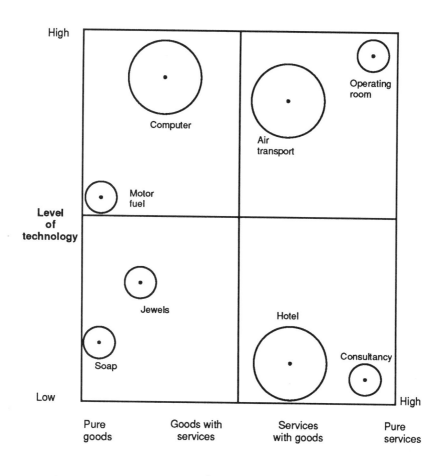

Degree of tangibility

to a membership relationship.[185] Normally it is in any organization's interest to promote a feeling of membership whenever possible, and this taxonomy is particularly useful for those organizations who have not yet thought about developing this feeling of identification in their customers.

Lovelock also classifies services on the basis of the degree of *customization* and the extent to which service providers can use *personal judgment*. Some services have a high level of customization which, depending on the nature of the service, can be addressed by having service providers

FIGURE 2-11   Classification of services by tangibility and service target

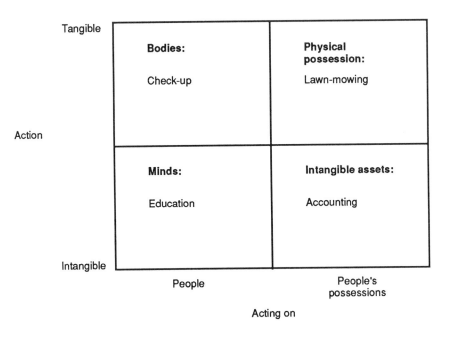

SOURCE: Adapted from Lovelock (reference 185)

exercise judgment (Figure 2-12). The idea that the employees in fast food restaurants do not use much judgment arises from the well-defined and controlled systems in which they work. In contrast, taxi drivers and waiters in four-star restaurants exercise much more judgment. Organizations in each of the four quadrants in Figure 2-12 need very different types of staff, highlighting the importance of hiring and training practices to good customer service.

Schmenner classifies services on the basis of the degree of *interaction and customization* — two constructs that Schmenner believes to be closely related — and *labor intensity* (Figure 2-13).[268] Schmenner notes that within this scheme, organizations tend to move toward the diagonal to improve control, and toward the service factory quadrant to improve productivity. For example, professional firms are hiring increasing numbers of para-professional technical staff to do as much of the clerical and technical work as possible. Managers must realize not only that changes are occurring, but also that high levels of labor intensity and

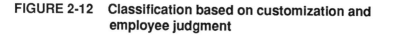

FIGURE 2-12   Classification based on customization and
               employee judgment

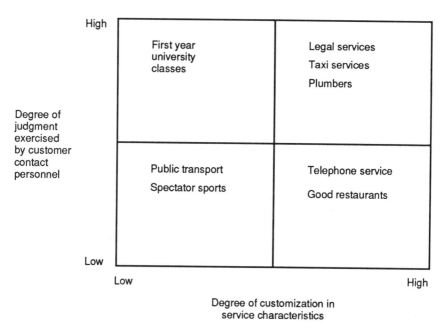

SOURCE: Adapted from Lovelock (reference 185)

customer contact put a premium on good workforce management, cost control and quality.

In Langeard's taxonomy, customers can be either *dominated* or *dominating*, and participate in the service either *actively* or *passively*.[164] Some interesting psychological implications stem from this scheme. Clients could be dominated by the service provider through lack of choice, urgency or a large difference in the level of competence between customer and server. However, most customers prefer not to be totally dominated; for example, it appears that many hotel clients are reluctant to let a bellman carry their luggage. There are many possible explanations for this shift away from services being performed for passive and often dominated customers. Customers want to feel less dependent on service providers so as to improve their self-image and feeling of control.[87] Many people dread getting service from a government agency. Even before we phone, we often feel deprived of all power to influence the speed of the outcome (let alone the outcome itself). Also, many people are more willing to be actively involved in service creation, as is evidenced

FIGURE 2-13   Classification by degree of labor intensity, and customization and interaction

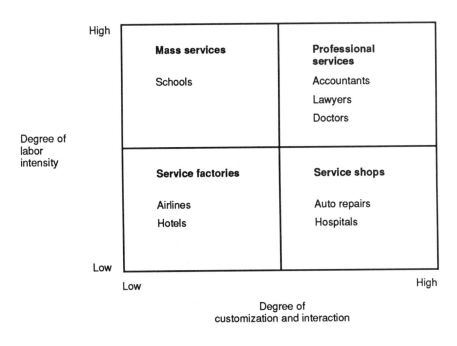

SOURCE: Adapted from Schmenner (reference 268)

by the growth of self-service in many industries. And many organizations offer discounts for self-service; for example, automatic dialing.

2.13   A three-dimensional classification

The scheme in Figure 2-14 brings together degree of *labor intensity, contact and interaction*, and *service customization*. Like its two-dimensional counterparts, this scheme can be used to see common traits of organizations sharing a region of the diagram, in this case, octants. It also makes it possible to compare organizations which share two of the three characteristics. Innovative managers might be able to modify a service characteristic accordingly. Pizza Pizza, for example, has a single phone number for ordering pizza in each city and keeps a computer data base of former customers. These service features are quite different from those of Pizza Hut and other pizza joints. Effectively, the Pizza Pizza data base allows the company to increase at least the perception of both its degree of customization, and of contact and interaction, and to decrease its degree of labor intensity. That is, it could be re-positioned in Figure 2-14.

FIGURE 2-14   Three-dimensional classification based on degree of labor intensity, contact and interaction, and customization

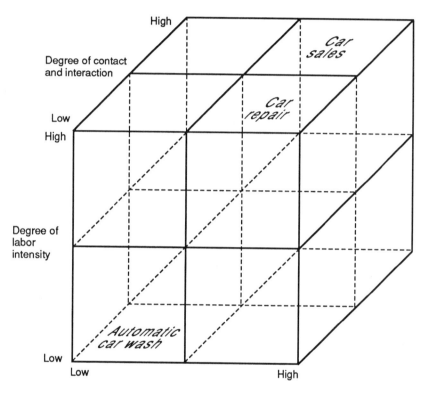

Degree of service customization

SOURCE: Adapted from Haywood-Farmer (reference 112)

2.14   Other classifications

An earlier section discussed a classification based on system inputs and resources as being either *materials*, *information* or *customers*.[217] Federal Express has differentiated itself from Emery by emphasizing the speed and accuracy of delivery instead of the packaging.

Mills and Margulies divide service organizations into *maintenance-interactive*, such as routine banking transactions, *task-interactive*, such as consulting and *personal-interactive*, such as nursing.[210] They suggest using seven variables to help classify services: information, decision, time, problem, awareness, transferability, and power and attachment. Within an industry, many combinations might be found. In accounting, for example, a company like H&R Block, specializing in completing tax returns, will have a very different profile based on these seven dimensions from a company like Ernst & Young, in the business of giving tax advice (consulting).

2.15   Conclusion

There are many other conceivable classifications; indeed, services can be classified on any basis that is possible to measure or estimate. The goal of classification is to recognize that different service organizations share one or more characteristics and therefore, managerial features. By understanding that there are common traits, the concepts in this book can be better applied, and more appropriate comparisons between services made.

The concept of any service is worth defining and periodically re-evaluating. It lies at the very heart of what a service organization is all about. A successful concept, by definition, will be attractive to the market. But a good concept is part of design, the topic of the next chapter.

CHAPTER

3

SERVICE DESIGN

A General Perspective

3.1 The importance of a good design

The design of a service is an excellent opportunity to give customers good value. Customers should be convinced that one or more of an organization's attributes make for a better deal than the packages offered by the competition. In this context, the term 'better deal' refers to the overall value of a package including price, location and so on, rather than to any isolated component. The difference being offered should be clear to customers, although they need not necessarily know the characteristics of the process. For example, credit card companies have differentiated their products by having cards of different colors, each of which gives a different level of service. Customers are quite aware of the service differences but unaware of how transactions are processed. In services, a good design is particularly important because the customer is involved in the process; error correction or poor design are much more obvious than in manufacturing processes.

Success in the service sector depends heavily on price, quality and service.[41] Each of these three elements is affected by service design. A sound design will make it possible to give the customer value by delivering an attractive level of quality, service and price. Quality and service must be built in — they cannot be added later — because the customer will assess both, often quite subjectively.

3.2   Integrating the service concept and delivery system

The concept, delivery system and level of service, all of which were discussed in Chapter 2, are closely related. Naturally, it is much easier and far more effective to ensure that these three are integrated in a unified whole from the outset rather than trying to fit one in at a later stage. Normally, the concept — the package of tangibles and intangibles — comes first. This package then has to be delivered in an appropriate way to the customer. Characteristics such as the attitude of the staff, the atmosphere, and the image of the facilities and the organization as a whole have to be designed in advance and controlled on an on-going basis to ensure a proper match between concept and delivery system. Finally, the service level has to be both built in at the design stage and then controlled, using suitable measures to determine how well the design is working. These measures should also be developed at the design stage because they are important in determining the success of the whole package. Airlines with frequent flyer programs get flooded with requests to trade a part of accumulated mileage for free airline tickets. Most airlines did not foresee this demand and therefore did not plan for it. The problem is amplified by the limited number of seats available on each flight. In some ways, this represents a service design failure.

Customer input is key to design because the service package will be successful only if enough customers are satisfied. Customers (or potential customers) can be surveyed, included in the design process through focus groups or test sites, or considered in other ways. Ignoring them is folly. Unfortunately, services that have a monopoly, such as government agencies, are more able to ignore customer dissatisfaction resulting from bad design because their customers have few viable options. They therefore do not face constant pressure to adjust the system for the customer. The importance of customers has been described in very simple, meaningful terms: design what they want, produce what they want when they want it and support what they bought.[41] It should be clear who to contact in case of dissatisfaction. Many utilities put a customer service phone number on bills, many governments have a central phone number from which any government agency can be reached, and even tax auditors now send letters that include their phone numbers!

Excellent service begins and ends with a good guarantee, a very good way to support the service package. Good service guarantees are unconditional, easy to understand, meaningful, painless to invoke and quick to pay.[104] A guarantee represents an intangible made tangible, a written contract guaranteeing that the service performance will be satisfactory to the customer. An unconditional service guarantee that promises complete satisfaction is an excellent marketing tool. But it also forces an organization to become more customer oriented, to set clear, attainable performance standards and to examine its service delivery system for possible failure points.

3.3 Basic service design

It is often the president who sets the tone for his or her organization's entire service orientation. There are huge perceived and real differences between Frank Lorenzo's hard driving, cost cutting approach (the now defunct Eastern Airlines)[61, 125] and Jan Carlzon's orientation to the customer (Scandinavian Airlines System).[35] Carlzon once had to catch a connecting flight in Copenhagen en route to Stockholm. He found that he had to go about half a mile from Concourse B, where the wide-bodied planes from overseas arrived, to Concourse A. Concourse B was used because it was closer to maintenance hangars. He also noted that he was not alone; many passengers made the same connection. Carlzon intervened; now planes are towed an extra few hundred metres but fewer passengers have to walk between concourses.

Although an orientation toward creating an effective service to satisfy customers is important, it is also necessary to be efficient by doing things properly. Striking the right balance between effectiveness and efficiency is important, necessary and challenging. The correct emphasis is often unclear. Fortunately, in many cases, higher effectiveness can lead to improved efficiency. For example, faster commuter trains provide a more effective service; increased usage resulting from higher effectiveness leads to higher efficiency.

Service failure, or lousy service, abounds because an unsystematic approach leads to bad design.[272] Careful design is fundamental to achieving excellence in service delivery. Although the unique characteristics of service might make the design stage more difficult, they also make it more important. Design is more than knowing the sequence of steps and the key characteristics:

> The design shows execution time standards that can be easily monitored and quantified. They allow the measurement of capacity and productivity through volume and throughput relationships.[272, p. 139]

A detailed design helps to control quality levels and process uniformity because it completes the global picture. One way to develop a detailed design is to create a 'service blueprint,'[272] which is simply a detailed step-by-step schematic description that looks and functions like an architectural blueprint, a critical path network or a flow chart for writing a computer program. Designing a blueprint involves four steps:

1. identify the process — specify inputs, steps and outputs
2. isolate fail points, the critical steps where additional efforts should be made to ensure perfect service
3. establish a time frame — determine standards and variances based on customer expectations
4. analyze profitability; based on market studies, consider what revenues and costs the system will generate.

A detailed blueprint for a service can be very elaborate, but it helps to ensure a systematic and coherent approach to the service package. Like all simulation approaches, it lets the user test and analyze without the time and expense of a real, full-scale or pilot operation. Pricing policies, expected profits from specific delivery systems, identification of customer contact points and potential modifications are the sorts of areas that can be analyzed. Blueprints also give tangible evidence of the process and are valuable training aids.

Overall Approaches to Service Design

3.4   Mapping relationships

As discussed earlier, the customer, who is often a participant in or present during the service process, should be the focal point of the entire service design. The characteristics of existing personnel, equipment, intended service and the proposed delivery system must be maintained in equilibrium (operations that are smooth and as planned) so that each aspect plays its intended role or has its intended effect on the service rendered. Figure 3-1 is an example of an equilibrium. Service is composed of three basic elements (core and peripheral services, service delivery system and service process) that are always present in variable proportions, and are hard to segregate. The customer's role can vary, as can his or her impact through interaction, but he or she influences each of the three elements. By being present, the customer perceives the process, judges the system and evaluates the quality of the service. For the system to be stable, the manager must act on this structure to determine which strategies he or she wishes to have for the organization. For instance, patients in a clinic perceive service to be of good quality when appointments are on time and they receive the doctor's full attention during treatment. It is only by understanding the relationships between these different aspects and how to control them that the manager can establish equilibrium in the enterprise.

For new services, designers have the luxury of starting from scratch. However, for existing services, or when a service is being significantly modified, the location(s), equipment or personnel already in place may

FIGURE 3-1   Design equilibrium

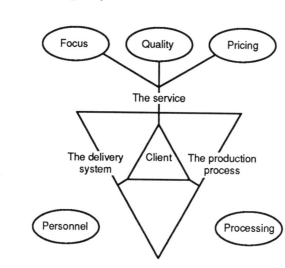

cause design headaches. Designers can overcome these problems to a certain extent by relocating, replacing equipment and or retraining. Ironically, major changes may pose fewer difficulties than more incremental ones. With major changes, the change is more visible; everyone recognizes its magnitude and is more inclined to take the necessary steps for implementation. There may also be a larger investment at stake, which may have been more carefully scrutinized. With incremental changes, fewer people believe the change to be significant and cannot justify the expense of making it; indeed, many may not even recognize that a change has been made. A poor design can be the result of a series of such moves. And changes may not be infrequent. Over the years, Stew Leonard's Dairy made 27 additions to its retail store, although by all accounts management was able to maintain the store's excellent service.[231]

One way to make the customer the focal point of the design is to pay particular attention to where the customer comes into contact with the service system or 'managing demand at the point of delivery.'[224] This expression implies that customers should be matched with the delivery mode. ATM customers value the sense that they are in control, the speed and the efficiency; users of traditional bank tellers value human contact, security and having it done for them.[164] If more than one delivery mode exists, an organization should determine how the modes match the needs of different customers and try to manage the match. They might offer incentives for customers to use a particular mode. For example, gasoline is marginally cheaper from self-service pumps than from full-service pumps. ATMs, because of opening hours and location, are usually more convenient than branch banks. Self-checkout in hotels is usually faster than regular checkout. Each delivery mode in these examples has benefits both for the customer and the service organization — fewer complaints, less space, lower costs. Of course, not all attempts to manage matches between customers and delivery mode have proven successful. Some educational institutions have experimented with closed-circuit televised lectures to increase class size without having to build a large lecture theatre. Students will line up before the class to ensure a seat in the live classroom rather than watching the same lecture on television.

Three elements (services offered, customer type, delivery mode) and three component processes (assembling service packages, segmenting customers, matching services and customers) should be considered when designing delivery systems. Northcraft et al.'s approach adds the component process dimension to Figure 3-1:

> ... demand management in service industries implies real time control of demand at the point of service delivery in order to increase service production and delivery efficiency. The limited attention paid to real time control of demand has been in the form of encouraging delegation of service provision activities to the customer or client. Demand management takes a broader view by searching for ways to increase effectiveness and efficiency through a better general match of service provision demands and service operation resources.[224, p. 66]

It is important to match service delivery and production to the minimally qualified or limiting resource, which may be a person or a physical asset. The concept is similar to the limit placed on assembly line output by the slowest step on the line. When dealing with human limitations, proper matching can increase motivation by making jobs more challenging. Remuneration might also be based on the complexity of the job. In some banks, tellers are specialized in some task (from basic operations to more complex functions). Staff in some fast food restaurants learn to perform tasks in a standard order. This matching process is called 'hierarchical mapping'; 'one-to-one mapping' and 'multiple mapping' are alternatives.

When an organization offers multiple services to several kinds of clientele, customers often prefer to get customized service.[216] The service delivery system might consist of a core of common operations, with specific requests dealt with on a customized basis. Airlines give their first-class passengers preferential treatment at check-in, although the basic process is not very different from economy class, but all passengers stand in the same line for customs and security checks. Everyone is familiar with fast food restaurants that customize a stock menu item (pizza) by allowing customers to choose what to put on it (toppings). Some even allow the customer to assemble the product. University academic programs are similarly constructed with core courses and electives, some from an approved list and others, open. Obviously this approach assumes customer ability to tolerate variation.

In service delivery, either customers come to the provider, the provider goes to the customer or the two parties deal at arm's length, perhaps through other parties.[184] This has interesting implications. Until the day that pest control over the telephone becomes feasible, this service will always have to be conducted on the customer's premises. Similarly, most passengers on cruise ships probably enjoy being on board much more than watching « Love Boat » on television. On the other hand, banking and stockbrokering originally required customers to be on hand, but can now be performed over the phone or electronically. Computer data bases make this sort of service delivery more feasible in other areas as well. Organizations tend to deliver service as economically as possible, provided that customers still accept the delivery system. Bar coding in supermarkets, now widespread, was postponed for years because of consumer suspicion.

3.5   The industrialization of services

Levitt was the original proponent of service industrialization, which aims to improve service efficiency and effectiveness by taking a systematic, standardized, 'industrial' approach to service design and operations.[173, 174] Levitt proposed that the traditional service attitudes of human variability and servitude be replaced by a combination of hard, soft and hybrid technologies. Hard technology consists of equipment such as automated car washes, ATMs, FAX machines and other self-serve machinery, as well as technician-operated equipment such as medical or automobile diagnostic equipment. Soft technologies, such as packaged vacation tours, fully systematized tax preparation services or packaged computer programs, are:

> ... the substitution of organized preplanned systems for individual service operatives. Often these involve some modifications of the tools (or technologies) employed, but their essential feature is the system itself....[174, p. 66]

Hybrid technologies, such as radio-controlled truck routing, information technologies and debit cards are combinations of hard and soft components. It became apparent to Levitt that the approaches used to manage service need not be limited to training people or buying equipment. When a superior technology for service delivery is found, the service concept might be altered considerably. Transportation used to be limited to horse and wagon; automotive power resulted not only in different ways of delivering existing transportation service, but also in radically new services.[11]

Levitt's main contributions were to develop the notion of improving service by using proper technologies and to stress the importance of soft and hybrid technologies. His most famous example is McDonald's, where everything is planned. Even the scoop used to fill french fry bags was carefully designed to control portion size, spillage and efficiency. And the bags were designed to give the impression of generosity.

Service industrialization often implies a move from low-volume, customized service to high-volume, standardized service. Fast food empires have little flexibility but do offer speed, cleanliness and identical service anywhere, anytime to large numbers of customers. (There is still room for à la carte restaurants because they serve a different market segment.[21]) In 1986, the Vag hairdressing company had about 40 beauty parlors, mostly franchises.[71] Vag has managed to switch customer loyalty from individual hairdressers to the Vag system through close central control. Head office trains personnel, sets operating standards and closely controls quality by ensuring adherence to standards. This service, for which there is no tipping, has significantly improved prices and standardization, but at the expense of personal relationships. Fantastic Sam's is another hair salon that has developed a similar concept.

Standardization can be achieved, when it is desirable, if the control of system characteristics and easy identification of customer problems (tax returns) or expectations (fast food) make proper planning possible. However, for some types of services, for example, consulting and other professional services, problem identification and problem solving are very complex, requiring expertise and customization. In these cases, standardization is much less feasible, although some is both possible and desirable.[113] Figure 3-2 illustrates this situation.

3.6   The customer as a productive resource

Instead of concentrating on technology, Lovelock and Young, among others, stress the potential contribution of the customer to service delivery.[186] This approach is attractive because it focuses on customer attitudes and involvement. Customer participation covers the complete range from total involvement to none at all. Watching TV is rarely participative; postal services are conducted with only minimal customer involvement. On the other hand, renting a carpet cleaner involves a great deal of customer involvement in contracting to rent the machine (at the agent's location), transporting it home, filling the machine with water and the right amount of the correct cleaning solution, cleaning the carpet, washing the machine, and transporting it back to the rental

FIGURE 3-2   Relationship between uncertainty of output and level of service standardization

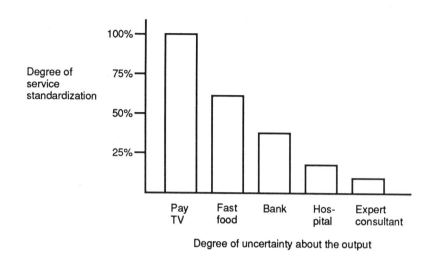

outlet. Organizations that facilitate customers doing it themselves — cook-it-yourself restaurants, brew-it-yourself breweries and frame-it-yourself establishments — are other examples. The success of these operations, and their relative rarity, present obvious opportunities both for service producers to enter into potentially attractive new businesses and for customers to have exciting new services available. Indeed, unless the activities performed by customers are substandard, disruptive or require remedial action by the organization, high levels of customer participation are to be encouraged.[212]

Of course, customers can usually choose how much they want to participate. This situation is comparable to customization, except that the customization is of the delivery rather than of the service itself. Some would argue that different delivery processes create different services. We agree that a change in delivery can radically alter a service concept. However, we do not believe that there is a difference in the basic service offered by, for example, self-serve and full-service gasoline stations.

Figure 3-3 shows the potential for improvement in productivity as a function of customer participation and contact. Not surprisingly, the greatest potential is in high-contact services with little participation. Increased customer participation is not the only way to increase productivity, nor is customer participation necessarily enough in and of itself. It must be balanced with industrialization and with proper use of information processing capability. Many significant improvements in productivity result from customers interacting with computers; service

FIGURE 3-3   Effect of customer participation and degree of contact on possible improvement in productivity

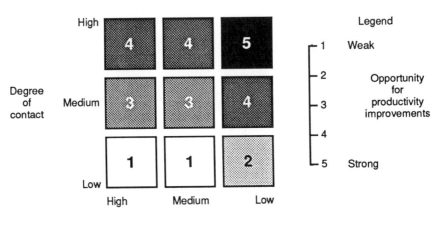

Degree of customer participation

providers must ensure that both the equipment and the software are user-friendly to realize these benefits. Figure 3-4 illustrates the situation.

A good customer behaves in the expected way within a given service system,[284] regardless of how productive or unproductive he or she may be. In a five-star hotel, it is normal for a bellhop to carry luggage to the guest's room. When guests try to carry their own luggage, it is met with

FIGURE 3-4   Implication of the customer's presence in the system

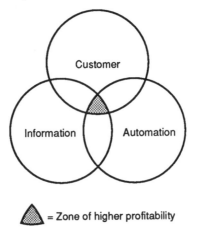

= Zone of higher profitability

disapproval by the desk clerks and bellhops. Bellhops sometimes take the luggage while the guest is registering to remove reasonable choice. This attitude illustrates the definition of roles in a service setting. Customers learn their roles first by observation and imitation, and then by active participation. Doing as planned implies that better productivity is achievable; therefore good customer education is important.

An organization should play a role in educating customers as to proper behavior. Most of the time, customers are willing to do as requested or shown, as is evidenced by the crowds that are prepared to wait patiently in line to buy tickets for a rock concert or sporting event. It is important for customers to learn their role quickly because it contributes to:

1. increased real and perceived performance, and service quality
2. greater customer satisfaction and loyalty
3. lower cost
4. better control over customers, which implies more conformity with the process as designed
5. the likelihood that customers will behave the same way in subsequent encounters
6. better knowledge of customer desires and needs.[209, 216]

As more services become international, socializing customers to conform with service processes takes on a different dimension.[179] For example, in western societies, queuing is usually well understood and accepted, although there are variations between countries. In many other countries, however, there is no concept of queuing — the one with the sharpest elbows and loudest voice gets served first.

Despite the advantages, not all organizations are ready or willing to invest in customer education. A number of reasons have been put forth: it is not an issue in manufacturing enterprises, managers have insufficient knowledge, and it has been judged that the investment would not have adequate return without also benefiting the competition.[212] Financial institutions that adopted ATMs early on incurred much higher customer education costs that did those that adopted them later. Innovators of new technology frequently face this disadvantage.[305]

Customers must also perceive the advantage in order to be motivated to participate in service production; after all, customers see themselves first and foremost as customers and not producers. Lower prices, higher quality, faster service, increased customization, more control and enjoyment are possible advantages. Marketing efforts should focus not on improvements to the performance of the system but on the benefits to customers of participating.

Customers may want to prolong the service process after their involvement would normally end. Possible explanations include dissatisfaction with results, enjoyment and a perceived value of the use of time.

A singer will be called back to the stage many times after a great performance because the audience does not want to leave the atmosphere they have enjoyed for the past few hours. Fast food customers may linger because they still have 30 minutes before they have to get back to work or because of an unexpected thunderstorm. A dissatisfied retail customer may stop the entire process by complaining, either in person or on the phone. Clearly, managers must exercise some control over situations like these. For example, Benihana of Tokyo, a chain of Japanese steakhouses where the meal is cooked on a hibachi grill in front of the guests, has relatively uncomfortable seats, a hot table at an inconvenient height and few places to put a drink. At the end of the meal, the staff members bow formally, thank the guests and start cleaning up — clear signals that the performance is over. Customers who still do not get the message may be left in the dark (literally) or asked to leave. Dissatisfied customers can be taken to a separate place to discuss their complaints, which not only keeps the process clear for other customers but also keeps other customers from hearing the details of the complaint.

On the other hand, customers should not always be treated in isolation because, in many services, they interact with other customers; indeed, the quality of the service is closely related to the level of interaction, and productivity, to the desired behavior. Individual fans at sporting events may go from being reserved to enthusiastic exhibitionists in the crowd setting. The 'wave' phenomenon in stadiums and mob behavior at soccer matches are examples. Similarly, when people walk out in the middle of a movie in droves, it is an incentive for others to join them or, at least, reassess the quality of the movie.

Participation in the service can be physical (1), intellectual (2) or emotional (3) and can be oriented to doing the service (A), contributing to service specifications (B), or participating in either the performance of the service or the evaluation and control of the process (C).[164] The categories in these two dimensions (1-3 and A-C) are not intended to be mutually exclusive. They can make possible the construction of a 3x3 matrix which can help managers to identify the combinations that are appropriate for their service. A wave of vandalism and theft might motivate residents to form a neighborhood watch program in collaboration with local police. In this case, an emotional aspect related to service performance has resulted in an orientation to participation in law enforcement.

Clearly, a lot of careful planning is required at the design stage for customer participation to be successful. It takes sensitivity to what motivates customers and understanding how they will behave under certain conditions. Seven aspects should be considered in developing a new process:[186]

1. develop customer trust
2. understand customer habits
3. pretest new procedures and equipment
4. understand what determines customer behavior
5. teach customers how to use innovations
6. promote the benefits of the new service and encourage people to try it
7. monitor and evaluate performance.

Managers should carefully consider these suggestions before they implement or modify a process. There are too many examples of service delivery that failed because one of these aspects was neglected. Improvements in productivity may be a good reason to increase customer participation, but they cannot be achieved without a disciplined approach.

3.7 Taking advantage of high contact and low contact steps

Customer participation is usually associated with a high contact environment, whereas service industrialization is associated with low contact. High contact systems (HCS) involve the customer most of the time that the service is being produced and delivered, and frequently involve service personnel as well; low contact systems (LCS) are the opposite. Each type of system involves a different environment and is therefore appropriate for meeting different objectives — effectiveness for HCSs and efficiency for LCSs.[44] Efficiency is consistent with a regular, rigid, mechanistic structure as for LCSs, whereas effectiveness is consistent with a more flexible, organic structure as for HCSs. LCSs and HCSs differ in many other respects as well: location, layout, quality control, forecasting, staffing, etc. A pizza restaurant catering to walk-in trade (HCS) will select a location that is highly visible and easily accessible to customers. In contrast, a delivery-only pizza outlet (LCS) will locate where operating costs are low in a place easily accessible to delivery vehicles and near potential customers. High visibility can in fact be a disadvantage to an LCS.

Workers are oriented either to other people (customers and co-workers) or to the system itself. HCSs should be staffed by people-oriented workers, and LCSs, by system-oriented people. Because customer perception of the quality of service is often closely associated with the attitude and competence of the serving staff, these workers need strong marketing, interpersonal and operating skills. Many non-profit organizations, such as the Red Cross, rely heavily on volunteers. People volunteer for a number of reasons, but some do it as minor psychological therapy. Volunteers in this category should be assigned first to LCS positions requiring little training and later moved to other positions (see Figure 3-5).

FIGURE 3-5   Matching staff with organizational requirements — the case of non-profit organizations

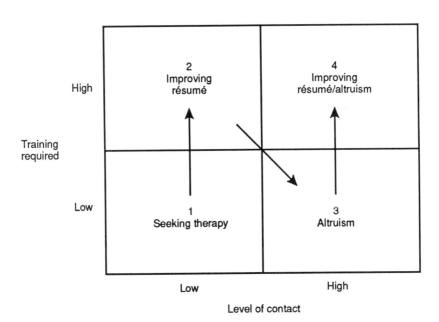

How can managers develop a coherent strategy to manage the high and low contact sections of their organizations? Here is one possibility:

1. identify the system as HCS or LCS by making a random series of observations of work to determine the activities of the group or an individual (work sampling)
2. determine whether the operating procedures fit the current structure
3. identify where in the system decoupling is both possible and desirable
4. decrease unnecessary direct customer service
5. use contact reduction strategies where appropriate
6. employ contact enhancement strategies where appropriate
7. relocate LCS parts of the service operations to lower cost facilities
8. enhance the customer contact provided
9. use traditional efficiency improvement techniques in LCSs.

Many managers must determine to what extent the operations involving the customer should be separated from those that don't. Some situations demand high contact (see Figure 3-6) and, therefore, coupled operations. Direct contact is unavoidable when customers must be physically or mentally present as part of the process. For example, a patient must be present to have his or her eyes examined. This contact is an excellent opportunity for the professional to offer additional services such as a follow-up appointment or trying contact lenses.

FIGURE 3-6   Situations in which decoupling is not suggested

1.   Face-to-face contact is seen as an essential marketing element of the service.

2.   Rapid exchange of information with the customer is required; service production and delivery are inseparable.

3.   Hiring additional supervisors would be impractical.

4.   Jobs are tightly prescribed by collective bargaining agreements.

5.   Tight coordination across task or orgnizational boundaries is critical.

6.   Resultant job specifications would be counter to company philosophy.

SOURCE: Adapted from Chase (references 39 and 40)

Even in an LCS, many tasks must be performed where customer interaction is unavoidable perhaps because the task itself is not easily divisible or costs do not justify hiring another individual to allow task division. Not all librarians, for example, are people-oriented. In some cases, they can be assigned to low contact tasks away from the public section of the library. An alternative or complementary approach is to reduce interaction by providing written information and directional signs concerning layout, location of material and procedures.

Although high labor intensity does not necessarily imply high contact, it does imply that workforce management (training, scheduling, control) is important, especially in large international organizations.[268] When labor intensity is low, technical aspects are important. This is the case for airlines, which try to schedule flights and maintenance so that aircraft are in the air for at least eight hours a day. Smaller companies manage to get 11 hours per day from their aircraft.

Figure 3-7 suggests that it is preferable to separate workers from customers whenever circumstances allow it. Customers are annoyed by workers who appear available to answer questions but say it is not their job, or who sit at desks ignoring the customers in the queue. When customers' phone calls are not being answered, they can't tell whether they are being ignored or not.

FIGURE 3-7   Situations in which decoupling is suggested

1. Face-to-face contact for all operations is not technologically required nor desired by the customer.

2. Separate workers are required to produce the service.

3. Tasks can be easily segmented into those requiring interpersonal skills and those requiring technical skills.

4. Information exchange between the service system and the customer can be accomplished by phone or mail.

5. The price of the service is more critical to the customer than convenience or customization.

SOURCE: Adapted from Chase (references 39 and 40)

When two (or more) related service channels are offered, it is possible to shift customer demand from one to another. Managers can likely make one channel high contact and the other low contact. ATM transactions cost less than transactions performed by human tellers. It's conceivable that customers might have to pay a surcharge in the future to use a human teller for a transaction that an ATM could perform. Sometimes customers consciously avoid face-to-face contact, in which case a low contact approach has a much better chance of success. For example, it is preferable to make available a telephone number that people can call anonymously for information about sexually transmitted diseases, and to place pamphlets in a variety of locations.

When the service requires no heavy or expensive equipment, it may be possible for a people-oriented staff member take it directly to the customer's premises. The alternative necessitates a reception area, possibly a waiting room, the right decor and good customer relations on the part of all staff. Doctors used to make house calls as a matter of course until specialized equipment took over from the traditional doctor's bag. Also, as demand increased, doctors didn't want to lose time travelling from patient to patient. But equipment is now becoming more portable, and with increasing concern over the cost of health care, there may be a resurgence in home medicine.

The design of HCSs must balance technology and employees.[43] However, this is also true of LCSs, because it is not always desirable to reduce customer contact. Whenever there is a provider-customer contact, even when the contact is over the phone, the two parties have to deal with the customer's needs as a team with different roles. Some service enterprises, for example, consulting firms, make a tremendous effort to match the personalities and competence of customer and consultant.

3.8   Design and the marketing mix

A seven-P marketing mix for services that expands on the traditional four Ps of marketing was discussed in Chapter 2. Although any service should strive for an internally consistent combination of elements for each P, the importance of the components will vary depending on the type of service involved. In high contact services, participants are an important component, as is process design, particularly because of its impact on customers. In low contact services, process design is also important, but more as a means for efficiency. For example, Emery Air Freight puts a lot of emphasis on managing its process in order to meet its promise of next-day delivery — all letters and parcels must be sorted within a three-hour period each day.[188]

One important element of high contact service design is managing customers' reactions to the inevitable queue. The question is: How can we make this 'wasted' time pass more quickly and pleasantly? Agreeable surroundings, dissemination of information about the service, moving some steps in the process to before or during the queuing period and offering some supplementary services are possible techniques.[184, 194] They may improve efficiency and provide important marketing opportunities as well as making the wait more pleasant.

Examples abound of turning a queue into a service opportunity. Relaxing music, a seat and a drink make the waiting time in a restaurant seem shorter as well as providing an attractive source of high contribution revenue. Restaurants can also offer waiting customers a menu, a practice which not only makes the time pass more quickly, but also speeds up processing time once they are seated. Customers waiting at the door of a disco may like to hear the music, see a piece of the action and be seen, but few discos provide these opportunities because space, especially non-paying space, is at a premium. The first of these examples represents increased contribution, the second increased productivity, and the third higher quality and a guarantee of capacity utilization; all these features are desirable.

At popular attractions, such as Disney World or world fairs, queues may last all day. A customer may spend over an hour in a single queue, sometimes under adverse conditions. Managers can offer entertainment to waiting guests, let the queue advance continuously (albeit slowly), let the customers know what is available or where to go once they are inside, or disguise the length of the queue (although this tactic has its disadvantages). The atmosphere inside service facilities is undoubtedly important, but managers should not neglect it outside either.

3.9   Service design in a nutshell

Heskett summarizes the integrative nature of the aspects of service design as follows:

> The selection and development of employees, care in assignment, and the layout and equipment of the facility (in a high-contact environment) are all integral elements of the design of the service encounter, which in turn is based on the company's assessment of customer needs.[121, p. 123]

Designing an excellent service is not easy, but it is possible. The challenge is to balance many concepts and realities, but adjustments are always possible, even if they are not always easy to implement.

4

CAPACITY MANAGEMENT

Operational and Psychological Components

4.1 The importance of managing capacity

Capacity management is important to service managers because of its impact on system productivity. Capacity places physical or other limitations on the number of customers that can be served and often on the type of service that can be provided. A 500-seat theatre can only accommodate 500 people. Productions with a break-even point of 600 people can be held there only at a financial loss. Although it usually reflects an opportunity to improve productivity, unused capacity may come at a cost, both in the price of the extra facilities and in the changed nature of the service. Teaching a class of 50 in a lecture hall designed for 250 is less intimate than in a smaller room. And performing in a partially filled theatre puts extra pressure on the players and other staff.

Managing service capacity is not easy. Once a facility is built, its size and features tend to be permanent unless significant additional expenditures are made. Every manager has to live from time to time with rooms that are too big or too small, with computer systems that can't handle the latest software or with equipment that doesn't have the desired features. There are exceptions of course. Some organizations can easily rent space and others don't use much equipment. Consulting firms might be cited as examples. For others, however, the cost of errors in utilization is extremely high. For example, it takes at least ten years to plan and build a major hydroelectric dam or nuclear reactor.

Fluctuations in service demand compound the difficulty of managing capacity. Fluctuations can be extreme but very regular, with differing periods: yearly (outdoor pools or ski hills), weekly (Friday evening shopping) or hourly (public commuter transit or restaurants), or they can have periods of different length. They may also be very unpredictable, as will be attested to by any grocery store manager trying to have exactly the right number of cashiers on duty at all times. Demand fluctuations and the general absence of inventory buffers put a premium on demand forecasting.

Customers are one source of uncertainty and thus of fluctuation, not only in demand, but in capacity as well.[285] In the case of a restaurant, it is difficult to forecast how many customers will arrive, in what size groups, when, what they will want to eat, what other services they will ask for and how long they will stay. The higher the degree of uncertainty in these variables, the more difficult it will be to operate at a satisfactory level of efficiency over an extended period.

How can a manager decide what the optimal capacity is? What level of capacity utilization is acceptable? Many managers in manufacturing facilities aim for utilization rates near 100%. Managers of job shops, however, in which flexibility is a key success factor, feel uncomfortable with such a high rate. The high level of uncertainty in many services facilities also supports a lower utilization rate and thus lower efficiency. The trade-off may be high utilization versus maintaining enough capacity to serve a 'special' customer on short notice, or it may be high utilization versus high quality. In many service industries, quality deteriorates beyond a certain utilization rate. Any commuter caught in a seemingly endless traffic jam, or any relative of a seriously ill patient awaiting a hospital bed will confirm that fact.

It is not easy to set optimal levels. Figure 4-1 illustrates a situation with an optimum near 70% — enough to keep human providers busy but with time to serve customers individually and enough capacity in reserve so as not to pose too many managerial headaches. The 70% figure, although arbitrary, has some support in computer systems; computer companies suggest adding capacity even when utilization rates are below 70% to avoid excessive response time. Each organization must decide for itself what capacity utilization rate it wishes to have.

The optimal utilization rate is very context-specific. Low rates are appropriate when both the degree of uncertainty and the stakes are high. For example, hospital emergency rooms and fire departments should aim for low utilization because of the high level of uncertainty and the life or death nature of their activities. Relatively predictable services such as commuter trains or service factories without customer contact, such as postal sorting operations, can plan to operate much nearer 100% utilization. Interestingly, there is a third group for which high utilization is

FIGURE 4-1   Relationship between the rate of service utilization (r) and service quality

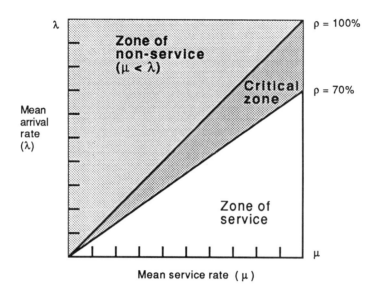

desirable. Baseball and hockey teams like sell-outs, not only because of the virtually 100% contribution margin of each customer, but because a full house creates an atmosphere that pleases custsomers, motivates the home team to perform better and boosts future ticket sales. Stage performances and bars share this phenomenon. On the other hand, many airline passengers feel that a flight is too crowded when the seat next to theirs is occupied. Airlines capitalize on this response to sell more business class seats.

Many enterprises prefer not to operate too close to capacity at all times. They fear that at peak demand they would be forced to make unacceptable compromises to service quality, or have to invest in expensive facilities and equipment needed only during the peak. Disruptions in mail service force courier services to lower their service level to regular customers, knowing that few of their new customers will remain once mail service is restored. Of course, for those new customers, service is as good as possible in an attempt to hold onto them permanently. Electricity companies want to encourage electricity use but meeting peak demand is very costly. Capacity utilization of 95%, which may occur only on the coldest or hottest days, forces them to operate marginally profitable facilities and to consider long-term investments very carefully.

Customers have expectations regarding capacity. The authors of one study concluded that 75% of incidents in service encounters can be traced to customer expectations exceeding the system's capacity to deliver service.[227] It is no simple task to balance attracting new customers with ensuring that the organization can provide them with service, let alone excellent service.

4.2   Some observations on queues

One logical outcome of demand exceeding capacity is the formation of a queue of customers waiting for service. Queues are everywhere in operations management, but in services, they have particular significance because they are often made up of potential customers.

As noted above, many customers become unhappy because system capacity cannot satisfy their expectations. Poor information or a misleading previous experience might lead to unrealistic customer expectations. When a system's capacity is not sufficient to meet those expectations, some customers have to wait. Waiting time is often considered to be valuable time wasted, although the effect of a wait depends very much on the individual and his or her circumstances.

Queuing phenomena have been well studied by operations research scholars, who have developed theory and simulation models to address queuing problems. These techniques are of undeniable benefit to managers. Any introductory text on operations management, operations research or management science has chapters dealing with these topics; examples of practical applications abound. Their main use is in giving managers tools to answer 'what if' questions quickly and cheaply.

Queuing has also been examined from the point of view of its psychological impact on customers. Larson noted that the actual or perceived utility of participating in the system depends on average waiting time, the waiting environment and the extent of feedback the customer is given about delays.[167] He concluded that the perception of waiting depends on various factors including the actual waiting time, the urgency of the service, the customers' perception of fairness, the pleasantness of the surroundings, and the adequacy, timeliness and tone of information regarding the cause and expected duration of delays.

Maister developed eight similar propositions about queuing:

1. unoccupied time feels longer than occupied time
2. pre-process waiting feels longer than in-process waiting
3. anxiety makes waiting seem longer
4. uncertain waits seem longer than known, finite waits
5. unexplained waits seem longer than explained waits
6. unfair waits seem longer than equitable waits

7. the more valuable the service, the longer the customer will wait
8. solo waits seem longer than group waits.[194]

Although none of these propositions has been rigorously tested, there are undoubtedly numerous examples to support them.

Figure 4-2 shows a number of relevant factors with the customer purposely at the focal point. The various factors can be summarized in the following statement, one which every manager might be wise to have engraved above his or her desk: the longer a customer waits (or thinks he or she waits), the less adequate the information provided, the less fair he or she considers the wait and the less interesting the waiting environment, the more likely it is that a customer will be dissatisfied with or leave the system.

FIGURE 4-2   Psychological factors related to waiting time

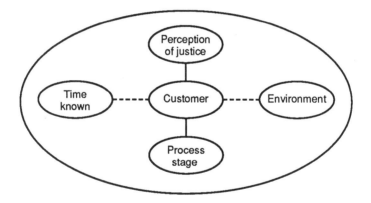

One airline received numerous complaints about waiting times for luggage in Houston. Studies showed that the wait was only seven minutes, one minute less than the industry standard, but that passengers arrived at the carousel only one minute after leaving the plane. The airline solved the problem by moving the carousel so that passengers had a six-minute walk and only a one-minute wait. Complaints virtually disappeared. London's Heathrow 4 terminal was designed with exactly this approach in mind.

Adjusting actual and perceived waiting times is only one simple tool available to managers. Another, often used in restaurants, is to tell the customer that his or her wait will be 15 minutes when the staff members really expect a ten-minute wait. This strategy, although ethically questionable, serves to put the customer in a good mood when the wait is shorter than indicated, and to protect the staff when the wait is actually 15 minutes. Lies are acceptable only if the result is to the customer's benefit. This strategy can backfire, however. During the wait for a delayed VIA Rail train, VIA staff announced that the new boarding time would be in about 30 minutes, upon which several waiting passengers left the queue to make phone calls or go to the bar. Several asked those remaining in line to watch their luggage. Boarding actually began, without public notice, only 10 minutes after the announcement. Imagine the feelings of the customers who had left the line. When they returned, they found the queue gone and possibly their luggage as well. Think of the dilemma of those asked to guard luggage. Should they stay and risk missing the train? Should they go but leave the luggage (which might be stolen)? Or should they board with the luggage (and risk being accused of theft)?

Other managerial tools include ensuring that the queue moves frequently and processing people at some point early in the queue. These approaches give the illusion that something is happening. For those who doubt their effectiveness, try allowing a gap to develop in front of you in a queue. Take one big step infrequently rather than frequent small ones. As long as you are at the front of the line when processing begins, it will do nothing to affect the total time you or anyone else spends in the line. But the people behind you will start trying to lead the queue from the back by applying subtle and not-so-subtle pressure to get you to move.

Sometimes a customer may choose among multiple, apparently identical queues. This set-up, common at grocery store checkouts, toll booths and fast-food chains, gives the customer a feeling of partial control (although 'the other line always moves faster'). Many banks have adopted a single-queue arrangement, which is faster and seen to be fairer but eliminates the element of choice. It was a reluctance to deny customers the illusion of control that delayed the widespread adoption of this queuing arrangement.

Single lines have disadvantages, too. If customers can switch lines, many of the theoretical advantages of a single queue fail.[257] Also, single queues imply identical servers, and implementing them makes it difficult to designate one for express transactions, cash only or business accounts. Having identical servers forces each staff member to be able to offer all services, therefore implying the same level of training for all. Thus, servers are likely to be over-trained for routine transactions and under-trained for the most complex transactions. Instead of eight to ten lines with many types of staff or a single line with only one type of staff, a compromise of approximately two lines and three types of staff (routine transactions, difficult transactions, flexible staff) is attractive.[3] This solution, already successfully implemented in some financial institutions, is shown in Figure 4-3.

FIGURE 4-3   Changing a queue from passive to active (better adapted)

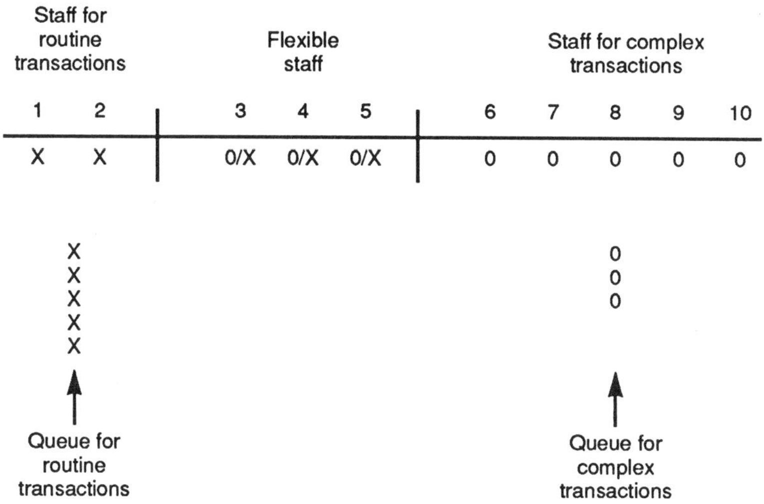

Staff for routine transactions		Flexible staff			Staff for complex transactions				
1	2	3	4	5	6	7	8	9	10
X	X	O/X	O/X	O/X	O	O	O	O	O

```
        X                                           O
        X                                           O
        X                                           O
        X
        X

        ↑                                           ↑

   Queue for                                    Queue for
    routine                                      complex
  transactions                                 transactions
```

SOURCE: Adapted from Ament (reference 3)

Altering the number of servers (tellers in banks, cashiers in grocery stores) is another managerial tool. The organization might have a rule like 'add another server if the line(s) exceeds three' and a corresponding rule for subtracting servers. Philosophically such rules look good but the second person in line may not appreciate it if the third in line gets served first at a newly opened counter, and no one appreciates it if his or her line is suddenly closed. Clearly, in systems which process customers through several points sequentially, such as a cafeteria line, adding capacity at non-bottleneck operations will not reduce overall processing time. Ideally, all stages operate at the same rate so that there are no bottlenecks. With good design and proper training, such systems can be developed. Most fast food operations are well balanced.

Queuing is also found in telecommunication systems. Figure 4-4 is a flow-chart for a telephone call entering a system. If all lines are busy, the caller will get a busy signal. Otherwise an operator answers the call or the caller is placed in a queue, often with a message asking the caller to wait so as to maintain his or her position in the queue. It is usually fruitless to have too large a queue because callers will soon hang up (unless the call

**FIGURE 4-4   System of service demand for routing a
telephone call**

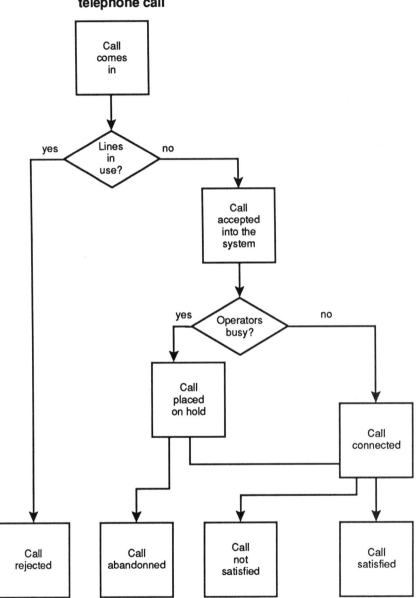

is extremely important or the party is very hard to reach). Some systems
play music to make the waiting time seem shorter. Other organizations
prefer to advertise to this captive audience or give out relatively interesting
information. A few organizations do this so well that callers sometimes

phone back and ask to be put in the queue to hear the rest of the message!

Defining suitable service levels is often directly related to the waiting time that customers will accept. One service bureau defined its acceptable service level this way: no caller should wait more than 30 seconds, normal callers should get a busy signal less than 10% of the time and priority customers should get a busy signal less than 4% of the time.[219] Their chore then consisted of determining the required number of servers for various call frequencies. This is a particular problem for emergency services and is relatively easy to solve using simulation, provided that representative historical data is available.

Controlling Supply and Altering Demand

The equilibrium between supply and demand can be expressed as an equation. Supply of capacity and demand for capacity are rarely in balance, although balance is usually desirable. One of the service manager's jobs is to try to keep the equation nearly balanced by altering supply and/or demand.

4.3   Chase demand versus level capacity strategies

One strategy for staying in balance is to adjust production levels to match demand patterns — the chase demand approach. Alternatively, the production rate can be held constant with demand patterns ignored. In manufacturing systems, inventory usually allows level production, although it may be an expensive strategy. Level production is clearly attractive because resource use is predictable and planning, scheduling, etc. become much easier. However, as Sasser noted:

> Although the chase demand strategy has many negative connotations for enlightened managers, there are some service delivery systems, such as amusement parks and resort hotels with highly seasonal or random fluctuations in demand, that survive only as a result of its successful application.[265, p. 137]

Clearly, managing staff level variations is a key component of a chase strategy. Using part-time employees and split shifts are two common tactics (for example, in fast food restaurants or public transit). A large pool of part-time workers available on short notice and/or staff with multiple skills add to managerial flexibility (Figure 4-5). Conversely, a staff of specialized, permanent workers restricts managerial flexibility. Unfortunately, many public sector services are inflexible for this reason.

**FIGURE 4-5   Overall flexibility in the management of personnel
and operations**

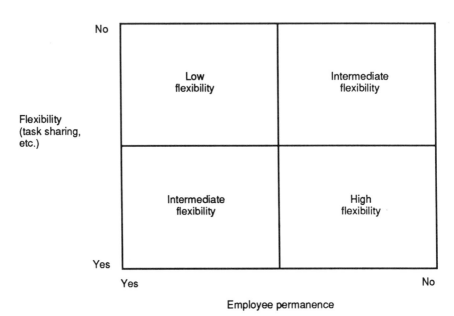

In its pure form, a level strategy provides the same amount of service capacity regardless of changes in demand. In contrast, a pure chase strategy changes capacity continuously so that it just matches demand. Naturally, neither strategy is commonly found in its pure state. Instead, many hybrid stragegies are used; some resemble level strategies and some look like chase strategies. Figure 4-6 illustrates two possible hybrids. Figure 4-7 describes how the choice of strategy depends on technology and customer participation in the service. Level strategies are used in operating rooms, on highways and in other situations that use a lot of fixed assets; in situations with highly skilled and paid staff, low turnover and high training costs; and in systems with low customer contact and interaction.[265] Service managers are all well aware, of course, that if demand exceeds capacity, service will deteriorate and business may be lost.

4.4   Influencing demand

As indicated above, the capacity supply and demand equation can be managed on either side. A number of variables can be used to affect demand. Price is an obvious one. Some organizations charge higher prices at peak times (or lower prices during low periods) to transfer

FIGURE 4-6   Demand variations as a function of capacity

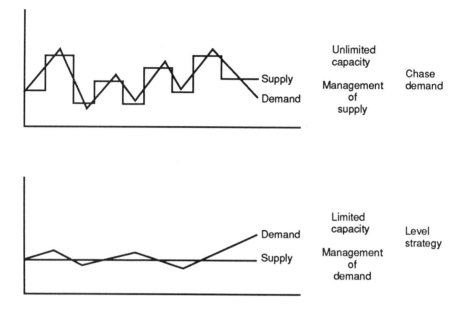

FIGURE 4-7   Influence of technology and client participation
on strategies for managing capacity

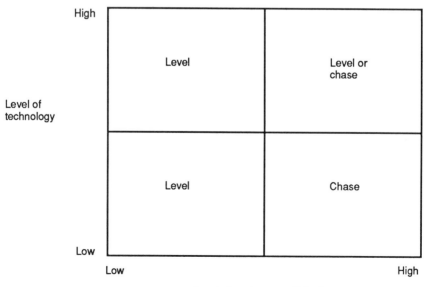

demand to non-peak periods (or to generate more revenue during peaks). Resorts, for example, offer mid-week or off-season specials. Although pre-Christmas sales are not unknown (especially in bad economic times), post-Christmas sales are much more common. Telephone companies and some electricity companies have time-dependent rates; others have usage-dependent rates — high use can be rewarded or penalized.

Indirect price incentives can also be used. Examples include free parking, reduced air fares if the journey involves a Saturday night stay, and time-dependent coupons handed out during off-peak periods or for use only during certain periods. Another example is to offer complementary services to complete a package — hotels cater primarily to business travellers during the week but offer special menus and activities to attract families on weekends.

Another way to affect demand for service capacity, although not necessarily for the service itself, is to design the service to be very efficient. Thus, the scarce resource can be very productive. Restaurants like McDonald's and Benihana of Tokyo are notable examples. One helpful design feature is requiring the customer to participate actively in service production. For example, at one time, all phone calls were channelled through operators but today self-dialing is almost universal. Similarly, fast food operations have eliminated the need for table service by actively involving customers.

Reservation systems are another way to manage, if not alter, demand. Reservation systems can give the service organization valuable advance notice of demand so it can adjust supply accordingly. They also reduce a major problem found in non-reservation systems — customers waiting in a queue for service and becoming angry and frustrated as a result. Of course, although customers may not be happy waiting, they usually expect to wait for a non-reservation service. Not so when a reservation is accepted. Now there is an implicit obligation. The customer expects to be served on time, so waiting takes on an added dimension. Doctors are notorious for not meeting appointment times. The implicit message from the doctor is: my time is worth more than yours. One Quebec medical facility's practice was to give ten pediatric patients appointments for 10:00 a.m. The last to be seen, at 12:30 p.m., was quite angry. In such a case, the doctor's time is fully and efficiently utilized, but at the patient's expense. Unfortunately, customer behavior often hinders the ability of service managers to plan. Restaurant, hotel and airline patrons are notorious for making reservations and then not showing up. Some of these service firms bill the customers, hold the reservation until a set time or deliberately over-book, as in the medical example above. In such cases, the customer believes he or she has a guaranteed reservation, while the service manager treats it as a statement of hours the facility is open. Needless to say, under these circumstances, misunderstanding is inevitable.

Before managers change the services offered, they should at least know the characteristics of their demand. How predictable is it? What causes variations and how can they be managed? Can the arrival rate of customers be controlled? How can demand be segmented and is it useful to do so? Figure 4-8 is one interesting model to help managers think about the possible implications of demand fluctuations and how demand might be satisfied (if meeting demand is intended).[185] Some services face large fluctuations regularly; sometimes they may not be able to meet demand, despite general expectations to the contrary. Emergency services and electricity supply are two quite inflexible services which should meet peak demand.

FIGURE 4-8   The nature of service supply and demand

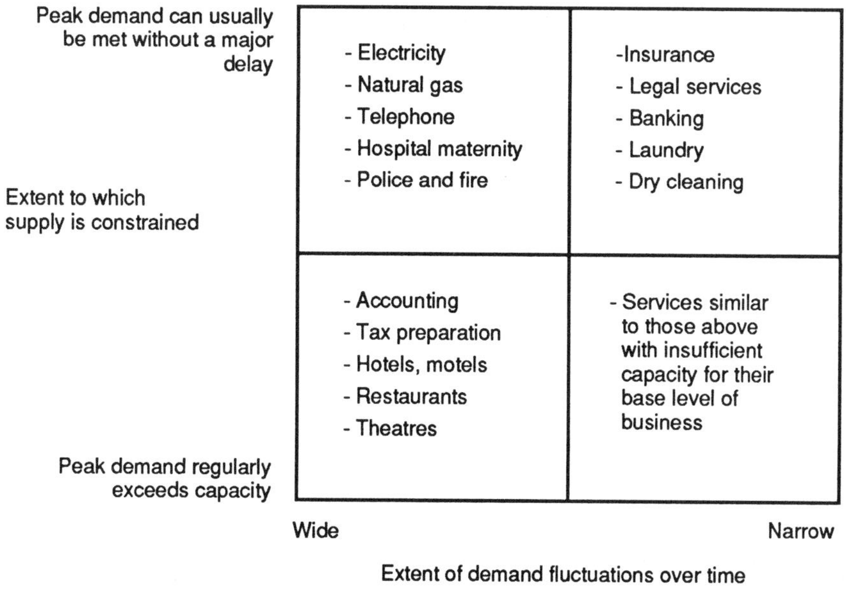

Peak demand can usually be met without a major delay	- Electricity - Natural gas - Telephone - Hospital maternity - Police and fire	-Insurance - Legal services - Banking - Laundry - Dry cleaning
Extent to which supply is constrained		
Peak demand regularly exceeds capacity	- Accounting - Tax preparation - Hotels, motels - Restaurants - Theatres	- Services similar to those above with insufficient capacity for their base level of business
	Wide Narrow	
	Extent of demand fluctuations over time	

SOURCE: Adapted from Lovelock (reference 185)

4.5   Modifying capacity

Unlike demand, which usually varies in small increments, capacity often has to be added in large blocks. A marginally larger client base may require a financial institution to buy a new office. A moderate population increase may require a new fire truck to meet acceptable service levels, and of course, a building to house it and someone to drive it. An extra kilowatt may require a new power station. It is unlikely that such a large capital investment will be made at the margin, so shortages are common. Many power systems are now facing very high peak period utilization and have told customers that shortages are possible. Even labor, considered by many to be a variable cost, tends to be added in large steps. An extra worker may be needed for only 15 minutes but labor laws often set a few hours as the minimum work period once the worker is called out. Naturally service organizations prefer to examine alternatives to capacity addition.

Although customer participation was discussed above as a means of reducing demand for capacity, it might just as accurately be thought of as a way to increase capacity, particularly if training costs are low. During one strike by hospital workers, patients' relatives were asked to provide the required daily patient care. Not only did this tactic provide service at a low cost, but apparently the patients' medical conditions improved much more quickly than usual. In this case, the quality of the service increased as well.

Capacity addition is sometimes necessary but there are a number of pitfalls to avoid. One danger is losing focus. Loss of focus can result from diversifying the product line, from directing managerial attention to activities other than satisfying customers activities (activities such as site selection and financing) or from simply being too big. Every organization has an optimum size and capacity utilization which are difficult to determine in advance but evident once they have been exceeded. Managers hate to hear customers complaining that service is not what it used to be — it's a warning that at some point they might lose them.

A second pitfall to avoid is adding the wrong type of capacity. Many airlines have at one time or another added aircraft that did not ultimately fit the needs of various routes. The typical problem was buying large planes becaue managers observed that the company flying the most seats on a route had a disproportionately large market share. Later it was recognized that flight frequency is a more important factor in determining market share than the number of seats flown.

A third pitfall is to add capacity in only part, or in the wrong section, of the service. Adding capacity to only a portion of a well-balanced service creates bottlenecks which restrict overall capacity. Naturally, adding capacity at non-bottleneck steps will neither increase overall capacity nor eliminate the bottleneck. Managers must know where the problem is and how capacity additions will affect it. Most managers think primarily, even exclusively, about core services. But the package is complex and peripheral services must be maintained, too. Not to do so threatens the organization's focus.

Competitors' reactions are another potential pitfall. Mining, smelting, forest products, chemicals and agriculture are known for their cycles. Many add capacity at the same time so the market swings widely from under- to over-supply. Services are no different. Addition of capacity in a balanced market can make every organization providing that service poorer.

Organizations can also undermine themselves. Providing fifth-class cruise passengers with first- or second-class service reduces the likelihood that they will upgrade their class (at a higher price) on the next trip. An organization should adhere to its stated standards unless the temporary changes are well controlled and part of a well-thought-through strategy. Otherwise, very profitable capacity might remain unused. Airlines that occasionally bump economy passengers to first- or business-class seem to manage it well. It is a last resort. Bumping is made quite clear so the customer is not confused. And the integrity of the service is maintained, reinforced by physical separation and visible evidence.

One option that can increase capacity is sharing capacity with another organization. Data bases and communication networks make it increasingly easy to share, as long as demand does not all occur at the same time. New service businesses have developed to provide shared office facilities to travelling businessmen. In these cases, overall capacity can be increased; in others, an increase in capacity for one organization comes at the expense of another. One bus service rented buses to another when the first faced a decline in passengers and the second, an increase. The deal required changing three panels on each bus — a mere 18 screws per bus.

One possible response to a capacity problem is to deliberately stock out. In retailing, this approach is common: try looking for a morning paper in the evening. However, cutting back need not result in a stock-out. Some electricity companies, notably New Zealand's, can shut off privately-owned devices, such as water heaters, electronically during peak periods; most home owners do not mind waiting a little while for hot water and storage tanks may make the company's smoothing of the peak invisible.

Good design can also help to increase capacity. Flexible facilities allow multiple uses. A simple example is the installation of movable walls in offices or teaching facilities. The seating arrangement in Toronto's Sky Dome allows it to be used for many different types of sporting and other events. Design can also determine where a bottleneck will be. On one championship golf course, the bottleneck is at the 11th hole.[114] Golf course bottlenecks are best at the 1st or the 10th holes so golfers wait near the club house where food and beverages are available. Had the problem been understood as the course was being designed, it could have been avoided. Simple simulation models are useful tools for such cases. Effective golf course management can also speed play. Cutting trees and grass, helping players find balls, placing flagsticks on easy parts of the green, and encouraging good golf etiquette are all useful ways to add capacity.

Hospitals, too, need extra capacity. A common approach to meeting departmental demand for nurses is to use 'flying teams' of highly skilled nurses, knowledgeable enough to help any understaffed department.[108] In the past, most hospitals relied on estimates and normal staffing levels to decide whether a department had enough staff, but newer methods allow better evaluation of departmental workload and therefore, of the need for additional staff. However, if this strategy is to work, the staff must be flexible. If personnel are not flexible, demand increases will generate increased waiting time or lower service levels. One social service had three stages: screening, evaluation and orientation, and therapy. Government funding attention on only one stage caused an imbalance and consequently a queue in later stages.

Clearly, intelligent scheduling can help to alleviate capacity problems. If two shifts are used, it makes sense, if at all possible, to overlap them at peak demand periods. Also, if demand peaks occur at lunch, it is advantageous to schedule staff lunches before and/or after that peak and to use the period just before the peak to prepare for it as much as possible. Similar adjustments can be made for annual peaks.

Another capacity-increasing strategy is to subcontract work out. The biggest danger in doing so is the loss of control over operations and the likelihood that customers will receive inconsistent or low quality service as a result. This can confuse customers and lead to lost business, and should perhaps be limited to non-customer-contact services. As was noted in Chapter 1, one reason for growth in the service sector is that manufacturing companies are buying services rather than providing their own.

Public services also face capacity problems. The Scottsdale (Arizona) Rural Metro Fire Department had some relatively small, cheap trucks that required few personnel but they had an unusually high pumping rate.[121] Fire data analysis showed that rapid response and application of large volumes of water as soon as possible were helpful in reducing fire losses. Part of the organization's ability to respond rapidly lay in its microfiche files of building layouts, which allowed fire department staff to study the layout while they were travelling to the fire. The fire fighters were able to get to know the building well before they arrived and get at the fire more quickly. This department's flexible, high-capacity equipment and operating practices meant it could meet demand effectively.

In any management of capacity, it is crucial to understand the problem fully. One author, in analyzing a specific traffic problem, wrote:

> Nonsignalized treatments such as parking control, regulation of turns and lane arrangement, are designed to increase capacity. Two of the most frequent violations that aggravate the congestion problems are intersection blockage and parking regulation violations.[244, p. 82]

By controlling traffic signals and reducing queues, the number of vehicles was increased by up to 20% and queues that back up through intersections were reduced by up to 91 %.

The above examples show that the proper use of tools to manage capacity can be very valuable in allowing service organizations to provide customers with the desired service level. However, it is frequently the quality of the service that is the key to retaining customers. Of course, capacity is a component of quality, but there are other factors and considerations which will be dealt with in the next chapter.

CHAPTER

5

MANAGING SERVICE QUALITY

Welcome to Quality in Services!

5.1 A preview of service quality

Many manufacturing companies produce only a few defective units per million. As good as that is, their customers demand even more — zero defects! Executives with experience in both manufacturing and services agree that reaching consistent quality in services is even more difficult than in manufacturing.[121] Many factors can cause service errors: labor, equipment, the service delivery system and the customers themselves. A consultant may do a brilliant piece of work with sparkling analysis and superb recommendations, but if he or she writes the report poorly, the client may well conclude that the study itself is flawed, or at least suspect. The converse may also be true, of course, as many a wealthy promoter knows full well! All steps in the service process, especially those involving the customer, must be designed carefully and performed well. The customer's impression is often closely related to the service package's weakest link and, unlike the situation for manufacturers, the customer's impression of the process is often more important than his or her impression of the final outcome. In Sherden's words:

> Product quality refers to whether a product or service functions as promised ... Product quality is the most tangible aspect of quality, and for some companies, the only aspect they consider.

> Service quality, in contrast, encompasses all the elements involved in delivering a product or service, from the initial contact through the actual sale to the subsequent servicing. Service quality can be thought

of as forming the context in which the product or service exists. Despite its intangibility, it is emerging as a new frontier of competition.[271, p. 45]

Numerous authors have proposed other definitions of service quality, ranging from 'conformance to requirements,' to 'creating value for the customer' and 'process versus output quality.' It is clear, however, that a customer has to be satisfied with each of the service components to be satisfied overall.

Many writers have stressed the need for top management support to implement change effectively. This is not surprising because top management deals with all functional areas, allocates budgets, establishes the reward system and sets organizational culture. All top managers are interested in achieving a suitable return on investments. In some cases measurement is relatively easy. In others, for example, improving service to customers who evaluate service quality very subjectively, the ROI is not at all easy to determine. As Figure 5-1 illustrates, organizations must reach an equilibrium between producing a level of quality that is too expensive (over-quality) and one that is below customer perceptions and expectations (under-quality).

FIGURE 5-1   Quality: A question of balance

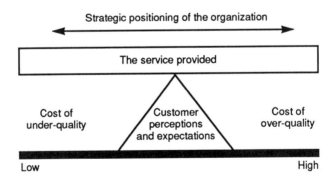

Quality in a service organization is composed of the following three elements:

a)   the level of service offered corresponding to the strategic positioning on the high-low scale adopted by the organization

b)   the expectations of the customer (the image of service quality that he or she anticipates receiving)

c)   the actual service offered as perceived by the customer.

A very useful way to deal with customer expectations is to analyze problematic and unpleasant situations (critical incidents) faced by customers. One study examined 205 critical incidents in 15 firms.[73] Although all 15 firms were manufacturers, some of the lessons are equally applicable to service firms. The author found that customers can overlook occasional incidents if they have confidence in the seller. Because of service intangibility, confidence may or may not be easy to develop. Many critical incidents can strengthen relationships and build confidence if the organization handles them correctly. Also, customers respond positively when they are properly informed about the incident and offered adequate compensation. Service managers might find it worthwhile to offer a free meal or a free ticket, depending on the nature of the service. Of course, if the complaint is a general one about service quality, an offer to experience it again may not be well received. Finally, although managers may well regard critical incidents as failures, they can also be regarded as opportunities to show customers what the organization can do for them. In other words, they can be viewed the same way manufacturing errors are viewed in Japan — as treasures to help improvement.

5.2   Getting to quality

Staff members are more likely to commit themselves to providing high quality service to customers when top management is clearly serious about it. Nothing makes a greater impact than guaranteeing satisfaction unconditionally.[104] As Al Burger, a pioneer in offering unconditional service guarantees, said, "Clients hired us to eliminate their pest problems not because we cost less, or worked faster, but because we guaranteed results. Unconditionally."[31, p. 124] Burger's guarantee was important because it was not added to an existing service as an afterthought for marketing advantage, but rather formed the underlying corporate philosophy around which the organization was built. With the potential of large payments to unsatisfied customers, a question quickly arises: "How can we design this organization to ensure that customers are satisfied?" Burger achieved spectacular results. Despite fees that were up to ten times those of competitors, the company had a disproportionately high market share. It paid out only $120,000 in 1986 on sales of $33 million. Burger believed so strongly in his philosophy that, when he sold his company, he specifically sought buyers who shared his values.[104]

The above example shows the value of a clear service concept aimed at getting results, the overwhelming incentive for using a company's services. Had Burger's company failed to live up to its promise, business would likely have dropped and the company would have had to pay out on its guarantee. It should be emphasized that in this example, although many factors play a role in customers' evaluation of quality (operator politeness and clealiness, types of machines used, techniques used, odor, etc.), the relatively easy verification of results and the impersonal nature of the service help to define quality.

It takes substantial effort to achieve quality. Not the least of these efforts must be in the area of the performance of both the customer and the server. Their behavior, judgment and interaction affect the service and its quality. In Chase's words:

> While technological devices can be substituted for some jobs performed by direct-contact workers, the worker's attitude, the environment of the facility and the attitude of the customer will determine the ultimate quality of the service experience.[39, p. 140]

Obviously many factors must be considered to achieve high quality. One paper proposed that each of the following five criteria must be met to achieve high quality:

1. services offered should be properly matched with the needs of the target market segment
2. the core service should be beyond reproach
3. the peripheral services should be at least satisfactory
4. all services should form a coherent package
5. continuous attention should be paid to all details.[76]

In other words, the service must be internally consistent and directed at a specific market segment (focused), and be delivered well. The numerous examples and concepts presented in this book help to show how these criteria should be applied to achieve the desired quality.

In high contact and interaction services, 'quality' may be confused with 'personalized.' What does 'personalized' mean?[284] Longer time with the customer? Offering advice? Small talk? Taking a personal interest in the customer? Smiles and eye contact with a friendly greeting? A basic service to meet customer needs and tastes? Although Surprenant and Solomon ask the question, they don't answer it beyond posing several possibilities. To what extent does service excellence in high contact and interaction services depend on achieving the right combination of all these details? The proper perception of customer expectations by service designers, coupled with service providers' ability to adapt the designed service to each customer, can be a potent combination despite the fact that such an approach increases service variability. Small grocery store owners use this approach. As a result, market shares of independent grocery stores have been rising for some years as the shares of larger, more impersonal supermarkets have dropped. Many authors suggest using a TLC approach (which can stand equally well for Tender Loving Care and Think Like a Customer) to achieve a proper level of quality.

One model of service quality includes three groups of components: physical (facilities, facilitating goods) and procedural, behavioral (attentiveness, speed, etc.), and judgmental (diagnosis, advice, knowledge). This model, represented as a triangle (Figure 5-2), proposes that to achieve high quality, an organization must strike a proper balance between the three groups of components. The question is, where should the organization be positioned in the triangle? The balance can — indeed must — be managed: getting it wrong can be disastrous. Too much emphasis on procedures often causes customers to feel they are being treated like numbers. It can also create a staff that is preoccupied with 'following the book' rather than delivering effective service. This attitude is often associated with bureaucracies, which emphasize avoiding errors and ensuring that the control system is properly followed. Public services are a prime example of this problem because extensive controls are coupled with little motivation to interpret the rules to satisfy the customer. Indeed, in many systems, workers who violate the rules, no matter what the reason, are punished.

FIGURE 5-2   Achieving quality in services

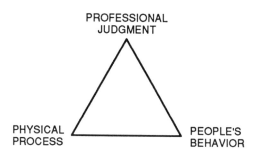

SOURCE: Adapted from Haywood-Farmer (reference 112)

An overemphasis on behavioral elements creates the risk of having staff members who are very personable but who lack the ability to satisfy customer needs efficiently. If such a scenario arises, it should serve as a signal that managers could improve operations by placing more emphasis on procedural and/or judgmental elements. Possibly, better training or having different staff would improve matters. Dull jobs where employees lack the whole picture, or complex jobs that they don't understand are the sorts of situations in which this problem arises. Employees try to compensate for their lack of motivation or ability by being very nice.

An organization emphasizing professional judgment favors flexibility over efficiency and pleasant behavior toward customers. Customers are perceived as less important than the problem the organization is solving. This is typical of professionals with unique expertise who may perform brilliantly in diagnosing and solving a problem, but may be rude to clients, and are often late in delivering results and doing paper work, much to the despair of both the client and management.

Clearly, different positioning within the triangle of Figure 5-2 is appropriate for different organizations. One way to decide what might be appropriate is to relate the choice of emphasis to the service characteristics shown in Figure 2-14.[112] Organizations with high contact and interaction, labor intensity, and customization require quite different approaches to quality from those that are low in any of these dimensions.

In short, it is clear that the more attention an organization pays to its service delivery system design, operating details, and staff training and motivation, the more likely it is to achieve its desired level of quality.

Perceived versus Actual Quality

5.3   Customer evaluation of service quality

Discussions of service organizations often emphasize the difficulty of evaluating service quality. Prospective customers are unable to measure quality directly. Before actually experiencing the service, they must use surrogate measures to make decisions such as which service firm, or which of several service options from a single firm, to accept. Organizations choose auditors and individuals choose vacation packages by relying on surrogate measures and perhaps testimonials from previous customers. The surrogate measures are often the physical evidence components of the service concept discussed in Chapter 2.

Naturally, impressions are crucial in evaluating intangible services. Customers often choose the cleaner of two service stations — a clean outside may signify clean washrooms. Similarly a repair technician who arrives in a clean truck, is polite and takes some time to explain the problem to the appliance owner is more likely to be called back than one who does not look or act as friendly but who may do a better technical job. Written reports face the same fate: if it looks nice, is inside a clean binder, spells the company officer's names correctly and is thick enough to justify the cost, its recipients are much less likely to dig deeply into it for flaws than if it lacks these characteristics.

Customer perceptions of quality are also based on what the provider appears to be doing during the service. Appliance technicians who comfort the customer by telling him or her that there are only three possible causes for the problem described and giving approximate repair costs have gone a long way toward developing customer confidence. Having the right tools, always giving the impression of knowing what's going on and suggesting ways to make a machine last longer or run better all make a good impression on the customer. Doing a good job is not enough; you must be perceived to be doing a good job. Marketing and human aspects are at least as important as operations in this context.

Customer expectations influence perceptions of quality. A taxpayer who phones a government office is happily surprised when employees will look up appropriate phone numbers for him or her, especially if that assistance is volunteered cheerfully. Organizations with excellent service reputations either live up to them or they don't. However, organizations with less auspicious reputations can benefit greatly when their service improves because customer expectations, justified or not, are lower than the service experienced. In the mid-1980s, TWA hired 2800 flight attendants to replace striking staff. Naturally, that number of new employees put severe pressure on training. Initially, the new staff did not have time to learn how to operate the ovens so no hot meals were served during that period.[191] But what did passengers expect when they heard that there was a strike? Because their expectations were lowered and they could at least fly (unlike Eastern Airline's customers in 1989), the customers did not perceive the quality of service to be unacceptably low.

Complaints about bad service are frequent but rave reviews about great service rare. Why? Is service really all that bad? Do we have a cultural bias toward complaint and against compliment? Or it is a measurement problem? Many services work so smoothly that the customer is unaware of even receiving a service, let alone a good service. This leads to an interesting and frustrating phenomenon: in superb services, quality may not even be noticed. As Levitt said,

> Unique to intangible products is the fact that the customer is seldom aware of being served well. This is especially so in the case of intangible products that have, for the duration of the contract, constant continuity ... Consumers usually don't know what they're getting until they don't get it.[175, p. 99]

Electricity, freight hauling and cleaning are examples of services we pay for and assume will be perfect. Under such an assumption, small problems might appear to be big ones. Smart competitors will take advantage of this unless customers realize how well served they have been. Organizations would be wise to tell them.

Some customers are willing to pay to get good service. Customers often use price to judge service quality, especially when the service is not well understood or when the risk is high. Wedding receptions often cost more than expected; the main reason may not be a conscious attempt to be ostentatious but rather a willingness of the decision-makers to pay a higher price to give them a greater sense of security. Hotels are more expensive but less risky than community halls. Similarly, many tourists travelling in developing countries prefer to purchase first-class tickets and go to hotels such as the Hilton rather than settle for cheaper transport and accommodation where they could mix more with the local population. Mingling with 'locals' gives a tourist a much more intimate view of the culture, but many perceive it to entail risks.

The criteria that customers use to evaluate services are very subjective. They vary with circumstances and from customer to customer. Providers who know what criteria customers use are in a much better position to design the service to meet those criteria or to tell the customer what to expect in light of their criteria. One tourist got a flat tire on his motorcycle 25 miles from the nearest garage while crossing a desert on a very hot day. A month earlier he had purchased two cans of a product that was supposed to seal the hole in a flat tire and inflate it to 20 psi. Although he hoped and expected that they would perform as promised, both cans failed. The author then installed a new tube but pinched (and punctured) it in the final operation. Finally, he resorted to his last option. He installed a tube in which he had had seven punctures repaired the previous day at an unattractive local garage. He had little faith in either the garage or the repair job. Despite his misgivings, he hoped that it would do the trick. It did: that service had performed well.

This example illustrates well the situation-dependent nature of service quality as perceived by customers. Under 'normal' circumstances, customers with flat tires might be interested in such service elements as cost, speed, timing and convenience. Under the conditions described, however, those criteria pale in significance compared to any solution that will work. Sasser, et al. allude to this type of situation when they present three models of quality evaluation: customers evaluate quality based on either one overpowering attribute, a dominant attribute with a minimum level for a few other criteria or a weighted average of criteria.[266] In situations with little choice, such as the one above, the first model is usually applicable. However, when customers face many interesting possibilities, such as deciding what to do on a Saturday evening, having fun might be the dominant criterion with the provision that travel distance and cost criteria are met. Managers who know their customers well will succeed in attracting the type of customers whose major service quality criteria they can satisfy.

We believe that frequency of use is an important situation dimension. When a vacationer visits a resort for the first time, an overpowering perceived attribute, perhaps a relaxing atmosphere, might dominate. The next time, knowing what to expect, the vacationer might assess the numerous activities offered in addition to the relaxing atmosphere (now less unknown), which might still dominate. Additional visits might cause a switch to the weighted average model. This shift is shown in Figure 5-3.

FIGURE 5-3   Relationship between the utilization frequency and/or duration and the evaluation model of service quality

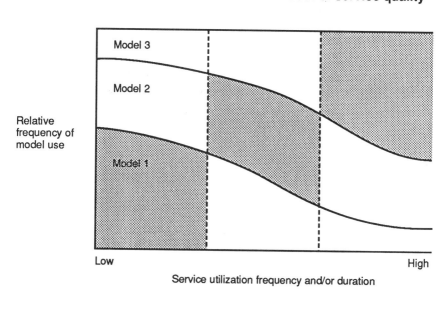

Model 1: one overwhelming attribute
Model 2: one dominant attribute but minimal levels of other criteria
Model 3: weighted average of all attributes

 = predominant model

SOURCE: Adapted from Sasser, Olsen and Wyckoff (reference 266)

Given the difficulty customers have in assessing and controlling the level of quality, it is not surprising that some organizations prefer to offer less than the customer thinks he or she is getting. How does the new home owner who is unfamiliar with gardening or construction know how much topsoil is required to ensure healthy grass within a month and for several years, or how close together eaves-trough nails should be? The customer's lack of knowledge creates opportunities for service firms to cut corners. The firm won't have to live with the consequences unless poor service is evident within the warranty period and can clearly be attributed to the service provider. As one builder put it, you don't make money by what you put into a house, but by what you leave out. In the long run, such an attitude is unwise. However, deceived customers might be forgiven for wondering if this is really the case. They neither know nor have much impact on how well a company is doing if they have no further business with them. And, at least in the short term, corner cutters may well appear to be quite successful.

5.4   Poor service quality is costly

In some cases, a quality level designed to be high corresponds to a low level of perceived quality. One hotel specialized in hosting meetings and put in a lot of extras, such as many flavors of coffee and expensive china, to please customers.[128] However, customer complaints increased; what they really wanted was quick coffee service and easy access to washrooms and telephones. Most services can give providers quick feedback when necessary; however, during the same crucial moments, customers often form their negative opinions.

Some industries, whether justifiably or not, are reputed to give poor service. Automobile repair by dealers is one. According to one author, 40% of this type of service must be re-done. Surely this high percentage does not result from perception alone. As the author states, "Today's horror stories will take years to die."[299, p. 116]

Such statements, and the widespread impressions they represent, are extremely bad publicity for a service organization. Because of the intangibility of service, a bad reputation is very difficult to reverse no matter how much a bad service has improved. Some authors report that each dissatisfied customer recounts his bad experience to 11 or 12 others. This can be extremely expensive, especially because each of them may tell others in turn and may well exaggerate the story with each telling. And the chain may continue for some time, reinforcing the negative image. Unfortunately, such negative publicity is not adequately counterbalanced by testimonials from satisfied customers. Equally unfortunate is the fact that only 4% of unhappy customers complain to the service organization, many blaming the individual server instead.[128] Without this direct feedback, management may never know a problem exists until it is too late. Offering a service guarantee is one excellent way to encourage complaints, thereby gathering valuable information to base improvements on.[104] Customers may blame service providers but they change their own behavior as service levels change.

In Chapter 4, we discussed the idea that a capacity utilization of 70 % is nearly optimal (see Figure 5-4). It is possible to conclude that customers are most likely to be satisfied at this level. As service systems drop below 70% capacity utilization, the service may deteriorate markedly as staff motivation drops. Alternatively, service may improve but customers may not detect the change. Passengers aboard a near-empty airplane almost certainly get better service than those on a full flight, although they may not perceive it as such. At very high utilization rates, the system may not be able to cope with the demands placed on it. In neither case are customer expectations likely to change much, so mismatches between expectations and perceptions (poor quality) are likely.

FIGURE 5-4   Customer perception of quality

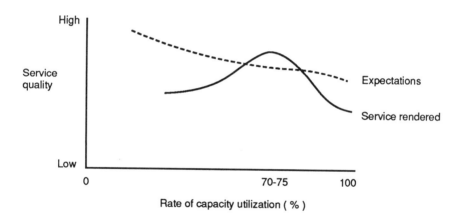

Rate of capacity utilization (%)

5.5   Measuring and controlling service quality

Most services have measurable, and therefore quantifiable, components. In assessing an organization's service quality, the components are important but they are not the only relevant factors. What other factors can a manager use to determine how his or her organization is doing compared to competitors? And how else can a manager identify with confidence where his or her organization's strengths and weaknesses lie?

One study of 2600 companies clearly demonstrated that financial performance is tied directly to the perceived quality of a company's goods or services.[299] Organizations that want to improve their quality level must somehow measure it. Methods of measurement include written questionnaires, typical in hotels and some restaurants, short interviews, often used by car dealers some time after purchase, or more rigorous evaluation techniques. Although aspects such as friendliness cannot be measured easily, asking customers to rate this factor on a scale of 1-5 can give valuable information to both managers and employees. As informative as these tools can be, we suspect that few are ever rigorously tested for reliability, validity, etc.

According to one report, service sector performance is made up of costs, hard performance measures (such as response time) and soft performance measures (such as attitude).[86] Managers in most service settings must consider all three types of performance in evaluating quality within their own organization. Within the past decade, many public services have focused increasingly on cost performance at the expense of the other two. This is analogous to moving toward one corner of the triangle in Figure 5-1. Such moves have not always produced the expected results, despite some significant cost savings. The union representing blue-collar workers in a large Canadian city recently made a commercial regarding the city's decision to contract out tree planting. The union admitted that private firms were doing the job at nearly half the cost but claimed that, based on five years of data, the tree mortality rate was about twice as high for trees planted by the private contractor. Assuming that these statements are verifiable and that there is no evidence of sabotage, how should a manager react?

In some cases, it might be better for the public not to be aware of certain quality measures because many people are naive about statistics and cannot be trusted to interpret them properly. Hospitals that use mortality statistics in their ads for heart patients use a hard, verifiable statistic that, unfortunately, may not tell the whole story.[260] Such figures hide differences in age, sex, race, lifestyle or general health of patients. Furthermore, they may say nothing about the range of observed outcomes. This situation is analogous to a large multi-site service organization using aggregate statistics either to promote all its units, including the very best and the very worst, or to apply pressure to those at the bottom of the rankings to improve their productivity. Using any measure without accounting for individual circumstances is dangerous.

One of the most noteworthy attempts to analyze and measure service quality has identified several possible gaps between management perception of customer expectations, service specifications, service delivery and external communication to customers. In this model, the fifth gap — between expected and perceived service quality — results from the other four.[311] Clearly good quality is attainable only when each of the other gaps is small, that is, when managers know what customers expect (gap 1), when those expectations are properly translated into specifications (gap 2), when the specifications are met in service delivery (gap 3) and when customers are accurately informed about the service (gap 4). In related work, the authors have developed a technique and a survey instrument to measure customer expectations and perceptions, and thus service quality.[312] This questionnaire (SERVQUAL) promises to be a valuable start to measuring service quality rigorously, although its range of usefulness has not yet been fully determined.[115]

Another approach is to look at financial data rather than operations. As organizations pass from the entrepreneurial to the professional management stages, they must improve their accounting systems as well as their operational measurements and possibly their structures.[215] This shift to a new management style can cause changes in the service concept or delivery. A systematic approach is required to relate the new control effort to the basic raison d'être of the firm. In the words of Bruggeman, et al.:

> Most of the time, management control is directed only toward momentary evaluation criteria. Company goals are mainly formulated in terms of costs, sales turnover, profits, return on investment, etc. In this process one frequently overlooks the importance of competitive advantage. By chasing the budgetary objectives continuously, one frequently forgets the need to be competitive.
>
> In service organizations service quality is an important competitive success factor.
>
> Management control cannot be an end in itself, but only a means to build a competitive service company.[29, pp. 77, 84]

The orientation towards service quality expressed in these words is meaningful only if it is put into practice. If the service is oriented toward customer satisfaction, the desired quality level might be reached. If not, the goal will likely prove to be only wishful thinking.

6

GEARING UP TO IMPROVE PRODUCTIVITY

Some Approaches to Productivity

6.1 The all-inclusive notion of productivity

As with most of the topics in this book, trying to cover productivity fully in a single chapter is an impossible task. In fact, the entire book is in a sense about productivity as well as quality in the service industries. Productivity means different things to different people. The common approach is to define it in terms of output (possibly sales) divided by some measure of labor (frequently direct labor only) input (often hours or wages). This popular but narrow view is often inappropriate. Productivity is an all-encompassing concept that, at least in theory, should include all system inputs and outputs.

Productivity measures the results of how a service is performed. These results can be assessed against plans as well as compared to competitors' results. Productivity is often measured by a number of ratios of useful and meaningful outputs divided by appropriate inputs to determine how well organizational resources are being used. This approach to productivity is thus oriented toward efficiency, or doing things correctly. Effectiveness, or doing the right things, requires different measures because it implies determining the extent to which organizational goals are being met in areas such as service design.

This chapter provides a brief overview of productivity. The reader is encouraged first to relate its concepts to those in the earlier chapters of this book which describe numerous approaches to enhance productivity, and second, to refer to a general text on operations management or one specifically on productivity for a more thorough discussion. For example, Nollet, et al. deal with the importance of productivity at the organizational as well as the international level, with productivity measures and with productivity's relationship to other operations management concepts.[222]

6.2 Looking at productivity from several angles

How well an organization does in absolute terms or over time is less important than its performance relative to that of its competitors. Every organization needs customers prepared to pay its price. There is really no substitute for a satisfied customer. If the relative cost of a service gets too high, customers will seek out alternatives. No organization has a guaranteed monopoly forever. Times change, and with them, attitudes, norms and technology. Government post offices once had monopolies but courier services, and later electronic mail and facsimile machines, eroded their power. In the future, other technologies may very well arise to pose additional threats. Many churches feel endangered by the popularity of other types of religious associations and by people who believe they can do without active participation in a church. This type of change represents a fundamental reorientation of societal values.

Figure 6-1 shows the customer positioned as an important link between organizational strategy and planning activities, and operations. Managers must focus on the customer when they decide what to do (strategy), when they decide how to do it (planning), and when they execute those plans to produce and deliver a service that meets customer needs efficiently (operations). The customer interacts to different degrees in the operations of the service. Consequently, systems must be designed to facilitate the customer's task, and personnel must be sensitized to customer needs and collaborate to meet them. A constant interaction between all levels allows the enterprise to adjust to variations, both internal and external.

Successful performers ensure that their service(s) meets their customers' needs at a satisfactory level (effectiveness) by providing services coherently and at a reasonable cost (efficiency). Organizations like Shouldice Hospital,[119, 120] Stew Leonard's Dairy,[230, 231] Walt Disney Productions[230, 231] and others[114] have created high demand through high quality. High demand, in turn, eliminates significant peaks and valleys, and makes the efficient operations of a level strategy much easier to achieve. In many industries, it is the little extras — that additional effort to excel — that separates the leader(s) from the pack.

FIGURE 6-1 Preoccupation with the customer

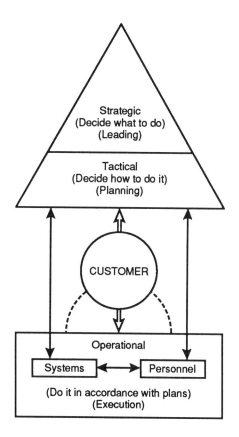

Before a manager can increase organizational productivity, he or she must thoroughly understand the service process, especially the interface between customers and server. Changing the process to improve productivity, for example, speeding it up or standardizing it, will probably also change the perceived quality of the service. Managers must take such effects into consideration to make changes effective as well as efficient. Increasing the use of fixed resources (productivity) in a service station by adding a convenience store or restaurant is different from adding a rust protection service.

The labor intensity of many services is often seen as a major hindrance to increasing productivity. The reason lies in the difficulty of substituting equipment for labor.[209] To some extent, this thinking reflects the traditional narrow view that productivity is associated only with (direct) labor. However, high labor intensity represents an opportunity to examine the process carefully for potentially large productivity improvements.[186] Do customers have free time while waiting for service? Are customers trying to bypass personnel to do the work themselves? Are customers very interested in knowing more about the service providers' tasks? Questions such as these pave the way for productivity increases by identifying opportunities for new services and new service workers, the customers.

Chase and coworkers proposed separating those elements of the service process requiring customer contact from those not requiring contact.[39, 40, 43, 44] One purpose for dividing a service this way is that different productivity improvement strategies may be possible in the 'back room' in the absence of the customer from those in the 'front room' with the customer. Chase, et al. proposed an equation to represent system efficiency[40]:

$$\text{Potential system efficiency} = f\left[1 - \frac{\text{customer contact time}}{\text{service creation time}}\right]$$

According to this equation, system efficiency decreases as the customer spends more time in contact with the system while the service is being created. Conversely, efficiency rises when customer contact is reduced. Although this equation unrealistically treats customer contact time as being totally unproductive, it does reflect the disruption that uncontrolled customers can cause to productivity. The increased productivity is reflected in the reduced resource use (represented in Figure 6-2 by a smaller area) needed to create a unit of service output (however it might be defined) after the change is made.

As discussed above, behavioral, marketing and operational factors must be examined simultaneously to keep the service concept focused. Another way to represent possible productivity improvements is the Venn diagram in Figure 6-3 which implies that it is easier to improve productivity when customer behavior can be influenced, operations can be industrialized and the technical core can be isolated from customers all at the same time (zone 3). The optimal region is not meant to imply that each component must be pushed to its limit, but rather that balanced consideration should be given to each. Innovative measures could prove to be very useful in this regard. For example, telephones were once hardwired into homes, most of which had only one or two phone locations. Problems of any sort required a visit from a service representative with the usual scheduling problems. During the 1970s, telephone companies began installing jack systems to encourage customers to bring inoperative phones in. Customers were given up to five jacks in their homes at a small cost, were able to contact the company at their convenience (during office hours) and were able to maintain their home's privacy; in

FIGURE 6-2   Concept of productivity growth in service enterprises

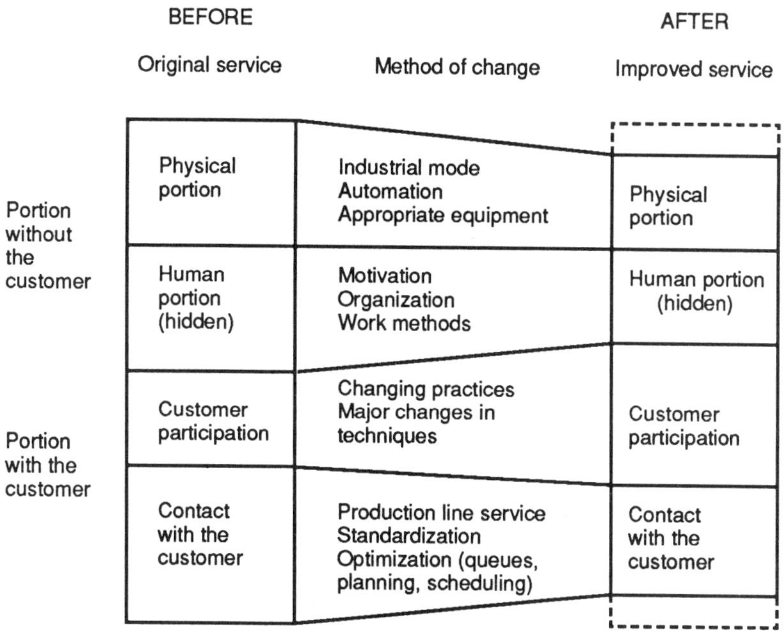

BEFORE   AFTER

Original service   Method of change   Improved service

Portion without the customer	Physical portion	Industrial mode Automation Appropriate equipment	Physical portion
	Human portion (hidden)	Motivation Organization Work methods	Human portion (hidden)
Portion with the customer	Customer participation	Changing practices Major changes in techniques	Customer participation
	Contact with the customer	Production line service Standardization Optimization (queues, planning, scheduling)	Contact with the customer

FIGURE 6-3   Degree of productivity achievable as a function of some dimensions of service improvement methods

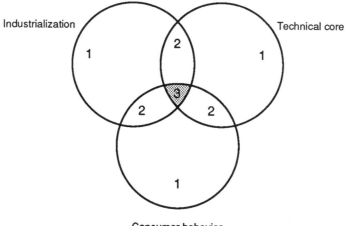

Consumer behavior

1 = Low productivity
2 = Medium productivity
3 = High productivity

exchange, they had only the minor inconvenience and small cost of taking in their phones. The company incurred extra installation costs but reduced service call costs, and was able to repair phones in the back room according to their own schedule and away from customers. Often customers are given a temporary replacement phone, a service that builds good will, and sales representatives have the opportunity to sell additional services while customers wait.

Standardizing the steps in delivering the service can help to accelerate the process, ensure that employees learn as fast as possible and increase the likelihood of meeting specifications. However, standardization may make service staff feel more like machines because it does limit their flexibility to meet individual customer needs.

Productivity can also be improved by delegating tasks to the lowest level of staff that can perform the task competently. In professional service firms, for example, as professional staff members grow towards partnership, they must learn to delegate some of their technical tasks to more junior colleagues. This makes it possible for them to concentrate on developing new business, managing the firm and performing only those technical tasks that really call for their level of expertise; at the same time, it develops junior staff members. Without delegation, productive time, which may not be recoverable from clients, is lost and the firm has a development vacuum. In some cases, of course, tasks that seem mundane are not delegated to others. For example, the president of one mass marketer of household items personally performs the task of preparing advertising copy because he perceives it to be a key factor of corporate success.

Altering the range of services offered is a standard means of changing productivity.[21] Adding services can spread fixed costs over a larger base and possibly attract more customers. Universities that add continuing education departments are attempting to do this. Eliminating services, especially lower margin ones, can lead to a tighter focus and higher margin. Elimination can be by branch, thus allowing both breadth and productivity, although retail-type services that adopt such rationalization must have a number of units in reasonably close proximity to allow customers access to the range of services. Many Canadian banks have concentrated certain activities in relatively few branches. Both increasing and decreasing services has the effect of changing the service concept; site-specific rationalization has the additional effect of creating multiple concepts, with consequent loss of focus and possible customer confusion. Some grocery stores and hotel chains have addressed this problem by establishing separate brand names and management for each of their service offerings. George Weston Ltd., for example, operates many types of grocery stores, each with its own concept.

Productivity (economies of scale) is often used to justify multiple site operations. However, according to a number of studies of airlines, railroads, urban bus systems, trucking, electric power and telecommunications, economies of scale are not as relevant as economies of density.[37] Transit companies that extend their systems into less populated areas to spread fixed costs might be unpleasantly surprised. Of course, history has shown that transportation developments can cause an increase in population density.

Armistead, et al. suggest looking at productivity from a different angle.[7] According to their model, three elements affect service productivity: the cost of input resources, the efficiency of the transforming resources and the utilization of the transforming resources. Management's impact on any of these elements is affected by three strategic determinants (volume, variety and variation). Figure 6-4 presents this situation. Naturally, managers must handle the three productivity elements simultaneously. Undue focus on reducing input costs (especially on only a few 'key' inputs) without corresponding attention to the utilization and efficiency of the transforming resources is unlikely to produce high productivity. Similarly, high productivity is unlikely to be achieved when attention is paid only to resource utilization or resource

FIGURE 6-4   The effects of strategic determinants on productivity

	Productivity		
	Input costs	Resource efficiency	Resource utilization
Volume	Quality factors Specialization	Learning Specialization	Accomodation of service mix
Variety	Reduced volume Range of skills	Learning General purpose technology	Time to manage variety Change costs
Variation	Overtime Subcontract	Requirements of pacing Standards Predictability	Capacity more fixed than demand
	Cost of Service Provision		

SOURCE: Adapted from Armistead, Johnston and Slack (reference 7)

efficiency. Volume effects (scale economies) have traditionally been seen as the main contributor to high productivity. Volume can lead to low input costs, efficient transformation and high resource utilization (Figure 6-4). McDonald's is a good example. In contrast, variety in the service offered is a major contributor to low productivity. Variety increases input costs, reduces resource efficiency and increases managerial complexity, thereby reducing resource utilization. Variation or process change, especially if it is unpredictable, also reduces productivity because organizations need to carry extra capacity and perhaps inventories in case they are required. Productivity can be increased by reducing either variety or variation.

6.3   White-collar productivity

This section presents two sets of ideas on white-collar productivity. These ideas are considered to be distinct from, but to complement, the concepts discussed so far. Although most of the concepts and models apply to it, white-collar productivity has a literature of its own, which is applicable to a certain extent outside the white-collar domain.

According to one author, the four most promising areas for white-collar productivity improvement are increased quality, utilization of new office technology, paying attention to and educating employees, and controlling overhead costs such as paperwork.[270] Twenty percent of quality cost comes from correcting errors, another 20% is incurred while trying to prevent errors that should have been eliminated at the design stage and 10% could be saved by eliminating ineffective or unnecessary tasks.[270] These suggestions could easily be applied to non-white-collar services or to manufacturing (although the savings might be different). For our purposes, we can conclude that design, equipment, people and procedures should be considered seriously when thinking about productivity improvement.

Berglind and Scales' model is quite different.[16] They identify five components of white-collar productivity:

1. focus (are the organization's activities properly oriented [effective]?)
2. organization (is the structure suitable and well integrated?)
3. process (are the activities performed efficiently?)
4. motivation (are the people constantly trying to do their best?)
5. management effect (is management playing its role properly?)

According to the authors, the fifth factor influences the other four significantly. This approach is inward looking in that it focuses on white-collar activities within an organization rather than as they relate to outside customers.

Based on these two models, one could argue that most factors influencing productivity can be related to management, the service provider, the customer or the task itself. This segmentation, represented in Figure 6-5, is quite wide but emphasizes the key role of people in the productivity of service organizations.

FIGURE 6-5   Key determinants of productivity

Measuring Productivity

6.4   Some limitations

For most processes, external factors, which managers have little or no control over, affect output levels and therefore productivity. This situation is particularly true of services because process control is often less strict than in manufacturing. The human nature of service providers and customers, and the service characteristic of immediate consumption reduce control and make it more difficult to identify meaningful measures. These issues are less significant in services such as automatic international telecommunications, where digits dialed by customers are stored until the number is completed and ready to be transmitted. Until memory limitations are reached, customer inexperience does not cause productivity problems and productivity is relatively easy to measure. Despite examples like this one, many problems remain:

> Even though the productivity of the service sector is an issue of great social importance, efforts at assessing output are plagued by measurement difficulties ... For service operations, this problem often results in a reliance on process controls rather than on output controls ...[211, p. 469]

However, as two other authors note:

> ... service organizations do not always manage those items which affect customer satisfaction to the same level as manufacturing organizations.... Effectiveness is needed as well as efficiency, and in many service industries this could be better achieved by emphasis on the processes, rather than by trying to become more 'product orientated.'[144, p. 38]

Measurement questions arise because of service intangibility. Is it preferable to try measuring a significant but difficult-to-measure factor rather than a more convenient or precise surrogate or alternative? How does measurement affect staff, customers and the organization? Are the right aspects being measured? Are they being measured appropriately? These questions are far from trivial. The old adage that you get what you inspect not what you expect has a considerable amount of truth to it.

Many white-collar employees resist attempts to measure their performance because they feel they have little to gain but a lot to lose.[24] This situation is complicated by the vague missions and objectives of such groups, the long time frames involved and the intangibility of output. Unless managers tell employees why productivity measures are important and how they would all benefit from having them, employees are unlikely to cooperate in establishing measures and providing data. This is particularly the case for professionals, who are usually flexible, are high-level decision-makers and have a considerable degree of knowledge-based power.

Even when employees are cooperative, arguments can arise in establishing adequate productivity measures. Often, families of measures must be developed, possibly with a weighting scheme, to realize a single productivity score.[182] But how many measures? London Life, a leading Canadian service company, created a list of 1200 productivity measures that were eventually distilled down to a manageable number. Incidentally, London Life's award-winning productivity program has helped make the company an industry leader in measures such as return on investment, profits per employee, growth rate, etc.

The weighted average approach is similarly useful when developing service quality measures. How does one decide what measures to use and how to weigh them? We suggest that there will never be any perfect answers, as they will change over time. Managers, after extensive and thorough consultation, must establish measures, implement them and monitor their effects. It helps during the planning stage to have a few people act as devil's advocates to pose the following questions: if this is implemented, what is the logical selfish reaction of staff? Is this reaction desirable?

Although productivity analysis is a valuable measure of performance over time, it is important that the right people do the measuring. Productivity analysis is often requested of external auditors. Because adopting measures of productivity can affect the service concept, these requests raise questions as to whether or not accountants are able to measure productivity adequately, judge the wisdom of a given productivity level, and do so at a reasonable cost.[28] Internal auditors, who are also usually accountants, face a similar dilemma. Despite their wider knowledge of the organization, many lack the proper scope of knowledge to inter-relate the various ideas and foresee the implications of potential modifications. The head of the internal audit group of a major transportation company once approached one of this book's authors to ask where to begin an audit, because he and his staff were trained in accounting and had had very few courses in other functional areas.

6.5   Towards developing useful productivity measures

At Westinghouse, white-collar productivity measures focus on the department rather than individuals, to ensure less bias toward measured activities.[258] Employees themselves try to determine which measures to use. To be acceptable, a measure must be quantifiable, consider inter-departmental dependence and agree with divisional objectives. If possible, a composite measure of all the significant ratios is used.

The system used at IBM has some similarities: measures should be simple, easily understood by staff, well supported by a base of sound data and able to identify efficient and inefficient areas of performance.[38] Both the Westinghouse and IBM systems insist on the importance of staff and on the simplicity and usefulness of the measures used.

However, many systems fail. One study of R & D productivity measurement systems postulated five reasons for failure:

1. too much emphasis on internal measurement; for example, the number of proposals or drafts written
2. too much emphasis on behavior, a measure of activity not output
3. measurement of outputs of questionable value to the organization, for example, quantity instead of quality or value
4. a measurement system that is too complicated and therefore difficult to administer and/or that has information overload
5. measurement that is too subjective.[26]

Obviously good measurement systems would have the opposite characteristics and would therefore focus on providing value to both the organization and its staff with benefits that significantly exceed the direct and indirect measurement costs. Some costs can be rather subtle. One study of group claims processing in a major North American insurance company found that 80% of the employees whose activities were monitored by a computer perceived that production quantity was the most important factor in their performance ratings. Coversely 85% of unmonitored employees said that work quality was most important. In the authors' words,

Individual productivity seems to be higher among those who consider it important regardless of its importance to the employer.

If it's not counted, it doesn't count.... People don't want to handle problems, because it slows them down.[99, pp. 42, 43]

Stories about measurement systems that have backfired abound: operators who disconnect customers because the time required to serve them reduces the daily average; buses that don't stop for passengers because doing so would put them off schedule[186]; professors who are unavailable to meet with students because doing so would reduce their research time. Sometimes customers conclude, and not without reason, that the person they are dealing with is not human. Designers of productivity measurement systems must consider the wider impact they are likely to have.

Boyett and Conn concluded that many measurement systems suffer from treating all white-collar work in the same way when five types of work should be considered, each of which deserves its own type of measure.[24] The five types are:

1. factory work, such as checking output for accuracy
2. support functions, such as production scheduling
3. recurring functions, such as payroll
4. quick response projects, such as short reports by staff
5. long-term projects.

In many settings, there is considerable overlap between these categories; indeed, a single employee may perform all of them. How then should that employee's productivity be evaluated? Moreover, many organizations employ scales that are easy to measure rather than more meaningful ones. For example, many use lines of code that a programmer writes as a surrogate measure of writing a program, without addressing the difficulty of writing the program, particularly of keeping it short and efficient in use of computer resources in terms of either time or memory. These are more salient measures of productivity and should be addressed. Managers must constantly wrestle with the dilemma of whether to give feedback quickly and cheaply, but using inappropriate scales, or more slowly and less precisely, but attempting to get at the heart of what is significant. Possibly a combination would be appropriate, although that makes it easy to ignore the more difficult significant measures. Given an either/or choice, we favor trying to measure what is most significant.

This section concludes with two success stories of service sector productivity measurement systems. Physical and occupational therapy are fields for which the development of meaningful productivity measures is widely perceived to be very difficult, if not impossible. Ventrone, et al. developed productivity standards and measures for one institution that could help managers to set reasonable goals for billable hours and evaluate each therapist's workload objectively.[301] To develop these standards, they used industrial engineering techniques such as work sampling, borrowed standards from other institutions, used short-time interval scheduling techniques and asked employees to keep records of their work hours for two or three weeks. As a result, this department of the Hershey Medical Centre was able to increase billings by 17%.

In a very different sector, the U.S. copyright office was able to improve its productivity substantially.[245] Despite a workload increase of 23% and a staff reduction of 19%, productivity increased by 15% over a five-year period. The approach used focused mostly on participative management. Managers implemented a monetary award system for exceptional team performance, emphasizing the importance of employee motivation and ideas. This productivity improvement scheme has not only had impressive results, but has also provided a clear course for the future.

6.6   Some final comments on productivity and its measures

A number of studies have concluded that profit-based accounting performance measures do not work well because of their short-term bias and the resulting effect on behavior.[86] Much wider measures are needed to properly reflect the strategic importance of the key competitive factors. This conclusion is considered to be more relevant to service organizations that to manufacturers, which compete largely on product features.

Productivity measures are meaningful signals an organization sends to its employees. Customers can sometimes detect what counts for the service provider. But is productivity really that important? Indeed it is, but not as an end in itself. Productivity is a result, but only one result, and the way it is achieved is what is important. Ultimately the means will affect the ends, all the ends. Many organizations have found themselves in trouble because they focused only on productivity. High productivity without customers is hardly a way to make money. Many service organizations can get rapid feedback from customers and reevaluate productivity as well as other results, such as quality. Customers can also usually find alternate suppliers rapidly. Although productivity is generally desirable, overemphasizing it may cause neglect of other important factors.

CHAPTER 7

ADDITIONAL CONCEPTS IN OPERATIONS, MARKETING, AND HUMAN RESOURCE MANAGEMENT

This chapter groups together ideas to reinforce their joint importance in managing service operations. Its purpose is to add valuable information to the structure developed so far.

Operations

7.1 More on technology

Many managers like their jobs because they feel in control. They perceive technology as useful because it is concrete. However, that view may be deceptive. As one group of authors concluded:

> A fundamental tenet of management is that we don't actually manage reality, but models or representations of reality. We manage budgets and schedules rather than dollars and time.[16, p. 42]

As has been noted frequently beforehand, service organizations are very diverse, and some are complicated to manage. Organizations like NASA are huge; they have many customers, often with conflicting interests and they put enormous expenditures and public image at risk. At NASA, the managerial task extends even beyond the farthest reaches of the earth. There are reported to be over 7000 orbiting objects of at least 10 centimetres that have to be continually traced[279]. Scientists estimate that the probability of a dangerous collision during any space shuttle is about 3%.

Technology is knowledge and procedure as well as equipment. Pizza restaurants may not have to dodge space objects, but managing their own brand of technology can still pose a challenge. Tom Monaghan, president of Domino's Pizza, likes to visit at least a few of his outlets every week to keep in touch with how their operations are running and to what extent the store managers are controlling the system and its technology.[145]

Although a relationship between technology and organizational structure has been demonstrated for manufacturers, the relationship is less conclusive for the service sector, and inconclusive for organizations involved in both manufacturing and services.[211] There may well be fundamental differences in the technologies used for each sector. For example, robotics are not only diverse in their uses (spot welding, picking oranges, guarding buildings, caring for the handicapped, assisting brain surgeons[32]), but also in how they are managed.

Service organizations and their customers also benefit from a range of communication technologies. Artificial intelligence has enhanced machine/human understanding to the point where replacing staff in unappealing jobs with machines is a distinct possiblity. Fibre optics and computers have reduced the cost of a telephone call. Other services, such as lecturing, have not changed significantly in the last century; they may represent opportunities for innovation in the future. Overall, service sector technologies have advanced quickly enough to challenge the ability of organizations, staff and customers to adapt. Communication companies, which operate in a highly competitive environment rife with technological change, can't afford to delay modifications to improve customer service and operational efficiency.

However, adopting new technologies may be very difficult. Barras demonstrates that the innovation process that user industries, such as services, employ once new technology is adopted tends to have three stages, which he calls a 'reverse product cycle':

> ... a first stage in which the applications of the new technology are designed to increase the efficiency of delivery of existing services; a second stage in which the technology is applied to improving the quality of services; and a third stage in which the technology assists in generating wholly transformed or new services.[11, p. 165]

For example, the operational efficiency of banks was increased progressively by mainframe computers operating in batch mode in the 1970s and by on-line systems in the 1980s; the emphasis promises to be on networks in the 1990s. Results of developments such as these can help service managers to forecast the types of changes likely to occur in their industries. It is interesting to note that organizations that should be centred on customer satisfaction (Stage 2 in Barras' terms) are often preoccupied with improving efficiency (Stage 1). However, it could be argued that improved efficiency will ultimately lead to improved customer satisfaction. Three main factors regulate the rate at which technology is adopted or diffused: the trade-off between price and technical performance, the expected technological or market risks and the market structure of the adopting industry (Figure 7-1). This model can help managers to evaluate whether or not to adopt a specific innovation or to what extent they can expect their industries to adopt it.

FIGURE 7-1   Factors influencing the adoption or diffusion of technology in the service sector

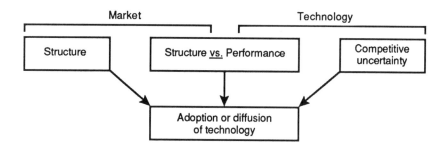

SOURCE: Adapted from Barras (reference 11)

Even small service organizations can benefit from technological improvements. For example, at Glemby Hair Salon, a customer can watch his or her face on a television screen as a hair stylist superimposes any of several hundred styles. This innovation, which costs less than $20,000, is an obvious improvement to customer service. It is estimated that it attracts an extra 40 customers per week.[288]

Technologies entailing equipment require maintenance services which grow with technological development; from a service viewpoint, technology becomes increasingly important. Although manufacturers design equipment with a veiw to reducing maintenance, some is always required. Services must therefore take into account such things as response time, down-time and cost. Knowledgeable technicians who can correct the problem in a hurry are essential. Both the maintenance service and its customers will benefit if emergency calls are kept to a minimum. This is why customers are often given the option of a maintenance contract at a fixed annual fee — it improves not only cash flow planning for both parties but also service, by encouraging preventive maintenance.

7.2   The dispatch function

The role of the dispatcher in service organizations is similar, though wider in scope, to that of the production controller.[302] Dispatchers may contact customers and diagnose problems, filter knowledge, disptach drivers, schedule staff, establish priorities, sell services and control information. With that kind of scope, as well as contact with customers, the role has to be filled by an appropriate person to be both effective and efficient. For example, not all taxi dispatchers seem friendly and knowledgeable. A taxi driver may even comment on this fact to a passenger. These comments could affect customer service. The dispatcher could also have a negative effect on the drivers who may respond by giving poor service. Services for both internal and external customers need dispatchers who combine proficiency with amiability. Dispatching is common in police departments, trucking firms, ambulance companies and airport operations. In some of these settings, errors or poor attitude on the part of the dispatcher can be life threatening.

In many organizations, the dispatcher has the information key to doing a good job in his or her head. This gives the dispatcher extra power (and the potential for a higher salary), but it is a liability for the organization that has to replace a dispatcher on short notice. What information does a dispatcher need? He or she must have knowledge of resource availability over time, the current status of resources, response times and the client's service history. The information could be organized as follows: receipt of request, resource allocation, data update, etc. (see Figure 7-2). These steps are similar to production planning in any environment. Just as computers are used to make valuable contributions to production planning, they can be used in dispatching to keep track of the status and availability of current resources, response times, client files

FIGURE 7-2   The role of the service dispatcher

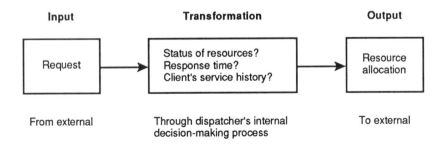

SOURCE: Adapted from Voss (reference 302)

and resource allocation. Dispatchers need only handle the interface with humans, and even that could be automated as users become more familiar with computers.

In most situations that involve dispatching vehicles, a key variable is the initial location of the vehicles, which can be fixed (fire trucks or ambulances) or variable (taxis or police cars). Fitzsimmons and Srikar studied the optimal location for ambulances in Austin, Texas.[88] They divided the city into 358 zones, computed interzone travel times, related the response time (a measure of service level) to the number of ambulances available, and developed a graph (Figure 7-3) which managers can use for making decisions.

FIGURE 7-3   Ambulance response times as a function of the number of ambulances in Austin, Texas

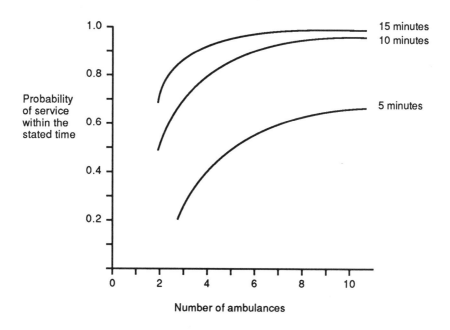

SOURCE: Adapted from Fitzsimmons and Srikar (reference 88)

Dispatching emergency vehicles involves criteria other than first-come-first-served for queue discipline and should allow for cancellations. Customers usually expect a first-come-first-served rule. Faculty members are often given priority codes for computer or library access which students consider unfair, especially as demand for the resource grows. However, when it is evident that the needs of individual customers differ significantly on the basis of time, such as in an emergency service, a queue discipline criterion based on that need is readily accepted. People with relatively minor ailments are usually content to get bumped from their position in the emergency room queue so that someone with life-threatening injuries can be served.

7.3   Procurement

Procurement is an area that is recognized as key in manufacturing, but considered less important in many services where purchases are relatively insignificant financially. In health care, education and consulting, personnel-related expenses dominate overwhelmingly, accounting for 70-80% of the total. Naturally, when equipment or facilitating goods are major budget items, managers will treat procurement decisions with more care. Some organizations overlook the potential for better managed operations while going to great lengths to reduce expenses. An experienced procurement professional would be a valuable asset in most service industries.

It is a major procurement decision for any service organization whether to make or buy goods and services. Almost any activity performed in-house (made) can also be performed outside (bought). Security, food, janitorial, legal and public relations services are frequently contracted out. Strategic considerations, such as controlling access to sensitive information or gaining knowledge from performing the activity, could justify conducting some of these activities in-house or purchasing additional services. This is where the procurement professional comes in; he or she can help to make that decision and, if relevant, choose an appropriate supplier. Figure 7-4 illustrates that the decision is not an either/or choice; there is a grey zone between the extremes — make and buy — that corresponds to activities that could or should be divided between the two.[168] For example, a firm's legal staff could do the bulk of the work, and use outside legal services for temporary overload or special projects. In making the make/buy choice, level of expertise required, cost of subcontracting, image, service life cycle, level of control required and capacity must all be considered. The higher its strategic importance, the more attractive the make option is.

When managers are not clear about whether to make or buy, it is often felt that they should buy in order to keep their service operations focused. There are usually many possible suppliers. Some may even be located far afield. Some organizations send key-punching jobs to Barbados for overnight service,[15] others send typing to Taiwan with a 48-hour turnaround. In each case, the contracted services are important but not central to the purchaser's business. Thus, buying the service allows the

FIGURE 7-4   Make or Buy?

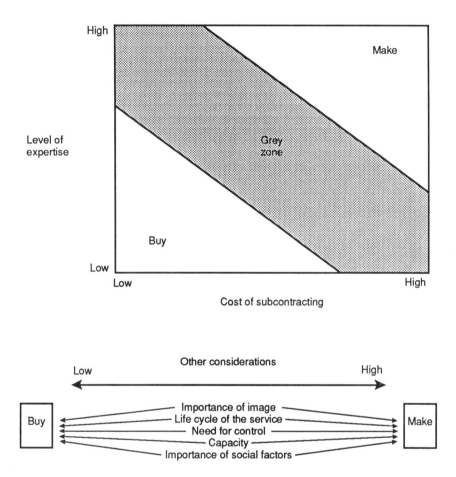

purchasing organiztion to focus its resources on its core activities. Also, these purchased services cost less than in-house or local alternatives.

Marketing

7.4   Zeroing in on the right segments

Officially, at least, marketing deals with markets with an underlying philosophy of satisfying customer needs and desires by providing suitable packages of goods and services. An alternative is to focus on what customers can do for the provider, in our context of services, by giving feedback. One owner of a small trucking business suggests:

Think of the market as a stream of information flowing into your business, information you can use to fine-tune your signal. You want your signal to be the one with the most information attached to it, the most intelligent about the market. Even the clearest signal is subject to wavering and static, however. It requires constant adjustment. You may have difficulty finding just the right frequency, and keeping your signal tuned properly. But no matter what the cost, you cannot make a better investment in your business.[110, p. 52]

Looked at in this way, marketing becomes a team effort with each party standing to gain — the customer by having needs or desires met, the provider by obtaining information and revenues, allowing it to enhance customer satisfaction further by developing even better services.

Marketing extends well beyond the parameters of the marketing department. This is particularly true of high-contact service organizations where there are numerous encounters between service staff and customers. The same is true of operations and the operations department. Very rigid organizational structures encourage employees to concentrate on performing narrow tasks and avoiding trouble, rather than on solving customer problems, which almost never fit into rigid categories. A major Canadian accounting firm tries its best to help clients any way it can, provided the help is defensible based on accounting theory, the professional standards established by the Canadian Institute of Chartered Accountants (CICA), and the law. This aggressive approach is quite different from the more conservative one adopted by many other firms which seek to avoid potential problems with the CICA and being seen as too opportunistic. In one author's view:

> ... successful service marketing is not usually a question of balancing out the conventional marketing equations, but of developing with customers, and potential customers, a relationship which demonstrates an understanding of their problems.[139, p. 93]

Marketing evidently poses special problems for non-profit services. Good marketing takes advantage of all justified contacts with customers to sell more services, to provide excellent service and to gather information from customers. This is just as applicable in the public sector as in the private sector. Indeed, knowledge of offered services and products counts most in non-profit organizations.[4] Unfortunately, many non-profit service organizations have a tendency to use a production philosophy. They first decide to produce a service, then they determine how to sell it, and only then do they analyze and segment the potential customers. All too often the results are services which address no real need or are awkwardly and expensively modified to meet customer requirements. Clearly a marketing approach would start with customer analysis and be much more likely to develop a suitable service the first time around. Organizations would benefit from reorienting their planning process accordingly.

Others types of organizations can benefit from a marketing orientation. For a company like American Express, serving different customer segments is very important.[197] Although American Express calls it a customer complaint department, it is used as an active marketing tool. Most of the department's staff comes from other areas of the organization and has at least six weeks of special training. The goal is to obtain empathetic, knowledgeable and efficient people.

Market segmentation is at least as important in service organizations as it is in manufacturing firms, but for different reasons. Lovelock states that:

> ... some market segments may be more desirable that others beause the customers fit particularly well with the organization's mission, reinforce the ambience that the service organization is trying to create, have needs that match the professional skills and interests of staff members, or pay higher rates and are more profitable.[185, p. 17]

Customers are sought not only for the revenue they provide but also for their potential contribution to a psychological aspect important for other customers or service staff. Many discos, for example, have their own particular style and regular customers that fit it. One group of regulars at a well-known disco was offered free admission and drinks because the owner discovered that other customers enjoyed watching them dance. A second example comes from the travel industry. All countries welcome rich visitors who spend a lot. However, rich tourists tend to avoid places where there is unrest. So some developing countries have started to target a different segment — young adventure-seekers. Although this segment is not as affluent, its currency is better than nothing, and satisfying them now may be a good investment for the future. In this case, the challenge is to try to satisfy both segments with one set of resources.

7.5 Pricing and selling tips

Many services are priced on the basis of cost. Although costs are obviously important to producers, and prices to consumers, value is perhaps even more important to consumers. Upscale hospitality services compete with their low-end counterparts on value, not price. Club Méditerranée (Club Med) is one such organization. It pioneered the all-inclusive resort concept, a package including accommodation, meals and recreation at a fixed prepaid price based on what the market was perceived to be willing to pay. Customers value not having to count pennies continually and worrying about whether they can afford dessert. You can even rent a complete Club Med site for a week,[147] and although the rent is high, it's an attractive option for organizations that want to reward their staff or hold a conference. Value depends on what options customers have and what they are willing to pay. Price is an important variable in determining value;[295] its image can influence potential customers, often counter-intuitively. For example, a consultant whose rate is low may be perceived to be less knowledgeable than one who charges more.

A retail organization is a good example of a service where high prices may attract a particular segment of customers. Presumably in their search for high value, they use price as a measure of quality or service. The importance of good salespeople in establishing an image of value cannot be over emphasized — few customers look only at the price when they buy and if they do, they will usually be able to find the same item more cheaply elsewhere. Salespeople who advise customers instead of pushing for a sale and treat customers with courtesy are a key asset to an upscale retailer. They are the organization's bread and butter.

On the other hand, poor sales cannot be blamed solely on salespeople. Unfortunately, although many believe that advertising can compensate for poor operations, this is seldom the case. For example, in early 1987, Wendy's experienced its first quarterly loss. In the words of its critics:

> ... management lost its focus and failed to pay attention to details. Service slipped, new products didn't meet expectations, a chicken subsidiary never took off, and a costly breakfast rollout rolled over and died last year.[54]

At the same time, Wendy's was relying heavily on advertising, but its ads appeared to be ineffective. Ads were switched rapidly, breakfasts and items such as baked potatoes were heavily promoted while hamburgers were neglected, and the ads became ends in themselves, divorced from the products and unfocused. In short, Wendy's lost sight of its real problems and focused on advertising.

Most customers will tolerate minor problems in service but not necessarily for long. A lot depends on the psychological cost to the customer of changing services. It is easier to switch fast food restaurants than auditing firms or psychologists. One reason why changing from one service provider to another is difficult is the sense of identity a customer has with a provider. Customer loyalty increases with their experience and involvement,[76] and likely with service intangibility. It's a bigger decision to change mechanics than gas stations. Changing service providers is more difficult when it involves a person and is contractual. It is hard to tell the milkman or the paperboy that you are changing suppliers, but it is virtually painless to switch car washes or supermarkets. However, even in the most difficult circumstances, customers will change services if they are pressed hard enough.

Human Resources

7.6 Motivation

Employees and customers are important to service organizations beyond simply being a source of revenue. Meeting goals is important for any service enterprise and this can be achieved only if the relationship with employees and customer is facilitated:

> If service organizations care about both employees and customers, the pay-off will be in terms of increased employee motivation and satisfaction; a high level of service quality as compared to the quality expected by customers, and therefore customer satisfaction; and, in turn, hopefully, customer loyalty and increased levels of business activity.[176, p. 74]

Although paying attention to a myriad of minute, seemingly unimportant details often makes the difference between an ordinary and an exceptional service enterprise, it should be emphasized that attention to details alone is not sufficient. A service must be fundamentally sound, that is, it must have a superior concept, motivated employees and an excellent operational system. Only then does it pay to pay attention to details. As Grönroos puts it:

> ... in the industrial society, manufacturing skills were the key to success, and production technology, technical product solutions, and raw materials created economy of scale and profitable operations, whereas in the service economy the employees are the *scarce resource*. Any firm can get sufficient technology, but in order to add the service elements needed in the customer relationship, a new strategic thinking, a *service know-how*, and new operational skills are needed.[100, p. 12]

This implies that managers should focus on service-oriented employees, on acquiring know-how early to gain strategic advantage and on thinking ahead, both strategically and operationally.

Motivating employees on an on-going basis is not easy. Every job has its dull aspects and most jobs get tedious after a while, particularly if they are limited in variety and challenge. So recognizing achievements above and beyond the call of duty should be the norm. It is customary in some organizations for the president or a vice-president to phone or send a gift to an employee who has done an exceptional job. Public recognition makes the approach even more powerful, as many companies have found. Some organizations invite their top sales representatives to a resort where they are wined and dined, and awarded certificates of merit and praise at a public ceremony attended by other sales representatives and company executives. As a result, the sales staff are highly motivated to do an excellent job in the following years.

For many years, Singapore Airlines has ranked near the top of international airlines. One of the reasons is that less than 2% of the applicants to positions as flight attendants are hired. The population from which the flight attendants are drawn includes many who are relatively unsophisticated. They may never have seen many of the things we take for granted, such as cutlery and many of the items on the menu. Consequently, many of the successful ones have to learn very basic skills — how to use make-up, how to use cutlery, how to serve gourmet meals they are unfamiliar with. During their training, they have to clean planes and accompany sales staff visiting travel agents before they can become flight attendants. The tasks learned in training help to develop an overall operational perspective as well as knowledge of what is really important to customers.[299] The airline must train them carefully — it is the attention to a myriad of minute, seemingly unimportant details that distinguishes this airline. The training gives them the motivation and ability to perform at the expected high level of service (Figure 7-5).

FIGURE 7-5   The three components of successful human resource management

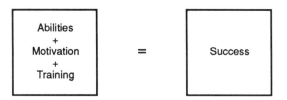

However, there is much more to good service than getting the technical details right. Surveys show that emotional tone makes as strong an impression on customers as having a problem solved quickly.[299] However, the staff does not create quality in a service as much as they deliver it by performing well. One poll identified perceived indifference on the part of service employees as the main reason (68%) why customers stopped patronizing a business.[81] This should be a powerful incentive for managers to keep their employees motivated.

Pride in doing a job well is a strong motivating factor. Being in contact with customers the employee has been able to satisfy can be a source of pride. However, many services are designed to minimize contact with customers in the interest of efficiency. Mechanics who repair the cars at automobile dealerships are usually isolated from customers by a service representative. But when a customer is able to talk directly to the mechanic, he or she usually gets a better explanation of what caused the problem and other useful information than when it is filtered through a service representative. Every minute spent talking with the mechanic costs the customer about $1, but there is much more involved than when the mechanic is simply working on the car. Not only does the mechanic take on a new role, motivating to him or her, but the customer also gets better service. There will probably always be room for small personal service stations staffed with real people.

There are other possibilities. Tasca was the best Lincoln-Mercury dealer in the US in 1986 and 1987, with sales of $53 million. They divide their service department into six color-coded teams which compete for monthly bonuses of $500 to $800.[214] Tasca's owner attributes the success of the dealership in large part to his service employees' commitment to excellence. They don't like to see a car come back because they have to fix it again. Trelltex Inc. has a similar approach.[77] They promise to ship goods within 24 hours, notify customers of any back-orders before shipping, ship the right product and make no pricing errors. If they fail, the customer gets $25. If they meet their promise, the group of order-handling employees shares $250 per month, less what was paid out to customers. After the program was introduced, errors went from about ten per month (at $200 each) to two or three. Employees do not need expensive incentives; they need basic motivation, which may take a variety of forms, even within the same company.

7.7   Setting the appropriate culture

By corporate culture, we mean the set of values underlying the way an organization is managed. The corporate culture depends on the values of the employees, especially those in top management. It also depends on the organization's history and the personal values of former top managers, especially the founder. Corporate culture is often exemplified by what might be called 'team spirit.'

Motivation cannot be sustained through programs such as 'employee of the month.' There has to be a meaningful permanent philosophy that employees will accept voluntarily. Slogans such as Avis' "We try harder" has to inspire employees to do the little extras that distinguish Avis from its competitors. In the manufacturing sector, Ford's slogan, "Quality is job 1" was backed by a change in attitude among top management. This attitude was passed along to employees and helped Ford to pass GM in profits in 1987.

Changing corporate culture and bringing in the right type of leadership is not easy. A good corporate culture can help employees to do their best for themselves, the organization and its customers. A poor one can make employees wonder why they should make an effort to please customers. When an enterprise has many services that are independent of each other, cross-functional group training can help to instill the same philosophy of excellent customer service in all employees.

Organizational leadership can have far-reaching effects within the organization and in the long term. Despite the fact that Walt Disney died in 1966, his philosophy is still felt at Disney theme parks by all 'cast members,' Disney's name for employees. The philosophy of Hewlett-Packard's founders was to maintain technological leadership; the philosophy has carried the company through decades of progress. In each enterprise, the founders were on-hand; they talked to employees and were close to the action; they really believed in what they preached and acted accordingly. The combination is one of the strongest incentives for employees to act in the same way.

Stew Leonard, founder of Stew Leonard's Dairy, has been very successful because of his 'Love that customer' philosophy.[171] The Director of Personnel looks for attitude; the rest can be achieved later. Team spirit is instilled in each new employee. The idea (Figure 7-6) is that good team spirit leads to increased pride in being part of the team, then desire for excellence (nothing less) motivates employees to work toward pleasing customers and doing an outstanding job. Success for both the employees and the customer are thus achieved.

FIGURE 7-6   Stew Leonard's recipe for success

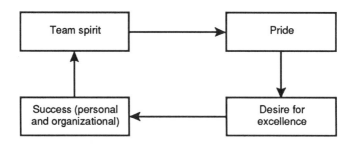

Not all organizations can evaluate the service provided by employees as closely as Stew Leonard can; until 1987, his company had only one outlet. In larger enterprises, quality circles could be helpful both in improving quality and in finding better means to relate operations more closely to corporate philosophy. However, there are a number of problems in using quality circles in services.[170] Intangible products are hard to evaluate; circle members change jobs frequently; multi-site operations hinder communication; and there may be no organizational culture that recognizes quality as a predominant goal. These problems do not eliminate quality circles from the list of possible approaches, but they do emphasize the importance of a coordinated and consistent approach to managing human resources.

CHAPTER 8

GROWTH AND STRATEGY

Growth

8.1 Growth is a strategy

The underlying assumption of most service organizations is that they will grow at some stage; many feel that growth is a measure of success. Growth is usually justified on the grounds of market potential, available resources, preference of top management, a desire to move in before the competition or to develop personnel. Growth usually requires a major reallocation of resources as well as potential changes in objectives. As such, growth is itself a strategy. However, there are viable strategies other than growth as evidenced by the many very successful firms that remain essentially the same size for years. Not all enterprises want to, or should, grow.

We deal with growth first because growth brings to light many of the long-term problems managers commonly face. We later discuss other respects of strategy.

Three distinct modes of growth can be identified. Many service firms grow by adding sites — multiplication. Others, perhaps locked into a single site for some reason, grow by adding services — diversification. Still others grow by purchasing an existing service business, and converting and integrating the purchased units — take over.

8.2 Multiple sites as a growth strategy

Opening a new site cannot be done haphazardly. Once the decision has been made, location must be given due consideration:

> Service organizations normally grow by opening new branches. The choice of where to locate a new outlet has been oversimplified in both practice and theory. Evaluating a potential location requires estimating three effects: the primary effect — what sales and profit the outlet will attain; the secondary effect — ... the impact of the new outlet on the performance of existing outlets; and the network cost effect — how the new outlet will affect the cost structure of all the outlets within the group.[64, p. 403]

Although operating more than one unit might create control problems, it could still be justified by the reasons listed at the beginning of this chapter. Because the service sector is turbulent,[68] there are ample opportunities for organizations that can operate in that context. The rapid and major changes that are taking place stem from over-capacity, new low-cost competitors and spiralling customer expectations. One strategic response to these changes is to develop new or significantly modified services. While it's true that competitive forces may reduce revenues and profits, a good concept and delivery system can usually be counted on to attract clients and provide some immunity from competition.

Although recent advances in computer and communication software have made multi-site management somewhat easier, major challenges remain. Some aspects, such as personnel management and quality control, are a significant challenge in a single site, let alone in multiple ones. Managers of multi-site operations require notably different skills than their counterparts in single sites.

Multi-site firms typically start off with a single site. At the single-site stage, the chief executive, often the founder and owner, is involved in all functional areas. He or she is responsible for managing the firm's resources, marketing the firm's services, and developing and maintaining the integrity of the firm's concept. Financial management, which may have been important during start-up, may well shrink as positive cash flows are achieved.

Often, organizations that are successful make the move to multi-site operations. When they do so, the managerial job changes markedly, especially if there are many new units or if the new units are far away. Expanding across international borders poses an additional set of challenges. Superior technical, administrative and financial resources are required.[80] It is preferable to standardize operations as much as possible so that solutions to problems can be easily transferred between sites.

This synergy can both attract clients and entrance productivity. As soon as a second site is contemplated, financing becomes an issue again, as does site selection, site development and unit start-up. They will continue to be important as long as growth continues. Marketing has to serve a geographically broader area. The chief executive, who can only be in one place at a time, looses touch with operations. Consequently, it is imperative that the organization have a strong concept before expansion begins. The strength of the concept depends both on design and on communication. The concept must be designed to be internally consistent and to meet the needs of a specific, targeted market segment. It must also be communicated to the unit managers and staff, who have to execute it on a daily basis. So before expansion begins, the organization must prepare training and operations manuals, arrange training sessions, etc.

It is also essential that the organization have an adequate control system so that it can be managed at a distance. The senior executive or other head office staff must be able to get the information they need when they need it to ensure that the units are operating properly. Information has to be available either on paper or electronically because, although the head office staff can and should visit periodically, they cannot be at the site at all times and cannot be expected to manage the unit. That job falls to the unit manager or franchisee.

Collier suggests ten criteria for evaluating how transportable an operation is: legal restrictions, ability to advertise, technical capabilities, channels of distribution, cultural and social norms, distance, buyer behavior, language, political stability and national synergism.[52] Despite its technical capabilities, Japan's internal distribution systems lag well behind those of most industrialized countries. Japan's language and culture are also quite alien to most North Americans. In Japan, a nod of the head that we would interpret as 'yes' may well mean 'no.' Consequently, most firms making their first international venture find it far easier to get their feet wet elsewhere in North America, in Europe or in Australasia first before trying to cope with so many changes simultaneously. This does not mean that expansion of service enterprises into very different cultures is impossible — far from it, as the world-wide success of many service businesses attests.

McDonald's emphasis on QSC & V (quality, service, cleanliness and value) is a good combination that is easy to export. In cultures such as Japan's, rigid adherence to procedures is normal and easy. The rigid procedures are not the hardest part for McDonald's to duplicate. In the Soviet Union, the supply system required to meet their standards of quality is a major challenge. The company had to train Soviet farmers to cultivate and harvest imported varieties of potatoes and cucumbers, and to manage their cattle. The company also built a food distribution plant with its own bakery, dairy, meat-processing units and microbiology laboratory.[20] McDonald's looked on this as a necessary investment to develop its concept in this new market while adhering to its well-delineated standards.

There are numerous internal factors in multi-site expansion as well (see Figure 8-1) which can either facilitate or hinder multi-site growth. For example, a highly specialized consulting firm might find it difficult to find suitable personnel. This characteristic would limit its growth by opening additional offices. Such a company would likely also be well known, so having an office near customers may not be a significant advantage. Many one-person consulting firms operate around the world from a single site.

FIGURE 8-1   Factors influencing the number of sites of a service enterprise

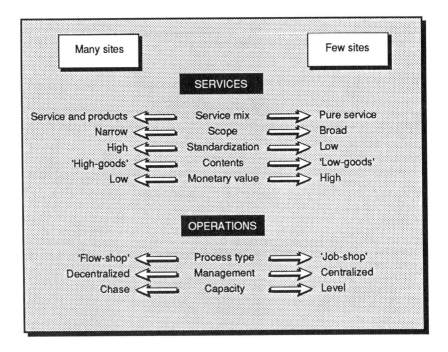

Figure 8-2 illustrates the factors involved in the decision to expand in a somewhat different way. In this figure, the size of the circles represents the relative importance of a factor in the overall design of the service. If personnel are key, as in the example of the specialized consulting firm, it is more sensible to operate few sites. Conversely, if equipment consti-

FIGURE 8-2   Relative importance of the factors influencing the number of sites of a service organization

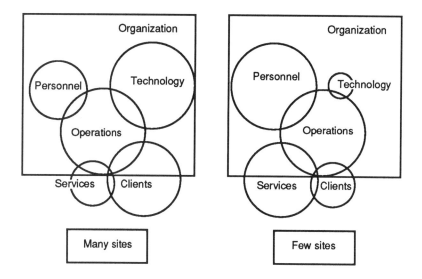

tutes a major portion of the service design, opening additional sites should be more feasible.

The importance of customers is an interesting factor. Fast food operations grow by multi-site expansion because the service must be readily accessible to customers. Many other services are of this type. For the consulting firm, however, a single site is feasible because the service can be taken directly to the customer or performed in a remote office without the customer being present. In other cases, for example in highly specialized medical services, the customer will go to extraordinary lengths to get to the service. Although this framework may at first glance appear to be very conceptual, it is helpful in assessing the importance of the many factors that influence the decision to add sites.

As noted earlier in this chapter, services can expand across international borders. Despite their intangibility, services have a bright future as potential exports.[153] The service itself is not usually exported; it is produced abroad and the profits are repatriated. An alternative is to bring customers to the country of origin. Tourism and medical treatment or legal action that requires international travel are examples. Many consulting and accounting firms operate internationally as do organizations operating in areas such as hospital cleaning and garbage collection. Among the more promising services for international development are advertising, transportation, shipping, software, data-base storage, construction, health care, filmmaking and banking. Trade in services is reciprocal; many firms in other countries can, and do, export services to North America. The coming decade may see explosive growth in service exports and major changes in the international players.

Growth by adding sites has extended to many services. Kinder-Care owns and operates all of its centres, although similar organizations tend to operate on a franchise basis (see below).[78] Its service concept is based on the feeling that parents want development and education for their children as well as care. Kinder-Care's operating procedures are highly standardized; they are printed up in binders and new educators are expected to become familiar with them. However, the standardization and low pay have resulted in high staff turnover (100% annually). Some criticize this approach and the mixed results which include a possible standardized attitude towards children; others claim that it is a good start for an area which was not well organized even ten years ago. Other organizations have pursued a similar concept, except that they are considering franchising, which may be inappropriate at the top end of this market.[278]

8.3   Franchising as a growth option

Any enterprise that takes its service directly to the customer must add sites to achieve significant growth unless it changes the service. Company-owned sites are easier to control and can be more profitable; they make it possible to test new ideas but they require operational expertise. These are good reasons to keep at least a few company-owned units in an expanding chain.

Franchising is a method of distributing a good and/or service in which the franchisor contracts out the right to carry on a business in a prescribed way, for a set period of time, in a specific location. In essence, the franchisor is selling a tradename and/or the right to operate under that name. In exchange, the franchisee usually pays an initial franchise fee, as well as annual royalty fees based on sales and a share of advertising costs. The franchisee agrees to manage the business in a prescribed way.

Franchising is a very common alternative to maintaining ownership of expansion sites, and with good reason: there are substantial advantages to both franchisor and franchisee. The franchisor can expand rapidly using investment capital from franchisees as financing and their hightened motivation as independent operators to boost sales. Depending on the terms of the franchise agreement, the advantages to the franchisee include a proven concept, lower start-up costs, wide-spread advertising, assistance with operations, materials at a lower cost and possibly territorial exclusivity. The two parties share profits and control. Studies have shown that franchises fail at a fifth the rate of new businesses and grow more quickly.[243] Many franchises are available for less that $250,000; some include a financing package to make them more accessible.

Many franchisors try to control their franchises closely, both to ensure a better chance of survival and to maintain the overall image of the organization. Based on the assumption that the franchisor knows the best way to run the business, control of operations should improve revenues as well. Franchises may be offered individually (each unit has a separate franchise agreement) or as a group, possibly a geographic territory or as a master franchise. Territorial franchises or franchises to non-operating investors represent a much higher risk to the franchisor. To maintain operational control, a franchisor may grant individual franchises or retain ownership of the facility and franchise out only the operation. An organization may be reluctant to grant a territorial franchise unless it is ready to relinquish more control than it would by awarding individual franchises. However, maintaining close control and growing quickly may be mutually exclusive, as shown in Figure 8-3.

FIGURE 8-3   Principal forms of franchising

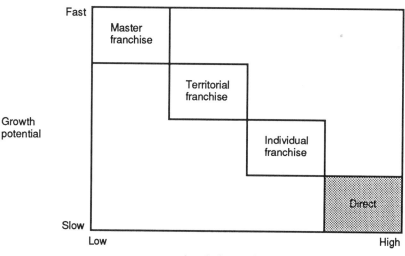

Franchising has become big business. McDonald's is a major franchising success story. As of early 1990, McDonald's had 11,300 franchises in about 50 countries around the world, including Japan and the

Soviet Union, and was growing at a rate of about 500 units per year. The company's current management believes just as strongly in private ownership as did founder, Ray Kroc. For them, private ownership is the key to ensuring superior quality, service, cleanliness and value (QSC & V). How does the philosophy fit in eastern Europe? Negotiations were and continue to be difficult. It took George Cohon, President and CEO of McDonald's Canada, 14 years to open a unit in Moscow. It was not a typical opening. McDonald's had to develop a large food supply infrastructure to support the unit. Sometimes discussions with the Moscow City Council's food service division had to start again from scratch because the whole Soviet negotiating team had changed without notice. Mr. Cohon explains why the Soviets finally accepted the deal:

> It might sound like an exaggeration to speak of 'technology transfer' when you're talking about a milk-shake machine, but what these countries are getting with the McDonald's deal is a whole culture of production that has proved itself to be among the most successful in the world. Quality control — in the sense that a correctly weighed portion of perfectly fried, precisely sliced, uniformly cultivated potatoes is a measure of quality — is an enormous challenge to Soviet production. Going into business with McDonald's is a shortcut to mastering that expertise.[20, p. 35]

McDonald's experience in transferring its expertise to the Soviet Union illustrates the importance of developing an infrastructure if necessary, and of being patient. These lessons are as relevant for franchises within a nation as they are in the international arena.

With over 2,500 units in the United States as of 1988, McDonald's was the country's largest owner of commercial real estate.[218] The organization has stuck tenaciously to its service concept, focusing on hamburgers. As one McDonald's manager was quoted as saying (somewhat tongue in cheek): "We have over 16,000 washrooms; when they are all clean we will consider diversifying."[93, p.2] Some observers consider the addition of breakfast and salad to the menu to be long-terms mistakes; however, the McDonald's name has proven to be stronger than theory.

Drugstore franchises have also grown significantly over the past 20 years, although many see this trend as part of the changing role (deprofessionalization) of pharmacists. Jean Coutu franchises account for 42% of drugstore sales in Quebec. Less than 25% of sales are pharmaceutical. Because of its size, Jean Coutu enjoys purchasing strength which means the organization can offer very competitive prices; impulse sales to customers originally attracted by its advertisements are also increased.

New units, either franchised or company-owned, usually duplicate as closely as possible the original service. However, this is not necessarily always the case. Disneyland in Japan is a close copy of the California original, including the design of the trash cans and the location of the drinking fountains. In fact, its biggest asset is that it looks like the USA.[101] However, the unit in Florida is much larger and has many more attractions than the one in California. In France, the government is an active player, through its subway and highway systems, and reduced amusement park taxes in exchange for which French is the park's dominant language. Walt Disney Company retains 17% equity and controls the park's management, whereas in Japan it simply gets royalties on admissions and sales.

The Au Bon Pain fast food chain is another forceful example.[187] Plagued by symptoms of disheartened unit managers, Au Bon Pain introduced a very successful partner-manager program to motivate its managers. Each manager has considerable freedom to exercise individual initiative in day-to-day operations and participates in a potentially lucrative profit-sharing plan. Apparently, managers are now inspired. Although service quality is high in each restaurant as measured by comprehensive corporate-wide criteria, each Au Bon Pain outlet has developed its own distinct character. This company is trading off a certain amount of chain-wide uniformity for manager motivation.

Most legislative jurisdictions have extensive by-laws that require prospective franchisors to fully disclose financial and operating data. Nevertheless, not all franchises are success stories. Many fail because of lack of finances, managerial inexperience, poor concept and/or a lack of attention by the franchisee.[106] The Frits chain, a Quebec fastfood operation which focused on hot dogs and french fries, is one example.[264] They appeared to have an advantage by focusing on a non-hamburger product line. There are over 15,000 hamburger outlets in the United States and only 315 hot dog franchises. But people weren't prepared to drive to a hot dog outlet over McDonald's, Burger King or Kentucky Fried Chicken. Furthermore, Frits outlets were 3,000 square feet, too large (and expensive) for this type of franchise. The biggest mistake, however, seems to be that there were franchisees who wanted to invest in instead of operate a fast food outlet. The few owners whose units are still operating have changed the name and made significant other changes at considerable personal cost and time. In essence, they have completely changed the concept; they got a location out of their original investment.

The Pop-Ins maid service chain failed for a number of reasons, key among them being mismanagement of virtually every aspect of the business.[106] Cash flow problems, inexperienced management and lack of support for franchises led to bankruptcy. It highlights the fact that once a franchise is sold, the franchisor's work is not over. The franchisor has to provide marketing, operations and legal support to maintain the value of the franchises. Without on-going support, there is no advantage to being part of a chain, franchised or otherwise.

8.4   Multi-service strategies

Some firms choose to grow by diversifying the service they offer. These enterprises often have a large fixed asset that is either unique or under-utilized. Ski resorts often expand this way. Their major asset — the mountain — cannot be duplicated, although alternative sites could be found. Ski resorts are also seasonal, and their assets create virtually no return during the off-season or years with poor snow conditions. So the option is to become a two- or all-season resort by developing summer attractions, accommodation and conference business. When done well, the results are striking. There are, however, many pitfalls. An all-season resort has to design a single set of facilities to meet the needs of several different segments of the market. Accommodation, and food and beverage facilities suitable for skiers may be less than ideal for the conference market. In addition, their cost structure may be different than that of more appropriate facilities. The net result could be a very difficult managerial job.

Fast food restaurants have expanded by adding a breakfast menu. The key to success seems to be a menu that fits the restaurant's overall fast food philosophy and uses the same facilities. If the time that breakfast is available is restricted, focus will probably not suffer. Keg Restaurants, a house with a concept that includes a 'good times' philosophy resisted opening at lunch, despite the profit potential, because its management perceived that the fast pace of lunch service was inconsistent with the company's relaxed image

Diversification can be fruitful, but managers must not lose sight of the original business. It has to provide both cash flow during expansion as well as a nucleus of loyal customers for the new facilities.

The focus of an operation is a major strategic decision. Some of the potential problems are that focus is not unidirectional, customer needs differ, classification schemes can be too broad and a service package is often more complex than it appears at first glance.[300] However, focus can be improved. Although classification schemes (Chapter 2) are usually used to distinguish between industries, better schemes, or the more intelligent application of existing ones, could be used to distinguish between competing firms within an industry instead. Repackaging services, zeroing in on the right customers, and separating front and back room operations are other possibilities. Unbundling a service may be warranted when customers want only a part of the package. Many restaurants began offering a salad bar as a side order, but discovered that many customers considered salad to be a main course. They responded by repackaging their service to offer a salad bar as either a side dish or a main course. Airlines cannot seem to make up their minds about bundling.

Some unbundle, charging extra for drinks and headsets. Other bundle, including all services in the ticket price.

Organizations must of course be careful about modifying their core service; it often constitutes the raison d'être of the enterprise. Peripheral services are much easier to modify. Hospitals are in the health care business and because of its specialized equipment and staff, it is extremely unlikely that any hospital would completely change its focus. However, a hospital might change from being a general hospital to a specialty one; it would still be focused on health care but the service concept would be different.

Multi-service concepts are one way to grow. Yet another way to grow quickly is by acquisition — acquiring a similar service organization and converting its units. This mode of growth can be used to expand nationally as well as internationally. Accounting firms like Touche Ross have used it. (Others, such as Arthur Andersen, have preferred to expand more slowly by expanding internally.) The acquiring firm buys sites, market share, customer base, concept, staff, equipment and/or management. The major danger is incompatibility between the two corporate cultures, including managerial style. It seems that only after the merger do the differences between apparently similar services become evident. This often happens in the mergers of law, accounting, advertising and brokerage firms. For example, one of Touche Ross' acquisitions in the early 1980s resulted in a loss of both staff and clientele of about 40% within 18 months, including some key managers and clients.

Retail operations that expand within other stores do not have to worry as much about inconsistent philosophies, as long as the customer base is similar. A post office operating within a retail store is a good example. A store within a store often leads to increased sales for both because it attracts more customers.[27] Overhead and fixed costs are also reduced. It is an alternative to diversification — the benefits are achieved without management being spread too thin.

8.5   Demands on management

Different types of expansion require different managerial skills. Adding sites takes shrewdness in finding, selecting and developing them. Adding services requires ability in managing complex operations. Acquisition and conversion takes talent in managing change. Figure 8-4 illustrates the relative degree or risk involved in moving from a single service/single location operation to a more complex one. In general, simple moves are less risky than complex ones. For example, Toys R Us first focused solely on toys but later added children's clothing to its product line. This change implied modifications to the layout as well as more personalized

FIGURE 8-4   Location and changing the service as risk factors

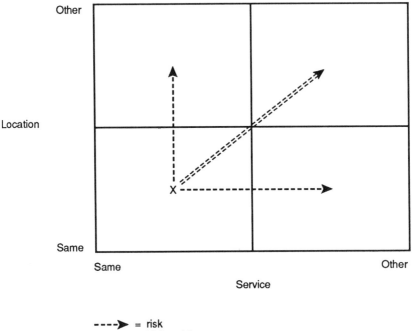

```
----▶  = risk
====▶  = higher risk
```

service,[268] and would have been much more risky had the company made the change in all its stores simultaneously or merged with a clothing retailer. But they were successful because they chose to execute expansion progressively and proceed in a closely controlled manner. The company enjoys a 20% share of retail toy sales in the United States, which translates into economies of scale and preferential treatment from suppliers, such as early delivery of popular toys.[70] Toys R Us must have done something right! In contrast, Three Buoys Houseboat Vacations was involved in at least three different businesses (houseboat manufacturing, houseboat rental and marina operation) and rapidly growing. Reduced sales, cash flow problems and increasing managerial complexity combined to force this entrepreneurial company into bankruptcy in 1989.

8.6   Manufacturing firms moving into services

If a manufacturer wants to put more emphasis on customer service, develop new services or acquire a service company, it needs a change of orientation from top management. A simple decision based on financial considerations is not enough.

Manufacturers moving into services have many options. Potts suggests that 95% of profits come from services after the peak of a product's life.[239] This can represent a source of profit for any organization prepared to deliver the level of service customers expect. Once the warranty expires, customers can choose to continue a relationship with that firm or find an alternate supplier. Car manufacturers have been able to retain customers by offering plans similar to those offered by health maintenance organizations. Customers pay a fixed annual fee as insurance against major repairs on the condition that they go to an approved dealer and have regular preventive maintenance checks.

Manufacturers can enter the service field in several ways.[42] Canton points to the potential benefits of expanding into services compared to manufactured items — lower costs of capital, distribution and energy, and reduced international competition.[33] A manufacturer can develop services within its current technology and market or develop new markets and/or technology at a greater risk (Figure 8-5). Firms like IBM or Prime Computers that service their own products through service contracts are in Quadrant 1. Not all manufacturers can offer a service that is related to their core operation. The Batesville Casket Division moved into Quadrant 2 when it diversified into the insurance business.

FIGURE 8-5   Changes in technology and market as risk factors

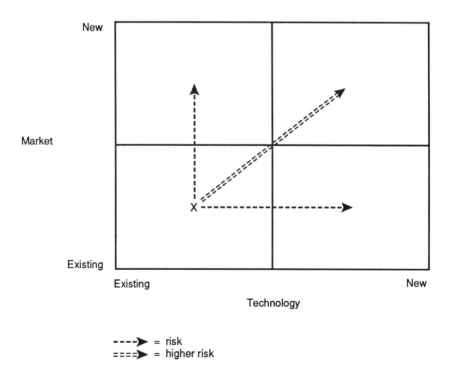

On the other hand, some manufacturers can use the same technology but aim for different markets. Ticketron expanded by decentralizing into offices in many retail stores, thus moving from Quadrant 1 to Quadrant 3. A move from Quadrant 1 to Quadrant 4 is very risky. Canton lists ten avenues for diversification into services, including: building on the firm's skills (DuPont selling its maintenance expertise), financing customers (General Motors Acceptance Corporation) and capitalizing on existing resources (Kimberly-Clark selling airplane maintenance developed for its corporate fleet).[33]

Chase and Garvin suggest that manufacturers can provide services by using their facilities as laboratories, for consultations, as showrooms and for dispatching. They also suggest that there are many more possibilities. In their words:

> Tomorrow's leading manufacturing companies will be the ones whose managers unleash the service potential of their factories. Competition demands it. Technology makes it possible.[42, p. 68]

These strategies require a sound analysis both of an organization's strengths and weaknesses, and of its fit with new opportunities. It also requires a broad strategic perspective from top management. This type of analysis leads to the second section of this chapter, an overview of service strategy.

Strategy

The strategy taken by top management is the overall direction for all decisions and activities in the organization. It is based on their assessment of organizational capabilities, what competitors, suppliers and customers are likely to do, and other anticipated changes in the environment. Figure 8-6 presents a framework that can be used to determine an overall strategy leading to a strategy for operations; the same model can be used for marketing, human resources and other areas.

A strategy deals with growth, but other options — maintaining the status quo or even reducing the size of the operation — should also be considered. Both internal factors (past experience, control, managerial competence) and external factors (service life cycle, market share, available funds) have to be taken into account. Figure 8-7 emphasizes that both growth and shrinkage are integral parts of an overall strategy. As one author put it:

> In sum, strategic management can be described as an ongoing, pro-active, future-result-oriented process of managing organizations and their environments through utilizing knowledge derived from various

FIGURE 8-6   Strategic planning model for operations in service organizations

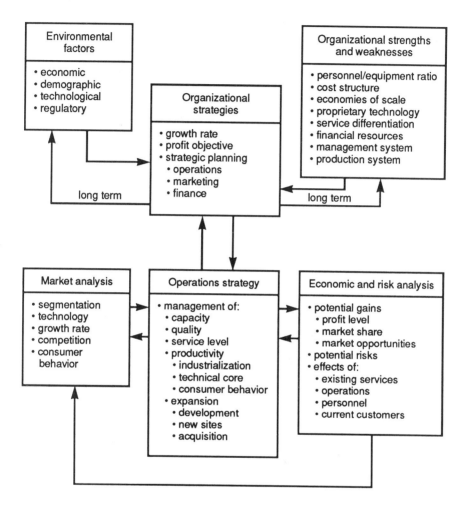

disciplines. All of these components are aimed at organizational survival, growth and profitability[247, p. 333]

Results are important. They should correspond to measurable objectives that enable different units in the organization to have similar targets. Resistance to change is an internal obstacle but there are also external problems:

> Indeed, the function of strategic management often includes the task of shielding, interpreting, or filtering market changes so as not to disrupt the operation in a dysfunctional way... We propose that, from the standpoint of the operations function, this 'strategic filter' acts to shape three

FIGURE 8-7   Determining future operations strategies

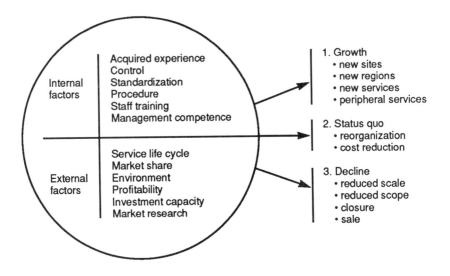

vital influences on systems productivity: the *Volume* of demand; the *Variety* of services to be offered; the *Variation* in the volume and nature of demand over time.[7, p. 98]

One study of a 25-branch distributing operation illustrates the types of problems that a change in environment can bring.[133] Many of the mistakes in distribution — wrong material, wrong place, wrong time — resulted from treating symptoms instead of causes, from not understanding the system fully, from providing bad information to poorly trained personnel and from a lack of leadership in distribution. In this case, identifying goals, including the logistics of strategic planning, watching for changes in the supply chain and getting to know customers well were key factors in solving the problem. Staff can't be expected to deliver a coherent service unless top management clearly identifies a strategy for the enterprise and demonstrates how all of the organization's activities relate to that strategy.

8.7   Relationship of strategy to customers, staff and structure

A strategy aims to design a service (and deliver it as designed) while paying close attention to the strategies used by competitors. An organization can compete on many levels: price, range of services and quality are the three most common. Even within a single environment, different strategies can be successful. For example, some companies try to enhance the interface between the firm and the customer while competitors may try to reduce the interface. Both strategies can be effective. Shouldice Hospital specializes in external inguinal hernia surgery on healthy patients. It enhance interaction between staff and patients to improve patient morale, orient new patients and give the hospital a good public image.[120] Other hospitals try to reduce customer-server interactions by promoting out-patient clinics and hospitals without walls (in which service is provided in the patient's home, and by using more para-professional staff. Despite these radically different approaches, both types of hospital provide high quality services.

Shouldice Hospital is a good example of an organization with an intimate knowledge of its target market. It attracts many foreign patients based on its reputation for patient care and excellent results. Its service delivery system fully support its strategy (outlined above), so each factor is coherently integrated: a clearly identified market, a consistent service concept, a clear strategy, and a reliable and coherent delivery system.

Heskett suggests that:

> High-performance service companies have gained their status in large measure by turning the strategic service vision inward: by targeting important groups of employees as well as customers.[121, pp. 120-121]

This position points out the importance of execution and management commitment in service delivery. Targeting employees could be included under 'internal quality,' which is closely related to operations strategy. In contrast, external quality is related to competitive strategy (see Figure 8-8).

FIGURE 8-8   Relationship between operating strategy, competitive strategy, and the production of products and services

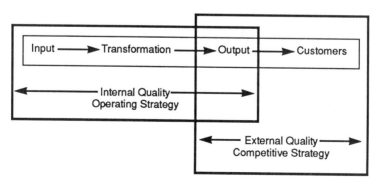

Once a strategy has been chosen, there are implications for the structure of the organization, which has to support the strategy. It could even be argued that structure is a part of strategy. Organizations that compete on price usually require tight control and are designed to provide it. Organizations that compete on fast response must be structured accordingly. One group suggested restructuring accounting firms along project (matrix) management lines instead of functional ones.[98] They did this to improve customer service through greater flexibility, possibly at the expense of efficiency. A study of 27 nursing sub-units revealed that high levels of structural instability and staff participation (facilitated by the structure) led to high performance.[1] Such outcomes are favored by organizational decentralization and extensive delegation; ultimately, the success of any strategy depends on the motivation and action of the service providers.

Thomas suggests six aspects for evaluating a given service strategy:

1. thoroughly understand the organization's specific service business
2. know the strategies to use against competitors
3. examine how to improve operational cost effectiveness
4. reexamine pricing strategy
5. develop and test new services with a coherent approach
6. consider acquisitions only if they really make sense for the organization.[295]

The elaboration of a strategy can be a complex process. However, general guidelines for determining a strategy in a manufacturing operation may also provide some useful hints for the service sector. Growth is one such strategy. However, one must be particularly careful about growing by adding the wrong types of services or expanding too quickly. Growing too much or in the wrong way, or trying to be all things to all people is not usually feasible. Unfortunately, the public sector, the subject of Chapter 9, often tries to do so.

CHAPTER
9

PUBLIC SERVICES

Increasing Performance: Mission Impossible?

The public sector is large in all developed societies. In North America, cries for 'fiscal responsibility' in government spending are common. This generally means a demand to cut back on public expenditure. At the same time, there are pleas, equally loud and often from the same quarters, for increased public support for a large number of causes. It is also no secret that public services are often run primarily, not for the benefit of the citizens who pay for the service, but to ensure that the governing party is re-elected. As Alter and co-authors put it in an article in *Newsweek*:

> Today's members [of the United States Congress] have become almost totally preoccupied with achieving a state of grace known as high visibility... for every one letter sent to Washington by a constituent, members of Congress send back an average of 12,000... Not only is most staff employed to enhance re-election, but most legislation also is introduced for that purpose... Congress is not unlike a failing railroad. The less freight it carries, the more people it employs... 132 of 253 House Democrats were chairman of a committee, subcommittee or select committee, and the Senate is even worse...[2, pp. 28, 29, 30]

This is the context in which public sector managers must operate. Efficiency and effectiveness are bound to be difficult to achieve simultaneously. In fact, according to Ross:

> The end result may or may not be the one that is most cost-effective, but it will probably satisfy most of the actors who built the consensus necessary to satisfy their constituents' interests. In the public sector,

rational decision making is usually equated with political self-interest.[255, p. 30]

However, despite the obvious difficulties of improving management of the public sector, there have been some success stories.

9.1   The nature of public services

A significant segment of the service sector is made up of public services, whose productivity trails that of services in the private sector. The management of public sector services is under constant scrutiny because many of the services are essential, they are considered to be public property and the competence of their management is suspected. This section examines some of the special characteristics of public services.

According to Drucker, the reasons usually cited for the poor performance of the public service — unbusinesslike managers, inept staff, and intangible objectives and results — are only excuses.[66] In his view, the real cause of public sector malaise is the way public services are funded. Businesses, in his terms, are paid for satisfying customers. If customers do not receive value for their money, the organization will ultimately lose them. Public services, on the other hand, are usually funded from an allocated budget. Budgets are linked only marginally to the outcome they are expected to produce; instead they are allocated based on promises and good intentions. They are not connected directly to what the customer means by results and performance, nor to customer use of the service. The general lack of post-service reviews in the absence of motivation and resources to do so, compounds the problem even further. Public services are often monopolies, established either by legislation or convention. For example, an organization's use of its own maintenance department may be so entrenched that it becomes almost impossible for anyone in the organization to look elsewhere for maintenance services. Their customers have little or no choice in whether or not they use the service and/or pay for it. Many budget-based services are found in private enterprise as well as in the public sector, with similar characteristics.[66] Virtually any service department of a private sector organization — R & D, accounting, personnel — is in this category.

Control of budgets and expenditures is a difficult and critical task. In the Canadian context, the office of the Auditor General and its provincial counterparts bear much of the burden of proof that funds are being mismanaged. Despite their collective efforts, the results of which are made public every year, many of the suggestions from the Auditor General's office lead to tightened control, but not necessarily improved operational efficiency.

The sort of mismanagement the Auditor General looks for is poor performance as well as misapplication of controls. However, the terms 'results' and 'performance' take on different meanings in public services. 'Results' means a larger budget and 'performance' is often equated with the ability to maintain or increase the budget. Contributions to the market or achieving a goal (the usual meaning of the term 'results') are of secondary importance.

In a system in which gaining control of larger budgets augments power, efficiency is not necessarily desirable.[66] Achieving results with a reduced budget or staff amounts to 'poor' performance and reduced power. It may even threaten the very viability of the service and certainly that of the individuals within it. To spend under-budget is a clear signal that the next budget can be cut. When planning projects in budget-based organizations, it may be useful to grossly underestimate costs to get others to 'buy in'; once in, it may be relatively easy to arrange for larger budgets to allow the project to continue. And, in such organizations, the increased budget represents results.

Effectiveness is even more endangered in public services than efficiency.[66] To ask a controversial question such as: 'Should we be in this business at all?' poses a serious threat to the budget, and hence to potential rewards, power and even survival. The defensive approach of adding, but never rationalizing, leads to loss of focus and ineffectiveness. Dependence on a budget discourages setting priorities and concentrating efforts. Spreading resources too thinly and failing to address issues promptly rarely works; too little, too late is usually neither effective nor efficient. Operating as a monopoly almost certainly leads to a loss of focus. A profit-based organization with a 25% share of its market could be considered successful by any measure. It can remain focused on meeting its customers' needs because it has no obligation to satisfy a broader constituency. In contrast, a monopoly rejected by 75% of its 'customers' would be on very shaky ground indeed. It would not likely have its budget renewed. The probable response would be to lose focus by trying to be all things to all people.

Without relying on 'return on investment' or some other measure of results, cutting back can be difficult. Because what the institution does is always virtuous and 'in the public interest,' and not measured by results, it is tempting to respond to pressure for results from customers or managers by doubling effort (and the budget).

In the public sector, the allocation of funds should be more closely related to performance. Organizational units should be held accountable when they underestimate costs. It is admittedly not easy to change a budget philosophy, especially considering that policital power plays a role in budget allocation. However, it is often possible to do more — or less — with a given budget.

9.2   Efficiency or effectiveness?

Virtually every politician denounces the mismanagement of funds, operational inefficiency and poor service — except, of course, within their own jurisdiction. However, few seem prepared or able to do anything about it. The problem is significant enough that former President Reagan issued an executive order in 1986 to increase productivity within United States government departments by 20% by 1992, a compounded annual growth rate of about 3%. How effective can this approach be in such a huge system? Some progress has been made.[82] Based on statistical sampling, United States Customs adopted an honor system at Houston International Airport, which increased throughput by a factor of 2.5. This approach has undoubtedly increased efficiency and probably the public's perception of the service, but it also allows dishonest people to circumvent the law, which decreases its effectiveness. Managers in this situation face two problems: one is to develop a viable system for measuring performance appropriate to their department and the other is to involve employees in improving productivity even if it means rewarding them. Measurement often determines results. As Brown and Pyers noted:

> The idea of performance measurement has broad support, but it is often opposed in specific instances of practice. Measures provide powerful signals about performance[28, pp. 741-2]

There are numerous stakeholders whose concerns should be dealt with. In this case, they are primarily internal ones. Although we acknowledge the difficulty of measuring white-collar productivity, many activities can be measured, at least adequately enough for internal management purposes.

Although the efficiency of public services is a major concern, their effectiveness can be even more of a problem. In this context, we are using 'effectiveness' to mean doing the right thing and 'efficiency' to mean doing it the right way. This suggests that effectiveness is related to quality, and efficiency to productivity; in fact, these four notions are intertwined.

Effectiveness is often colored by political choice. Vancouver's Expo 86 is an example of a project that was completed despite mounting evidence that it was unreasonable to do so. In 1978, when it was first approved, Expo 86 was projected to cost $78 million and was supposed to be self-financing.[256] By 1985, the estimated cost had escalated by a factor of 19 to $1.5 billion (52% per year compounded) with a projected deficit of $311 million. The project was initiated, and support for it was continued, despite many warning signs: Montreal had run up deficits of $285 million on Expo 67 and $1 billion on the 1976 Summer Olympic Games; the 1984 World's Fair in New Orleans was a financial failure; and it appeared that Vancouver's infrastructure could not support the expected number of visitors. However, then Premier William Bennett was committed to the project because it was politically popular with both the special interest groups that stood to benefit and the general public. Because people had 'bought in,' getting out (and admitting that a mistake had been made) was unappealing. Expo 86 lagged behind schedule throughout its construction and ultimately showed a deficit of nearly $350 million,[25, 92] but it was institutionally imbedded and was therefore difficult to abandon.

The deficit was officially paid for out of lottery proceeds, making these funds unavailable for other projects. It should be noted that the stated deficit is for accounting purposes only, and does not take into consideration lasting benefits such as increased tourism, long-term inter-firm trade relationships and other business from an enhanced awareness of Vancouver and British Columbia.

Expo 67 and Expo 86 clearly show how important a role political agenda plays in public sector decision-making, as well as the fact that the more resources there are invested in a project, the more difficult it is to withdraw from it. Managers of projects like the Olympic Games face extreme pressure. Not only are they under constant public scrutiny, but they also face absolutely unalterable deadlines. At one point during the construction of the site for the Montreal Olympics, there were apparently more large cranes on half a square mile than in all of Europe! There were numerous reports of expensive equipment being rented for months, just in case it might be needed. The political stakes were high enough to overcome any rational economic argument. Despite the acknowledged irrelevance of sunk costs in making decisions about the future, once a decision has been made to proceed with a project, it is very likely that it will be funded to completion. Keep in mind, however, that although the overall return may be too low, the return on a small incremental investment at the margin may well be acceptable. For example, a tall office building is virtually useless without an elevator. Once the large investment has been made in the building, the return on a relatively small extra investment in an elevator system is very large, even though the project as a whole may never give an adequate yield.

Large projects can attract successful managers from the private and public sectors and do well financially. The 1984 Summer Olympics in Los Angeles and the 1988 Winter Olympics in Calgary made that clear. The policital side of these projects is obvious but it may be at least as important in regular government activities. For some, the experience can be disheartening. For members of the United States cabinet, the situation is quite different:

The new appointees will spend an average of less than two years in their public-sector jobs, and many will return to the private sector disappointed in their performance and frustrated by a complex web of agencies, committees, and political actors that often seem to defy rationality.[255, p. 28]

Welfare, education and defence are big-ticket budget items in both Canada and the United States. The corresponding departments are often acknowledged to be both inefficient and ineffective. Their vastness makes it difficult to consider global improvements. The effectiveness of funds allocation and operations management is often only measurable long after implementation. For example, consider how long it takes to evaluate a new education system; and once it is found to be flawed, how long does it take to modify it?

Needless to say, politically influenced funding policies greatly affect the efficiency of resource use. Municipal bus companies in the United States are reported to have twice the optimal number of buses because of assistance programs that subsidized the purchase of buses.[37] These programs resulted from political pressure to increase funding of public transportation by Washington. However, the assistance package did not give municipalities funds to operate and maintain the buses properly. And, although having more buses leads to better service, there is a point at which the marginal extra service is unwise economically. Too often, unfortunately, it is the squeaky wheel, rather than the most needy one, that gets the grease. Resources may be added where they are not really needed.

The opposite situation is also frequently observed. Cutting costs makes sense when there is sufficient slack to do so. Governments are in business to provide a wide range of services to a broad cross section of society. Strictly from a cost point of view, full resource utilization is ideal.[129] So there may be pressure to cut back services that aren't used to capacity. The danger with this approach is a significant reduction in service quality.

In all fairness to politicians, their divided loyalty to constituents and colleagues makes it hard for them to allocate funds effectively. It is very difficult to get a truly global perspective of an entire province, state or country because of both the scale and the scope. On the other hand, because senior bureaucrats are not directly accountable to the electorate, they should be in a better position to make the most of available resources. The level of service depends not only on the availability of the resources, but also on the efficiency with which they are used. Public officials and other managers can have a direct influence only on operational efficiency. A unit could quite possibly perform well, considering its constraints, but be seen as performing poorly because the public or elected officials have unrealistic expectations of it or make unreasonable demands on it. Despite improved performance on the part of the

Quebec income tax department (ease of contact, politeness and help-fulness), the public still treats the department with suspicion. Alternatively, a program may not make much sense considering what it is supposed to do (Figure 9-1). Some programs are designed largely for political reasons, which may affect efficiency or effectiveness. Canada's goods and services tax exempts some items, notably food, because it was considered unconscionable to tax food. The exceptions create potential loopholes and make collection and policing more difficult.

FIGURE 9-1   Efficiency and effectiveness within the public sector

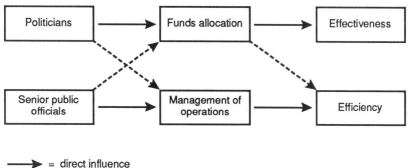

⎯⎯▶ = direct influence
----▶ = indirect influence

9.3   Human and technical challenges

Rightly or wrongly, the civil service has a reputation for job security and bureaucratic red tape. However, civil services often have poor records in industrial relations and efficiency. It is not surprising that automation to improve productivity is not usually well received. Canada Post introduced 30 mechanized processing systems at a cost of over $1 billion to increase processing rates from 1,200-1,500 letters per hour to 30,000.[45] Breakdowns and difficulties in maintaining a balanced line are some of the technical challenges Canada Post faced. However, the new technology also met with significant resistance on the part of postal workers, resulting in strikes and a very poor working environment. Despite Canada Post's experience, most automation efforts have improved efficiency and, when planned properly, many have improved working conditions as well.

The decision to adopt a new postal code format in the United States was rooted in a desire to improve efficiency and was based on decision tree analysis.[297] By highlighting how much companies who adopted the new code early on saved, the US Post Office has been able to encourage organizations, with moderate success, to add the additional four digits. Analysis predicted annual returns of $1.5 billion, thus justifying the $350 million investment in extra equipment and up to $300 million in annual operating costs. It also indicated that all other options examined, such as buying various configurations of other types of equipment, were better than cancelling the ZIP + 4 system. In this case, the introduction of new equipment apparently caused no problems to labor relations, probably because the same basic operations could be performed without major disturbances to the working environment.

To make any change successfully, it is important to thoroughly understand what motivates employees. It can be subtle. Police patrols are a case in point. Police have insisted on doing car patrols in pairs citing safety — their own and the public's — as the reason. However, the support and companionship of a patrol partner is probably an important social factor underlying their position. After all, police work is often boring, frequently dangerous and brings officers into contact with some of society's most difficult citizens.

Automation is not necessarily required to improve operations. For example, the City of Tampa rented goats to trim steep slopes around the city; the result was lower labor costs and enhanced safety. However, it is often much easier to concentrate on the technical, rather than the human, aspects of technology, especially when the need is to motivate people in a system that does not reward them for performance. A lack of motivating factors is often imbedded in the system and sometimes results from a collective agreement that makes it difficult to promote an employee on any grounds other than seniority. It's common enough that recently-hired employees outperform more senior employees after only a few weeks on the job, only to have their performance subsequently decline because of peer pressure.

9.4   The growing importance of bureaucracy

Earlier we discussed the political implications of managing public services. In addition to politicians, managers and administrators also have considerable power and do not necessarily act in the best interest of the people they are supposed to serve:

> The principal complaint about professions in government is that they hinder bureaucratic responsiveness. Each profession has its own world view, filtered through the education, experience, socialization, and specialized knowledge of its members. This world view may not be congruent with the 'public interest.' Critics hold that the professional bureaucracy often proceeds with its own notions of what is good for the people rather than seeking and responding to the interests

and demands of the general public, agency clientele, or elected officials.[147, p. 574]

According to these authors, the gaps between four groups (estates) of public sector employees that are perceived to be on a continuum — scientists, professionals, administrators, politicians — are narrowing. In particular, the distinction between professionals and administrators is becoming smaller, and the two groups combined are gaining in relative size and power as a new group — professional administrators. This study was done in the United States and may not be universal; the shifts are likely related to the cultures of the organizations involved. Three features of professionalism[117] among public employees — better education, specialized training and freedom — are a major reason. Bureaucrats have considerable control and power within their organizations whereas professionals have a valuable store of knowledge.[254] This is an attractive combination.[146]

Note, however, that professionalism is not necessarily essential for power. In some situations, the power of non-professional employees is considerable.[216] Morris identifies three types of dependency between customers and servers: benefit-based, monopolistic and professional. Welfare beneficiaries, because they do not pay for the service, have a benefit-based dependency. Although they have little direct power over the operating system, they can fight in the political arena if they are sufficiently organized. Customers dependent on a true or quasi monopoly, such as a public regulatory body or a utility, find switching to an alternate service either impossible or very expensive. Customers who depend on professionals lack the knowledge and/or expertise to perform the service themselves or to judge the quality of the service. In none of these dependencies is there any incentive to satisfy customers; customers will always be loyal if they have no viable alternatives.[216, p. 87]

Bureaucrats and politicians often find that strict adherence to rules and procedures is a strong defence against criticism. One author goes so far as to define bureaucrats and administrators by their unwavering reliance on rules.[201] It is easy to look busy shuffling paper and processing cases according to established procedures. Appearing to be busy suits most people in the system, but not necessarily users who value results. Complexity also slows down the processing of cases. Poor management, bureaucratic ineffectiveness and political accommodation have been identified as three main causes of complexity.[163] Effective operations management can help to reduce it.

Many people suspect that bureaucracy is excessive, that the size of the public sector is out of control. Is it measurable? One author suggests the following four criteria (they are equally applicable to the private sector):

1. excessive centralization of decision-making
2. too many layers of staff involved in policy, technical and legal advice, a situation which constrains the discretion of managerial decision-making
3. proliferation of levels of decision making within the hierarchy, leading to a lack of responsiveness
4. thick procedures manuals and numerous committee meetings and advisory groups.[131]

Meaningful solutions are being sought to offset these problems and the perceived low level of service in the public sector. For example, many large cities have decentralized their administrative offices to create smaller units that are more effective and responsive to local demands.

New Solutions for Old Problems?

9.5   Evaluating performance and improving operations

Despite training programs, managers at the United States Internal Revenue Service had to admit a few years ago that its tax advice was wrong in 3% of cases.[8] In one informal study, Canadian tax officials were found to have an even worse record.[226, 259] Insufficient training and incompetent personnel might be the cause. However, the complexity of tax law resulting from trying to please various special interest groups, efforts by lawyers and tax accountants to find loopholes and the equally assiduous efforts to plug them could also be the culprit.

Controlling income tax returns is mandatory — the financial and political stakes are very high. One study revealed that a U.S. tax inspector can generate additional tax revenue worth about three times his or her salary by finding deliberate or accidental errors in submitted returns.[8, 151] Similar control of beneficiaries of social aid in Quebec has saved the provincial government substantial sums. To be effective, any operations system must have suitable built-in controls.

A system that performs well does so because of a combination of staff working hard and intelligently. Performance is often constrained by tradition. For example, mail is delivered anywhere within Canada or the United States for the same rate despite the fact that it costs less to move mail between two nearby cities, such as Vancouver and Victoria, B.C., than between two communities, such as Valdez, Alaska and Flamingo, Florida. Similarly, long-distance telephone rates subsidize local calls. Deregulation has made it possible for new entrants to the communications field to compete in the highly profitable local markets, translating into significant savings to customers living in the right areas. Deregulation of mail services might have a similar result.

Many of these kinds of choices are made for political reasons or to ensure equality — the same price for all. However, the time may be ripe to look at public services from a different perspective. For example, what were the objectives when the decision was originally made? Are they still valid?

Once the public gets accustomed to a service or approach to service delivery, it is difficult to make significant modifications. For example, in the United States, university tuition fees are much higher than in Canada and there are many private institutions for which tuition is a major source of revenue. In Canada, universities are largely funded from the public coffers and tuition is kept low so that low-income students can go to university; in other words, it is a social, rather than an economic, choice. Reconsidering what universities are trying to achieve in both the short and long term might mean changing the Ministry of Education's funding philosophy. In Quebec, tuition fees were frozen for over 20 years; they then increased by over 240% over a two-year period. The calibre of education was perceived to be lower; many educators and administrators blamed this on low revenues. For instance, classes in social sciences were over-crowded to maximize use of available resources. Despite widespread concern over the quality of higher educa-tion, other provinces have yet to follow suit. It is a difficult decision because the quality of education is hard to measure in the short term and it is difficult to demonstrate that increased expenditure means better quality. Governments are also reluctant to increase expenditures because of fiscal restraint and the already huge amounts spent on education.

Total quality management is an interesting and potentially very use-ful approach to improving operations performance. However, it appears to be difficult to implement, in part at least because the goal of managing public systems well to provide good customer service conflicts with the interests of the entrenched bureaucracy.

In Washington, D.C., two major issues facing the Police 911 service were matching staff with demand and improving call-handling performance.[157] Demand was high — over two million calls per year for police, ambulance, fire and other emergency services. It was also highly variable, with significant peaks on Fridays and Saturdays and between 3:00 pm and 11:00 pm, and with calls that varied in length from ten seconds to 18 minutes. Staff could answer any busy line without regard to the order in which the calls were received. Carefully analyzing operations using data bases, time studies, work sampling, queuing, simulation, and linear and integer programming as well as an overall improvement in methods, scheduling and equipment led to a reduction in the average waiting time for emergency calls from ten seconds to three seconds and a reduction in the proportion of calls on hold from 33% to 12%. These improvements were accomplished without increasing the staff. A similar approach was successfully applied to the Canadian Trade Marks Office.[125]

One study concluded that Canadian cities, particularly those with populations below 50,000, could reduce fire service costs without affecting service levels (response time) by adding part-time fire fighters.[202] On the other hand, a completely part-time staff gave an average response time 25% higher than a completely full-time staff. Grosse Pointe Park, Michigan has merged its fire and police departments.[46] Simulation studies, later confirmed by actual performance, indicated that both response time and costs would be reduced. New Zealand has taken another approach — it has reduced and specialized its police force by assigning all traffic control duties to Ministry of Transport staff. One apparent result is that citizens have more respect for the police force; although they still get annoyed over seemingly trivial enforcement of traffic laws, they rightly blame someone other than the police force. Another result is that highly skilled personnel are concentrated in jobs that require skill, and less skilled (and less costly) staff is used for traffic control.

Not all politicians and administrators are prepared to make such drastic changes. Administrators often prefer to avoid political scrutiny by granting workers benefits, such as more vacation or free time. These advantages are less visible to the public and the image is that they are less costly than a salary increase. In addition, they are easier to reduce than a high salary. For instance, a typical fire fighter spends 34% of his or her time fighting or preventing fires, 53% on standby and 13% on vacations.[308] As costs increase, the option of contracting out the service will become more attractive.

9.6   Privatization and contracting out

Contracting out and privatization have become popular ways to reduce the cost of the public sector. There are factors other than cost to consider, however. As the portion of work that is contracted out increases, managers can lose control of how the service is delivered. One way to deal with this potential problem is for public service administrators to set standards for contracted work. This begs the obvious question: Why aren't they already doing this as a matter of course? One reason is the difficulty of measuring services. How do you evaluate the cleanliness of a park or the level of public safety after guards have been hired? However, most public services can be measured in some way. Police departments can use cost per man-hour; an accounting division could be evaluated on a cost per transaction basis. This emphasizes quantifiable rather than non-quantifiable information. Although any measurement might be better than none, it may be a mistake to accurately measure an insignificant factor that is easily measured instead of trying to estimate a more important factor that is difficult to measure. Perhaps contracting out would serve as the stimulus to spur managers in the right direction. And if it lets private contractors to do what they are best at — achieving the standard as economically as possible — it would be an economic advantage to the general public. One danger of contracting out, however, is policing contractors whose costs, and hence required cash flow, might be expected to change with economic conditions.

Contracting out is hardly an either/or decision (Figure 9-2). It is quite possible, even desirable, to strike a balance between contracting out and doing it in-house. Edmonton, Winnipeg and Montreal have reached such a balance in garbage collection[203] and snow removal.[183] For instance, Winnipeg contracts out about 30% of snow removal to the private sector by public tender. Both the exact timing and required capacity are quite unpredictable. When it snows, operators are called from the lowest bidder to the highest and then demobilized in the reverse order.

FIGURE 9-2   Steps towards privatization of public services

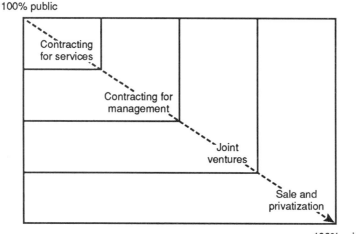

This ensures that sufficient capacity is available to handle a major storm, but it also rewards the lowest bidder. Overall, it is difficult to say what the appropriate proportions are for each city. They depend on economic, political and social factors.

Contracting out can put pressure on civic workers by establishing new standards.[203] For example, North Vancouver was able to demonstrate that a two-person crew could collect garbage from 694 homes per hour, compared to the 705 homes per hour serviced by three-person civic crews.

Some circumstances are more controversial than garbage collection or snow removal. Some American legislative jurisdictions are considering contracting out prison management.[63] Over 3.3 million Americans are under some form of correctional supervision and 25% are in custody. Privatization is seen as an answer to three problems: soaring inmate populations and caseloads, escalating costs and public correction bureaucracies that have failed to protect the public from convicted criminals. However, is it necessarily a good thing if the private sector can do the job more cheaply? To what extent will constitutional rights be protected? Is the process fair? What about the potential for corruption and money mismanagement?

There are innovative answers to these questions in sight. A panel made an extensive study of earlier judgments in the United States and devised a grid that would designate an appropriate punishment.[141] This move is supposed to ensure conformity between judges. Are judges prepared to give up some of their power and autonomy? The answer is, to some extent; after all, doctors are increasingly using computers to analyze a patient's symptoms.

The public purchase of private services is not unlike contracting out by private enterprises. Unless there are good reasons to make instead of buy, buying often makes more sense.[169] However, once a decision has been made to produce in-house, contracting out later can be very difficult, both managerially and politically. Public administrators should consider this reality the next time they want to increase the work load of civil servants. Efficiency and effectiveness can be improved by judiciously contracting out some public service work.

Overall, social and political factors, together with the bureaucratic orientation of the public sector, make any drastic changes challenging to say the least. However, in the years ahead, there might be more interesting options proposed as the general public increasingly demands performance from the public sector. Public sector response to concerns over deterioration of the earth's physical environment and resources is a case in point.

CHAPTER 10

HEALTH SERVICES

The Ever-present Preoccupation with Cost

10.1   A difficult situation

Discussions about the trade-off between the quality and cost of health care have become common not only within the health care field, but also in the media and the policital arena. The controversy is fueled by such evidence as long waiting lists for treatment of serious conditions, cases of people suffering or even dying because they cannot get service and by dissatisfaction with working conditions among health care workers. Private and public health care facilities alike face daunting problems. Although private hospitals are typically less financially robust, public hospitals have many more external pressures on them. And, with an aging population, lifestyles that many consider to be unhealthy, few attractive alternatives to hospital care, attitudes favoring costly high-technology treatment of illness and a widespread attitude that death is unacceptable (although clearly inevitable), the situation is unlikely to improve rapidly. This chapter discusses the problems faced by hospitals and proposes some possible solutions. Because hospitals dominate the delivery of health care in North America, the chapter focuses on them rather than other types of health care organizations. Although private and public hospitals differ, most of the material presented here applies to both.

   Goldsmith describes the situation facing hospitals as follows:

   Declining margins, excess capacity, mature product portfolio, bureau-cratic overburden, poorly planned and executed diversification moves, rapid CEO turnover — a familiar litany of symptoms of U.S. industries in trouble ...this list describes the $200 billion American hospital industry.[97, p. 104]

The author goes on to cite the managerial complexity of hospitals, a general absence of scale economies in the industry, the increasing number of activities and people that do not add service value to patients, poor marketing, a focus on marketing while ignoring operations and unwise investments as causes of this malaise. He predicts that as many as 1,000 United States hospitals could close in the near future. According to this article, to survive and respond better to public demands, hospitals should use strategies with four components:

1. renewed and deepened collaboration with physicians
2. solutions to the productivity problem
3. refocusing ambulatory and chronic care services
4. managing for medical value.

Hospitals have evident management problems. In their lay-outs, organization, staffing and systems, hospitals tend to be focused on treating in-patients, but there may be ten times as many out-patients using the facilities. Their focus has therefore not kept up with changes in the market. High costs result in increasingly complex cases being treated outside general hospitals, often in private clinics owned by physicians. As a result, the general hospital loses its bread-and-butter cases and is left with the most complicated (and costly) procedures. Overall, the decision-maker should concentrate on the value of treatment, not the cost *per se*. A particular procedure that is more expensive than an alternative should be preferred if it is medically safer, has a lower probability of re-admittance or allows the patient to return to work sooner.

But how much is too much to spend? And who should decide? When a close relative is in a public hospital, an individual is likely to conclude that no treatment is too expensive for the patient, especially if the costs are covered by insurance. Yet when the same individual is asked to pay higher taxes to support the increasing costs of health care, his or her view of the situation is usually quite different. The societal choice is far from being the sum of all individual choices.

10.2   Difficult managerial controls

Managing a general hospital must rank among the most difficult of managerial jobs. As in any type of organization, particularly the public ones discussed in Chapter 9, prestige in a hospital is associated with accumulation of assets or size of budget. In hospitals, the competition is both among departments and among individual physicians. Departments compete for bed allocations and physicians for places in a queue — to ensure that their patients get admitted first.

The high cost of sophisticated medical equipment, for example, laser beams, ultrasound, computer enhanced diagnosis and nuclear magnetic resonance imaging, is a major contributor to health care costs. Hospitals are becoming as automated as many factories; but in many, information systems and personnel training have not kept pace with technological developments. Equipment acquisition cannot always be justified from an economic viewpoint. Factors such as institutional prestige, improved health care and attractiveness to the medical fraternity often predominate. Needless to say, it is impossible to put a precise value on improved health care, although insurance companies and courts increasingly recognize that pain and injuries are worth more than mere lost wages.

Hospital administrators, like those in any organization, often have to live with the institution's history, structure, facilities, equipment and personnel.[62] In hospitals these constraints are compounded by the reliance of the entire system on physicians. This group of professionals has the unquestioned right to make medical decisions, many of which may cost the hospital a lot of money. However, in many hospitals physicians are not employees but simply users of the system — indeed, they can be thought of as the hospital's real customers. This independence, as well as the physicians' loyalty to the profession of medicine (or a medical specialty), both of which are typical of many professionals, reduces the extent of the hospital's control over its main 'workers.'[117] The physicians' central role in health care delivery and the possible difficulty of replacing them makes hospital administrators very physician-dependent.

10.3   Controlling costs

Insurers, especially public health insurance plans, typically establish schedules of insured diagnoses and the allowed fee for each diagnosis. Medicare in the United States, for example, defines 467 diagnostic related groups for billing purposes.[178] Such organizations try to reduce costs as much as possible. The result is that hospitals reimbursed by them have a fixed revenue (for a particular type of patient) which generally does not keep pace with inflation.[178] Accordingly, the hospital has an incentive to improve efficiency. Physicians may face reduced incomes, either because the hospital's revenue is restricted or because they bill the insurer directly and thus face the same reimbursement schedules as hospitals. Physicians may react by markedly reducing the extent to which they provide free services or by relocating. Many Canadian doctors moved to the United States because they felt that they could earn higher incomes there despite much higher malpractice insurance premiums.

An article by Young and Saltman outlines five variables that influence health care costs: case mix, number of cases, resources needed per case, resource cost and efficiency of resource use (Figure 10-1).[310] Their discussion concludes that administrators can really control only the efficiency of resource use, with partial control of the number of cases and costs. Therefore, cooperation with physicians becomes of paramount importance for controlling costs. In many cases, simply letting physicians know the cost of a procedure reduces the frequency with which it is performed.

FIGURE 10-1   Major factors affecting costs in health care organizations and the extent of possible administrative control

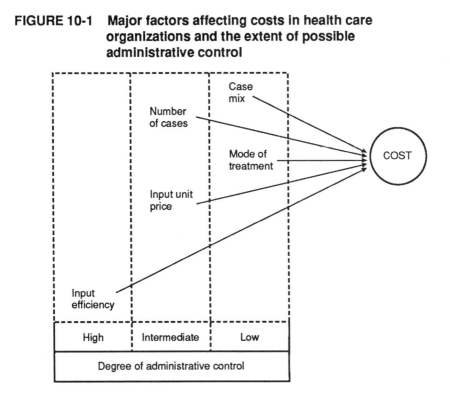

But once again, who should decide whether expensive operations such as organ transplants, which can cost more than $200,000, should be performed? As Egdahl stated:

> Great variability exists in the use of health services, depending on their availability, which creates a conflict between society's cost containment objectives and physicians' needs for patients and income.[74, p. 130]

Furthermore, a surgeon must treat a minimum number of cases to maintain his or her competence, and adding surgeons will increase the frequency of surgical procedures in an area. When these facts are combined, there might be a tendency to perform more elective surgery. Similarly, the length of hospital stays varies extensively among United States hospitals. Thus costs and use of medical resources tend to be determined by capacity, not demand. This situation is accentuated by the importance of health and the powerful advisory role of health care professionals. Full facilities have led to increasing numbers of surgical procedures (between 20 and 40%) being performed outside hospitals, often at half the cost.[74]

Controlling hospital budgets is further complicated by social missions which include caring for the poor or the elderly. Caring for the poor increases the likelihood that fees will not be fully recovered, or that they will be from closely controlled sources such as Medicare. Attending to the elderly uses beds that could be used for higher revenue-generating procedures. Consequently, public hospitals may not look kindly on private hospitals like Humana, because the latter may skim the market by focusing on the most profitable procedures and attracting richer people; they are even reported to offer elaborate menus and fast service.[150] Private hospitals are also criticized for doing less than their share of research and academic work. On the other hand, they can offer truly outstanding service.[120]

According to Wood, hospital costs have four components: admission cost, daily housekeeping costs, direct medical care costs, and operating suite, recovery room and other ancillary services costs.[306] This cost structure makes shorter hospital stays more profitable. In Wood's view, hospital costs should be billed directly, allowing for more efficient cost control. Costs are difficult to control because hospital information systems are often inadequate for managers to pinpoint costs accurately. Often, variable costs are not identified separately and allocated fixed costs distort decision making.

Possible Solutions

10.4   Improving capacity utilization

Some argue that the only way to control health care costs is to reduce existing capacity and medical staff. Ontario typically controls costs by closing hospital beds. British Columbia tries to control them by restricting the number of physicians that can bill the provincial health care plan. But are such controls realistic in a society with an aging population and the desire to be in better health? It could be argued that, except when redundancy can really be demonstrated, it makes more sense to use the expensive buildings, equipment and staff extensively while maintaining a reasonable operating level.

Maintaining an optimum operating level within a hospital is at least as difficult as in any other type of organization. Lead times for resources are long whereas those for patients can be very short — virtually non-existent in emergencies. It is likely that one or a few departments will be operating at or above capacity, while others will be under-utilized, possibly because of a particular case mix or because they might require resources already fully used in another department. For example, in-patients compete with out-patients for laboratory analysis resources. Although high invididual variability in service times is unavoidable for many types of treatment, the capacity problem has important implications:

> As bottleneck activities impede patient flow, patient waiting times and dissatisfaction increase. In addition, dissimilar processing capabilities may increase the provider's idle time, decreasing productivity and lowering morale.[6, p. 207]

These authors suggest alleviating the problems caused by differences in supply and demand by using the well-known demand-smoothing (level) and supply matching (chase) approaches (Figure 10-2) discussed in Chapter 4.[265] One method, successfully used by more and more hospitals, is to require that pre-admission papers be completed before childbirth. This not only accelerates a process many consider to be too long (especially given the possible circumstances), but it also takes it 'off line,' making it possible for the departments involved to plan their work loads more effectively. Although childbirth affords relatively long lead times, this same approach could be used for any sort of service delivery system except in emergencies.

FIGURE 10-2   Improving capacity utilization in hospitals

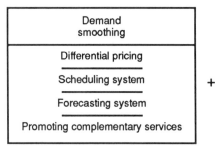
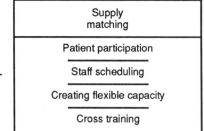

SOURCE: Adapted from Sasser (reference 265)

Because of the importance of physicians to health care and the dependence of resource use on their decisions, it is not surprising to find periods of over- and under-utilization of resources. It would be better, however, for physicians to maintain level work loads. What is needed is a close examination and analysis of work loads by department. Only with the results of such an analysis in hand can a hospital formulate a plan, if desired, to alter the situation.

Like hotels, many hospitals discharge patients in the morning and admit new patients in the afternoon (except for emergencies which arrive more randomly). However, some authors suggest that reversing this order would give greater flexibility and control in the operation of service departments such as admissions, increase convenience to patients and their families, reduce the average length of stay and increase the efficiency with which in-patient time is used. However, in public systems, hospital funding may be based on head counts, which are typically made at midnight; this factor explains, at least in part, why the current order persists.

One attractive way to increase overall capacity utilization is for departments to share beds. Higher utilization distributes fixed costs over a larger number of patients. A system with fixed allocation of beds to departments is inherently inflexible — at any given time there will probably be empty beds in some departments and extra demand for beds in others. Shared beds can be moved from one department to another depending on demand. The question is which departments can share beds economically and to what extent should beds be shared? Obstetrics and cardiology, for example, use quite different facilities and are usually located far apart. Beds shared by these two departments would have to be fully equipped for both, which could be expensive. Cardiology and intensive care would probably be able to share beds more economically.

Other factors constrain the successful use of such an approach; two of these are the number of patient groups (often identified with the number of in-patient departments) and the needs of the population being served (Figure 10-3). At one extreme of the flexibility spectrum, each bed could be shared, but this would be an expensive option because of the equipment and cross-training required. Some specialized organizations do manage this by focusing so narrowly that all patients can be considered identical, at least for operations planning purposes. At the other extreme, with no shared beds between departments, lies the all-too-familiar situation of empty beds in some departments and lists of patients waiting for beds in others. One study in a medium-size metropolitan hospital revealed that bed sharing between two major departments would have allowed the hospital's bed use to increase from 89.5% to 92.1%.[91]

FIGURE 10-3   Factors affecting the use of shared beds

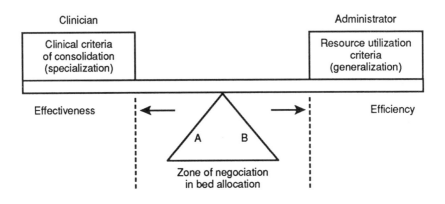

The location of the pivot point, which represents the point where the interests of the clinician couterbalance those of the administrator, is a function of:

A. the number of classes of patient
B. the needs of the population being served

The optimum number of shared beds depends on both clinical and administrative factors. Financially, the theoretical (or practical) optimum number of shared beds depends on additional revenue opportunities and the associated costs. Complicating the decision is the fact that not all shared beds have equal value. The marginal contribution of the first bed is large; that of subsequent beds is less as demand drops but costs remain. This situation is represented in Figure 10-4.

10.5   Productivity improvements

Most changes in hospitals in the last decade have been justified by so-called productivity increases — a term that has become quite un-popular because it is often associated with lay-offs or extra work. How-ever, cost increases cannot continue to escalate for long at the rate they have exhibited recently at several of our institutions.

Productivity improvements can result from increasing either effective-ness or efficiency. When a physician decides that a test or procedure is not necessary, although it may well be part of medical tradition, patient treatment becomes more efficient because the overall contribution margin increases. If the procedure is potentially harmful to the patient, omitting it may well improve the effectiveness of care as well. Use of a lumpectomy instead of a radical mastectomy in a breast cancer case is an

FIGURE 10-4   Factors in determining the optimal number of shared beds

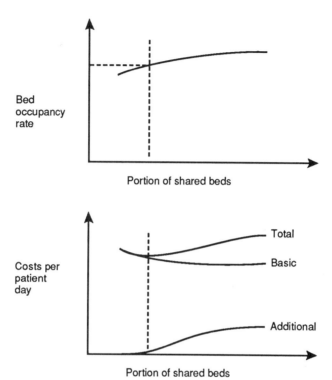

example of improving both effectiveness and efficiency. Another is the use of early ambulation following hernia surgery. It should be pointed out that physicians who innovate in this way may incur some risk by not following accepted medical practice, especially in our increasingly litigious society.

One author has suggested that hospital administrators consider a productivity improvement program only if they are not intending to use the program to reduce staff and only if middle management turnover is low.[58] The author suggests identifying those aspects to be improved, providing feedback to those involved, developing plans using team-building sessions and rewarding people for improving productivity.

Whatever techniques or programs are used, those involved must agree on a limited number of acceptable ways to proceed. It should also be understood that people will be asked for a fair day's work for a fair day's pay. Historically, methods such as work sampling and pre-determined time standards (such as MTM) have proven to be successful.

Approaches like nursing requirements planning (NRP), which is similar to aggregate planning, have proven to be successful in comparing work loads and establishing departmental staffing levels. However, NRP has not been popular with nurses, many of whom claim that it leaves little room for professional judgment and forces staff to work faster. The implication is that patients receive a lower quality service because it is less personal. One in-vitro fertilization clinic faced such a response upon increasing its productivity through the use of new technology.[130] This organization was able to double patient throughput with no staff increase by replacing its laparoscopy technology with ultrasound. The new technology was medically superior but the extra load on staff made it very difficult for them to provide the same levels of relaxed emotional support without burning out.

Managers require standards to control the productivity of expensive resources. Because services can be performed in many ways, it is easier to focus on aggregate measures for control purposes. Such indicators as the total number of tests performed per full-time equivalent worker by shift can be used to compare output from shift to shift. Such measures should be used with caution, however. Naturally, only the most meaningful measures for managers and staff should be used. In the testing example, factors such as the types of tests performed (and therefore time required), the testing lead time, test accuracy and other duties for which staff members are responsible are crucial to accurate interpretation of results. There is also a cost-benefit consideration — if data collection costs exceed the benefits to be gained, it may not be worth collecting the data. Although data is required for control purposes, managers must realize that in many areas of health care, service quality may be more important than productivity considerations.

As health care management develops, there will increasingly be room for new techniques such as statistical process control (SPC), a technique that is still in the process of being fully understood, accepted, implemented and used in the manufacturing sector. Because it makes it possible to chart measures against departmental norms, SPC is a powerful visual indicator for both managers and staff. Figure 10-5 shows how work load in a laboratory could be visualized. In this figure, UCL (upper control limit) is the acceptable normal maximum work level and LCL (lower control limit) is the lower acceptable limit. Too many points near LCL would indicate that an insufficient number of tests had been performed. Results consistently near either limit might prompt management to investigate possible consequences and causes: Is the department over- or under-staffed? Was the staff working as hard as normal? Was there a particularly high demand for tests? Has test quality been maintained?

FIGURE 10-5   Using SPC in hospitals

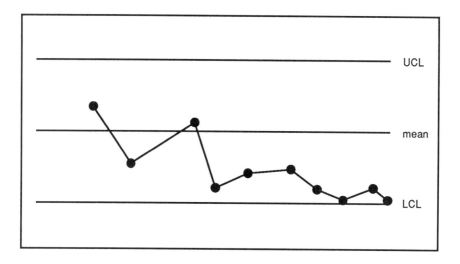

Some productivity improvement measures are easy to adopt and yield high cost-benefit ratios. For instance, older people normally need smaller medication doses than younger adults. A control system that can carefully regulate administered dosages can not only save money on drug costs but also improve patient health. And who would seriously oppose such a system? Similarly, the average error rate in dispensing medication was found, in a number of U.S. hospitals, to be approximately 10%, including errors such as wrong dosage, wrong drug, wrong patient, wrong time and wrong mode.[189] Unit dose systems, in which pharmacy staff prepare individual doses for each patient daily and nurses check the medication before it is administered, can reduce error rates to about 2%. This is still a frighteningly high rate, but at least it should be recognized as a dramatic improvement, and may pave the way for even better performance. Whatever productivity measures are used, managers should recognize that they will affect staff behavior — as with quality control, you get what you inspect rather than what you expect (Chapter 6).

One contributing factor to productivity problems in general hospitals lies in the meaning of the word 'general.' By their very nature, general hospitals treat a broad spectrum of conditions. As a result, they are inherently unfocused.[274] In contrast, specialty hospitals can be highly focused, allowing them to provide extremely high quality care at a high level of productivity. Would we do better to build numerous specialty hospitals and reduce our dependence on general hospitals? Would we do better to manage the general hospital as a collection of 'plants within a plant'?[274]

Overall, health care systems face increasing costs and demand for services at the same time as they face pressures to constrain the costs. Better and more economical ways to deliver the services must be found. The basic medical service is provided by health care professionals to the patient; administrators, financial people and other white-collar support staff do not contribute directly to patient care. They might make the health care professional's job easier (or harder), but they cannot replace professional care providers. It could easily be argued that to improve hospital productivity, the number of support staff should be kept to a minimun. Such an approach is reminiscent of the Japanese approach to factory management, where the number of (productive) line workers is high relative to the number of (unproductive) staff workers.

The climate in most hospitals will have to change before such a strategy can be implemented. Government demands for tighter control and more reports will make it increasingly difficult to do so. Third parties who pay for health care may make adequate care almost universally accessible, but they do not necessarily contribute to productivity improvement and higher quality care. Providing universal access to basic health care is the start towards a truly humane society, but there are significant costs associated with such a system.

CHAPTER 11

TRANSPORTATION SERVICES

Important Data to Get the Proper Perspective

Although the title, 'transportation services' covers transport of both people and goods, and could be extended to include transporting electronic information as well, this chapter will concentrate on passenger air travel and urban transit because these are familiar systems. However, other modes of transport are also experiencing interesting changes, both in technology and in how they are managed.

11.1   Increasing capital intensity

Because services are less amenable to being transported than non-services, transportation is one of the slowest growing segments within the service sector.[51] Unlike many services, transportation is very capital intensive and is becoming more so as equipment becomes simultaneously larger and more sophisticated. This economic factor has a significant effect on the management of this segment of the service sector.

Technological advances such as containerization, ship navigation systems, very fast trains in Europe and Japan and air traffic control systems are significant improvements, but the growth rate would be higher if better transportation systems and equipment were given higher priority. Given Canada's geography, in which a high proportion of the population lives in a long, narrow band along the United States border, one might expect that transportation services would be particularly prominent. However, Canada has recently seen significant cut-backs in passenger train service, seemingly continuous traffic jams in the larger cities and insufficient capacity during the busiest times at the most crowded airports.

Computer technology has had a major impact both on transportation equipment manufacturing and on the operation of transportation systems. As the first wide-bodied plane, the Boeing 747 represented a landmark in passenger transport. When the plane was conceived in the 1960s, it required 75,000 paper drawings. In contrast, a subsequent Boeing model, the 767, required none; everything was done through computer aided design and computer aided manufacturing (CAD-CAM).[142] Computers have also intruded into service dimensions. A flight plan that used to take an 1.5 hours to prepare now takes a computer 15 seconds to complete. Not only is the result obtained much faster, but the route selected is likely to be safer, faster and more economical.

Some changes can have a revolutionary effect on the service offered. The Concorde, for example, produced nearly 20 years ago, still seems ahead of its time. Today, analysts are hopeful that the new 'propfan' concept will save up to 85% in fuel consumption and be much quieter than propeller-driven engines.[160] But even revolutionary changes can take time. At this point, industry experts expect the propfan engine to be available by 1993; however, past experience has shown that many problems, managerial as well as technological, can thwart such plans.

The investment involved in a fleet, as well as the military interest in aerospace technology, brings non-economic criteria into prominence. Wardair Canada, recently acquired by Canadian Airlines, purchased 14 Airbus A-310s, each with 194 seats, for over $70 million per aircraft.[84] The purchase costs of aircraft and spare parts, and the number of jobs associated with these purchases, make such decisions more and more political, especially in a country like Canada where public participation in major business is common. Air Canada's acquisition of aircraft from Airbus could imply a significant shift of jobs from the current maintenance facilities in Ottawa, Winnipeg and Toronto to Canadair in Montreal. Such a move would have a significant impact within the Canadian political context, which is generally very sensitive to job losses and to job shifts between regions.

The huge investment in capital equipment and the fixed nature of personnel and operating costs give airlines very high fixed costs. Variable costs per passenger, on the other hand, are very low, perhaps less than 10% of the regular airfare. The result of these economic forces is that airlines compete by means of services such as low fares, route structures, departure schedules, frequent flyer plans, and ground and inflight services in an effort to ensure high utilization. One hopes that maintenance costs are sustained. At the extreme, inadequate maintenance of airplanes can result in tragedy, not to mention poor service.[50]

11.2   The existing capacity problems

This section deals with several capacity problems experienced at specific airports. These problems are much more interesting to read about than to experience first hand. Particularly important for those interested in managing services are the managerial issues behind the problems.

Major air traffic congestion occurs in many parts of the world. More than 8,000,000 passengers per year fly through Tokyo's Narita Airport. Unfortunately for travellers, Narita has only one runway, and it operates at full capacity. In Japan, where consensus decision-making dominates and land is extremely valuable, even if the government could convince the potato farmers who own the land surrounding Narita to sell, it is estimated that by the time this happens and a second runway opens, that one, too, will already be at capacity![232]

The air traffic situation is little better in Europe's busiest centres. Air traffic is worsening but the control system is run with outdated equipment by controllers suffering from low morale.[199] Each country runs its own control system, a fact that may well lead to significant variations in technology and controller training. At one extreme is Athens, whose controllers had to deal with up to 1,000 flights a day on busy days in 1987. Working without computers, and with virtually no radar, they followed each plane's progress by moving hand-printed strips of paper across a table. The potential for disaster is obvious.

European airlines now handle over 1 billion passengers each year; the airlines pay over $3 billion annually for airport services and continued access to air corridors.[19] About a third of this amount goes to European governments. European airfares are high because of the high volume of air travel and extensive government ownership, a situation that introduces a significant political dimension into management. Despite the high economic stakes, as we saw in Chapter 9, governments may well use different criteria from those used by private enterprises to make decisions about capacity.

Many travellers feel that the situation is little better on this side of the Atlantic. But how bad is it really? One indicator is that the last major airport to open in the United States was Dallas-Fort Worth in 1974.[158] Another is the paralysis experienced by Pearson International in Toronto in late 1988 and early 1989[303] because demand for takeoff and landing capacity exceeded supply during peak periods. The main problem is that the airport, already Canada's predominant one, is likely to be in even higher demand in the future, not only because of the large and growing Metropolitan Toronto population, but also because it is a major transshipment point for Canadian and international carriers — almost an unofficial hub. Ironically, Mirabel, which the Canadian government built in the 1970s, remains under-utilized and unpopular because of its location some distance from Montreal and its outlying population centres. Furthermore, the Canadian government cancelled plans to build a new airport at Pickering, east of Toronto, because of public pressure. The public seems to want to have its cake and eat it, too. Travellers want easy access to large airports serving many carriers, but local residents do not appreciate busy flight paths over residential areas. Plans to expand Pearson International by adding a runway faced this resistance in the late 1980s. The opening of Terminal 3 in late 1990 has not resolved the issue.

The problem has other dimensions, too. In 1984, although the United States experienced significant flight delays, those airports without sufficient room for expansion (25% of the total) could not even use the $65 million minimum cost of a runway, even if they had the money. In the early 1980s, President Reagan fired thousands of striking air traffic controllers; by 1987, there were 20% fewer air traffic controllers trying to cope with a 26% increase in passengers, and they were using technology that had changed little since the beginning of the decade.

In December 1987, about 54% of all flights in the United States were delayed at least 15 minutes; 30% (175 per day) were delayed for reasons other than weather.[208] The capacities of the three major components — number of flights, the airport and air traffic control (see Figure 11-1) — are almost never perfectly balanced. Although a balanced capacity is not essential, delays are likely if the number of flights is too high to be accommodated safely by the system. Unless there is a reliable forecast of a significant increase in demand, there is no point in having a large capacity excess in either the airport or air traffic control.

Service quality in air travel has become a national issue in the United States.[56] As a result of public complaints, United States airlines now have to report monthly statistics on such items as luggage lost, connections missed, on-time performance and reservations not honored. For airlines with a good record, this is a fantastic opportunity to show that excellent service (at least as measured by these statistics) still exists. In December 1988, all United States airlines showed a higher percentage of on-time arrivals than for December 1987, partly because of major efforts to improve the reported statistics. Flying at less economical speeds, giving priority to landings rather than take-offs and departing on time are measures that can increase the proportion of on-time arrivals.

FIGURE 11-1   Reaching an equilibrium in air traffic capacity

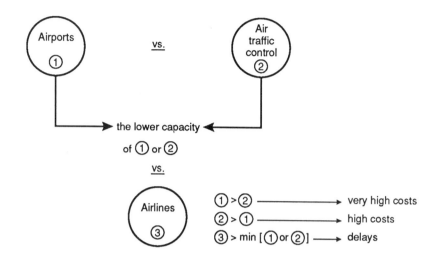

Improvements notwithstanding, demand for airport services exceeds supply in 22 of the busiest United States airports, and peak demand for en-route centre services exceeds supply in approximately 125 of the 652 air sectors.[208] Commuter aircraft, which can give better service, can also add to the problem. At Logan International in Boston, for example, small aircraft with capacities of up to 30 passengers account for 40% of flights but only 5% of passengers.[5]

Several solutions to these problems, some of them politically unpopular, have been proposed. One is to increase landing fees at peak periods, despite the fact that such a move may be perceived as unfair to smaller airlines and private aircraft. A similar approach is to base landing fees at the busiest airports on airplane size, with smaller craft paying proportionally higher fees. The present fee structure is based on capital cost recovery by allocating capital costs to expected flights. Because capital costs are largely fixed, having more flights should result in lower fees per flight. Queuing theory predicts that when congestion is severe, a small reduction in the number of flights could cause a disproportionately larger reduction in delays. Unfortunately, the reverse is also true.

Another solution, yet to be accepted, is to change the queuing rule to favor larger aircraft. Any change in queue discipline may be seen as unfair and may be difficult to implement. Indeed, just what measure of size is relevant — weight, wing span, seating capacity, number of passengers? How long should small planes wait before they are allowed to land or take off? How should a balance between airlines with different numbers of flights be achieved? How long a time period is relevant (assuming we work in time blocks)? Should priority always be given to landings rather than take-offs? These questions and others like them show that the solution does not necessarily lies in changing the priority rule; efforts must be made to understand the whole picture. Because of the presence of a political agenda in these questions, it is not surprising that an easy solution remains elusive.

Currently, Canadian airports are under the jurisdiction of Transport Canada, a department of the federal government. Federal officials are seriously considering allowing local public or private interests to manage and promote some aspects of airports, particularly those related to handling passengers and baggage. The feeling is that local groups are better able to manage. For example, Terminal 3 at Toronto's Pearson International is managed privately. However, so far at least, Transport Canada retains responsibility for safety, primarily through air traffic control. However, in Canada, political interests are always important. For example, Montreal has two major airports, Dorval and Mirabel. According to recent studies, one would be sufficient as the demand is not forecast to materialize until at least 2000. Studies to determine which airport should be closed concluded that both should be kept open. Many jobs are at stake; Dorval, located very near Montreal, is a popular location; and Mirabel, which has always been controversial, is a significant political agenda item.

How Airline Companies Manage

11.3 Preliminary considerations

Most airline executives readily admit that competition is fierce in this industry. There have been mergers and bankruptcies and these will no doubt continue. And there is a lot of competition based on price, route structures, schedules and in-flight service. However, the tremendous demand for airline service makes this industry the envy of many in other industries. Increasingly intense competition among international airlines will probably reduce the number of airlines, especially in Europe, but the competition in the industry as a whole is not as dramatic as one might suspect.

To what extent does the current situation result from poor decisions made in the past? Jan Carlzon, CEO of the renowned Scandinavian Airlines System (SAS) visited a few other airlines and asked their executives: "How do you arrive at a decision to buy new planes? Is it really more profitable than using the planes you already have? Or does it make your service better?"[34, p. 45] The answer? "Well, we never analysed it. It was so obvious that we should buy new planes. We've always done it that way!"[34, p. 45]

Japan Airlines, Swissair and Singapore Airlines are examples of companies that are successful not only because of strong government support, but also because they have long-term commitments to invest in the right equipment and to give exceptional customer service.[240] Other authors attribute the low profitability of carriers such as Lufthansa and Swissair to their membership in the International Association of Air Transporters (IATA).[53] This group of over 100 airlines sets fares to guarantee its members a specific rate of return over costs, thus reducing pressures to control costs. Consequently, most IATA members are able to make profits; competition tends to focus on service and on trying to increase market share rather than on reducing costs.

On the other hand, smaller, efficient, price competitive transporters have been forced into bankruptcy. This was the fate of Laker Airways, which competed head to head with many major carriers. With very low prices, Laker needed high occupancy levels to cover its fixed costs. It was able to achieve the needed load levels until its competitors decided to match Laker's prices. Naturally after Laker went out of business, they quickly raised prices to the prior levels.

The alternate strategy of using the fleet heavily can result in horrendous service. Indian Airlines is reported to have the highest utilization in the world.[50] This results in frequent flight cancellations or delays, sometimes of days, daily schedule changes and 'preponed' flights, which are rescheduled on short notice to depart earlier. Apparently, passengers arriving at the originally scheduled times for flights that have been 'preponed' are ineligible for refunds! Surely a company offering such service would not survive without government protection.

Airline operating costs are largely fixed, so flying partially filled aircraft is costly. Energy costs represent 20-25% of operating costs and salaries, about 30%.[238] Airports charge fees for take-offs and/or landings. Take-off and ascent use more fuel than level flight or descent. The added costs for take-offs or landings mean that the cost per passenger-kilometre decreases as the distance travelled increases (see Figure 11-2). Given these considerations, care must be taken to match aircraft type with the planned number of passengers. Some aircraft are more efficient over short distances whereas others are designed to be more efficient over longer distances. On the other hand, route structures and equipment availability may require airlines to fly some routes with few passengers. The final leg of an Atlanta-Buffalo-Toronto flight once had only one passenger. The airline could not save money by arranging alternate transportation because the aircraft and its crew were needed for another flight originating in Toronto.

FIGURE 11-2   Costs per passenger-kilometre as a function of distance travelled

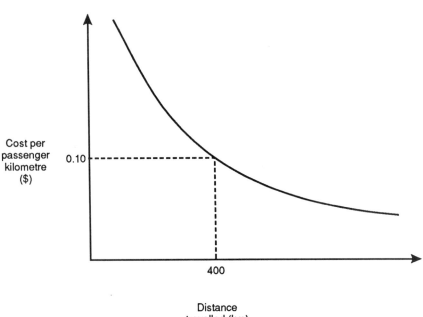

The high cost of take-offs coupled with studies revealing that airlines with more available seats on a route tended to have a disproportionately high market share resulted in many airlines purchasing wide-bodied aircraft in the early 1970s. Subsequently, it was discovered that passengers were not so much concerned with the number of seats available, but rather with the frequency of departures. An airline could compete successfully, especially on short routes, with a rival flying wide-bodies aircraft relatively infrequently by flying smaller aircraft more frequently. Smaller aircraft tend to cost less, be more fuel efficient and enhance operational flexibility, although they may be slower, less pleasant in rough weather and less conducive to in-flight service.

11.4   The hub and spoke system

Federal Express originated the hub and spoke system in 1973. They opened a super-hub in Memphis where all parcels are received, shorted and dispatched within four hours. Despite its distance from the geographic centre of the United States, Memphis was selected because of its inexpensive labor and its airport, which can handle numerous take-offs and landings within a short time span. Federal Express is aided in its strategy by the nature of its over-night freight delivery business, which requires activity at night when airports traditionally have large capacity excesses. Memphis is operating at full capacity, dealing with Federal Express' approximately 130 take-offs per day transporting about 700,000 packages and sorting them, usually within 2.5 hours. The company has decided to open a second hub in Indianapolis to switch more packages to trucks from airplanes. Federal Express' controls are so tight that 98.8% of flights arrive within 15 minutes of schedule and a customer can be told where a package is within 30 minutes of making an enquiry. Because of its tracking system, "Federal Express has actually become ... a fifty-to-500-mile-an-hour warehouse."[275, p. 17]

The hub and spoke system is similar in the passenger airline industry. Passengers are brought to a transfer point (hub) from which many flights will originate within a relatively short period (along the spokes). This approach promotes better service and cheaper operation by allowing airlines to match airplane type with route length. This strategy is widely used in the United States; many non-American airlines use their country's capital city as their main hub.

Air Canada and Canadian Airlines both use this strategy. The result has been the emergence of several smaller regional airlines operating in close cooperation with the majors. The smaller companies typically serve short routes with small aircraft and integrate ticketing and scheduling of their feeder flights with those arriving at and departing from major centres. As a result, more attention is being paid to the quality of regional aircraft and on some routes there is now competition where there used to be none. Fare structures favor flights within the same airline group. Even when there is no price differential, passengers tend to select the same airline or group when they have a choice.

Despite their scheduling and cost advantages, hub and spoke systems do have a downside. The emphasis on using the hub may eliminate direct flights between two spoke cities, thus lengthening some passengers' journeys and decreasing their safety, although only marginally. The desire to use the hub as a tranfer point in a relatively short time span leads to increased congestion, both in the air and on the ground. This congestion is exacerbated by passenger desire to travel in certain popular time slots. Spending some time in a hub like Atlanta (Delta) in the late afternoon will underline the point dramatically. Unfortunately, travellers experience time-consuming, costly delays. Overall, the preoccupation seems to be with improved efficiency rather than improved customer service. But the efficiency is not necessarily passed on to the customer:

> As airlines have come to dominate the cities used as their hubs, they
> have used their market power in those cities to raise fares.[261, p. 81]

Ruppenthal goes on to insist that an airline is a complete system rather than merely a collection of planes; large size therefore confers important advantages. A similar concentration of economic power has been observed in many other industries. In the 1930s, the United States had hundreds of small breweries but now only a few large ones remain.

In contrast, one author contends that numerous studies have demonstrated that once an airline has a few aircraft, it benefits from no real economies of scale.[53] Therefore, differences in airline costs should be attributed to different types of aircraft, route densities and scheduling, rather than to mere size. According to this view, there is no reason why this industry should be oligopolistic.

11.5   Frequent flyer programs

Have you ever tried to reach an airline by phone at a convenient time to get the free frequent flyer tickets you are eligible for? It is often very difficult to get through, and getting the tickets you want can be even harder, especially if your desired departure date is in the late spring or summer. Not only are phone lines heavily used but there are also a number of restrictions, including the very limited availability of seats, often only 12 to 18 in economy class on a given flight. Because the same destinations are popular at the same times each year, some frequent flyers are bound to be disappointed.

Frequent flyer programs were developed as a marketing tool to attract the full-fare business traveller in the early 1980s, when the industry had unused capacity. Initially, they worked well; however, they were easy to copy and their marketing impact has diminished. Now that the climate has changed, airlines retain their programs mostly for defensive reasons. No airline dares to be the first to abandon its program, not only because some passengers would switch to other carriers, but also because accumulated benefits represent a significant accrued liability, and airlines would have to set a deadline for redeeming all benefits. The accumulated benefits are simply too large to handle in a short time frame, because the current restrictions on seat numbers would prohibit some members from using their accrued benefits.

A frequent flyer is one who flies more than 12 times per year.[172] There are approximately 20 million such passengers in the world.[161] Only 2% of them are not members of frequent flyer programs, and only 4% are members of only one. A full 48% are members of more than four programs! Air Canada's Aeroplan has 310,000 members and Canadian Airlines' Canadian Plus has 750,000. It is difficult to manage these large groups efficiently while simultaneously satisfying customers.

Frequent flyer programs could cost United States airlines over $1.25 billion in lost revenue alone, a figure that we consider to be conservative.[132] But, basically "an airline is only as smart as its least intelligent member."[132, p. 57] Fortunately for airlines, only about 50% of benefits are claimed, although attempts to close a program might well increase that proportion. On the other hand, upgrades under the plans are costing more than expected, because full-fare passengers are often displaced by frequent flyers travelling for the basic economy fare.

Frequent flyer programs raise some interesting ethical issues for travellers whose flights are paid for by third parties, often employers. Who owns the travel benefits? Frequent flyer programs have been estimated to result in cost over-runs of at least $4 billion through such practices as paying higher fares (57%), unnecessary travel (16%), and extra time and expense from taking indirect routes (16%).[132] Some organizations such as VISA instruct their employees to take the least costly route. Others require that employees deal only through in-house agencies. The number of frequent flyer points available has become the second most important criterion for choosing a flight, behind the schedule, but ahead of service and cost.[161]

11.6   Reservation systems

Reservation systems are another important component of the airline system:

> Each megacarrier maintains a sophisticated reservations system to juggle ticket prices and ensure maximum revenues for every flight. On a single day recently Delta used its computer to make 79,000 fare changes, adjusting them up and down as tickets were sold. American adjusted 106,000 fares the same day.[159, p. 68]

These changes can be justified by the fact that 60% of bookings for business travellers are subsequently changed. With so many changes and the high contribution margin on tickets, it is not surprising that passengers who buy seats late often get a better bargain than those who booked earlier.

More than 70% of airline tickets are sold through travel agents. Because agents' commissions vary according to the volume of business booked with a given airline, and because many major cities are connected by numerous flights from several carriers, many agents do not really take the time to study airline tariffs. This practice is unfair, not only for passengers and corporations looking for the best deal, but also for airlines listed at the bottom of the screen. Carriers who use the large reservation systems owned by American and United have sued them for alleged unfair discrimination.[261] According to the suit, the reservation systems were programmed to give preference to the owner if the system owner and another carrier had competing flights. Naturally, the travel agents usually accept what the computer schedules. The reservation system can thus be used as a substantial competitive weapon.

Developments in operations research have given managers the tools to improve their use of reservations. For example, one study developed a generalized network flow model technique to optimize the allocation of seats on a flight with more than one class and intermediate stops.[65] It is likely that developments along these lines will continue in all areas of transportation, including airlines and urban transit.

11.7   Flying where the passenger comes first

One older passenger recently complained that the in-flight service he received did not justify the $1,000 he had paid for his full-fare ticket. Seeing that passengers in the other sections were being served faster and with what appeared to be better food, he realized that his full-fare ticket did nothing but guarantee him a seat in the economy section (which he called third class!). His perception of the quality of the service might have been different had he paid the lowest possible fare of $259 for the same flight. It is well known that there are fewer staff members per passenger on planes than there were in the late 1970s. This difference cannot be attributed to excessive staff levels at that time or to technological improvements. It is the result of using larger planes and higher occupancy rates while attempting to keep labor costs low. The effect has been a reduction in service, especially on full flights of short duration when staff are particularly rushed.

Many airlines have reduced the distance between seat rows by about two inches (5%). As one author says, "no amount of efficiency or courtesy is going to make a cramped passenger feel good about the service."[189, p. 61] Cramping can lead to ill will between passengers in adjacent seats, particularly when the front one wishes to recline his or her seat. Cramping is also a factor when seats are narrow. It seems that when making such economical decisions, airline executives do not take into consideration the fact that some minimum level of comfort has to be retained for the whole service to be considered satisfactory. It is difficult for passengers to separate the quality of the service given by flight attendants from the effects of the cabin lay-out, and even if they can, the cabin staff will have to work harder to offset the negative impact of a cramped seat. For most passengers, a cramped flight is not enjoyable, especially if it is full. Because full flights are becoming more and more common, this may be the time to reconsider lay-out decisions made earlier. In fact, this may already be happening. The economy class seats of one Canadian airline provide enough leg room and seat width: a standard briefcase will fit under the seat, and even when reclined, the seat ahead does not hit the passenger's knees.

SAS's Carlzon drastically changed SAS' orientation by emphasizing customer service, including good connections for business travellers.[35] As he puts it, ten million customers in contact with an average of five employees each makes 50 million moments of truth (points of direct contact with the customer). The key people are those staff members who interact with the customer directly; they should be given more authority to make decisions and act without always having to ask a superior.

Carlzon provides numerous other examples of a customer-driven approach. During a visit to Boeing, he asked executives about some of the characteristics of planes designed to please passengers. He found that aircraft manufacturers want to please airline executives first, who focus much of their attention on technological innovation rather than better customer service. In any event, if all companies purchase very similar planes, possibly because of little choice, none will achieve an advantage.

When Carlzon became CEO, SAS had just purchased four new aircraft from Airbus, each costing $30 million, with seating capacities of 240 and lower operating costs than McDonnell-Douglas DC-9s (110 seats). Many executives would have said, 'Let's use the Airbuses' despite the fact that the higher seating capacity would mean more stops. Scandinavian passengers wanted the direct flights available with DC-9s. Under Carlzon's leadership, they got them. That is a customer-driven approach!

Urban Transit

11.8   The impact of subsidies

The cooperative nature of public transport makes services better the more they are used, since frequency and route coverage can be increased and the access times reduced for all users.[22, p. 111]

Despite this reality, unless they are motivated to use public transit by factors like parking problems or longer transit lines, most people prefer to drive to work. An excellent system, which might receive priority by means of dedicated traffic lanes or traffic light controls, could do well with few subsidies. However, subsidies appear to be increasing.[22] Governments in 17 countries increased their share of payment for the annual operating costs of public transit within their jurisdictions by 20% from 1965 to 1982. Why have they done so? For reasons such as ensuring a better environment, improving efficiency, preserving the urban character, making the best use of existing facilities, providing reliable transport to those without access to a car, satisfying the specific needs of disadvantaged citizens and avoiding a sense of unfairness felt by captive users as services become more expensive and/or deteriorate through no fault of their own. Not surprisingly, governments provide funding for objectives important to governments, not primarily to ensure system efficiency or low prices.

Many United States cities had good transit systems in the 1940s. However, in many cities, governments allowed private organizations to take over the public transit system. The results have included reduced quality of service and gradual deterioration of equipment. In contrast, road maintenance has been relatively well funded, showing clearly where priorities lie both for governments and for the citizens they represent. Public funding of roads is considered a necessity because it would be politically unacceptable to tax direct users for the actual costs.

New York City provides a striking example of severe equipment deterioration. Equipment reliability is often measured by mean time (or distance) between failures. From 1968 to 1980 in New York, this measure dropped from about 28,000 to 8,200 miles.This had an enormous negative impact on the quality of the service provided. During the same period, the number of delay minutes increased by 400%. It is easy to see how unreliability in a public transit system leads to reduced patronage. A few late arrivals at work many be all it takes to discourage the marginal rider, and that rider's fare, which is virtually 100% contribution, is lost. A downward spiral quickly develops.

Fortunately, similar situations have been reversed. In 1981, the Houston Transit Agency was experiencing serious problems: buses broke down every 513 miles (on average), the accident rate was four times the national average, the operating cost per revenue mile was more than twice the national average.[148] Only four years later, the agency had improved dramatically in all these measures and more, to become one of the best in the United States (Figure 11-3). How were they able to achieve such a feat? Management developed a super-crew concept in which teams of particularly skilled mechanics restored one bus at a time to excellent condition. The compensation of bus drivers and mechanics became tied to organizational success. But, before deciding on a recovery strategy, the organization determined the real reasons behind its problems and established ambitious, measurable goals. Achievement of these goals was recognized publicly; the result was a positive corporate image among employees and the public alike.

Public transit performance can be measured in many ways. From the large number of measures actually used in many transport systems, a 1978 Organization for Economic Co-operation and Development

FIGURE 11-3   Changes in the performance indicators of the Houston transit system

	Fiscal 1981	Fiscal 1985
Accidents (per 100,000 miles)	9.2	2.5
Miles between mechanical road calls	513	6104
On-time buses	39%	96%
Cost per revenue mile	$5.54	$3.39
Millions of passengers	47.7	67.9

SOURCE: Adapted from Kiepper (reference 148)

(OECD) report recommends 18 essential and 25 desirable measures.[22] This study classifies the 43 recommended measures into seven groups: service production (9), service reliability (5), safety (1), maintenance (11), cost (10), revenues (4) and ridership (3). The measures are further categorized into four types of potential application: internal assessment of trends within an operating unit, comparison between operating divisions, service planning to estimate the implications of expanding or contracting service levels, and external assessment and comparison to other organizations. These sorts of measures could be used anywhere; however, depending on the existing problems and where managers want to put the emphasis, some are more appropriate than others.

Cash grant subsidies to operators appear to have less impact on efforts to improve operational efficiency than do subsidies to users because the whole point of transit service is to be cooperative.[22] One study found that public ownership, public management and high subsidization were associated with significantly higher increases in operating costs for a decade.[118] Conversely, another study of 20 cities' transit systems, which were partly publicly and partly privately owned, concluded that ownership *per se* does not affect efficiency.[229] This latter finding provides hope for public sector managers who believe that it is possible to improve a system others have written off as too difficult to manage.

11.9   Improving customer service first

In recent years, transit systems have started to refer to rider as 'customers' instead 'users.' This change is more than purely semantic. 'Customer' implies a person who has a real choice between public transit and other forms of transportation, and the term places the emphasis on this important person. 'User,' on the other hand, places the primary emphasis on the system. For most customers, small fare increases are insignificant compared to perceived changes in the service. What really matters is the perceived value of the transit system compared to alternatives. The important criteria appear to be expected waiting time, relative cost, reliability of the schedule, amount of inconvenience, probability of getting a seat and social acceptance.[72] Although these criteria will be used by most customers, their weight will vary from person to person and for a single individual over time.

Travel time is often the most important criterion. Interestingly, people tend to underestimate travel time by car and overestimate the time by public transit, probably because they feel more at ease in their own vehicles. Often, particularly in the case of city buses which compete directly with cars, public transit is noticeably slower. It is undoubtedly faster in subway systems, which avoid congested roads altogether. Often total time seems longer, not because the ride is slower, but because there may be significant waiting and walking time:

> Transportation planners have quantified the miseries of 'empty time' waiting. They have found that bus passengers perceive a minute of delay at curbside waiting for a bus to 'cost' two to three times that of a minute of time spent in the bus. This higher cost of waiting is used in models to design bus routes.[166, p. 898]

One study examined the value passengers place on their time in relation to their hourly pay rate: in-bus time is valued at one third their pay rate, walking time at one and one half times, and waiting time at two to three times.[72] Thus, one minute of waiting time is perceived to be worth six to nine minutes of travel time (see Figure 11-4). This reaction is most likely caused by the perception of time wasted; doing nothing (waiting) is seen to be more 'expensive' than engaging in a slow activity (walking). And, as if this were not enough, people tend to remember only their worst experiences in public transit systems. Unfortunately, service reliability is more difficult and costly to measure than service production.

One phenomenon most public transit systems experience is extreme peaking in demand. Ridership is very heavy for relatively short periods in the morning and late afternoon on weekdays as people go to and from work, but much lighter at other times. Systems typically schedule their equipment and drivers to meet these peaks. Minibuses would appear to be a reasonable way to deal with this demand pattern: they allow higher frequency and flexible, more personal service at lower cost during low demand periods. In short, they are a way to adjust supply in small increments to meet demand (see Chapter 4). This may be a viable solution in many systems but it is not a panacea; in particular, it does not look as

FIGURE 11-4   Perceived relative cost of bus travel

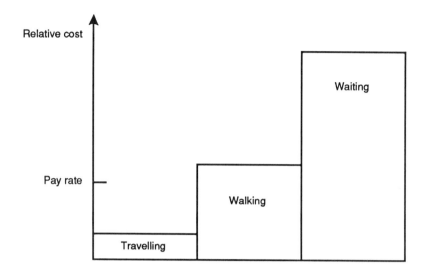

promising during the peaks. In London, the transit system reverted to double-decker buses because minibuses could not handle the volume and contributed more per passenger to traffic congestion and air pollution. (Of course, in that particular system, double-decker buses create a certain image worth retaining.) The option of large buses for peak periods and small ones for non-peak periods, while desirable, raises the capital costs to unacceptable levels.

Technological advances have resulted in some improvements for customers. The Toronto Transit Commission decided to invest $35 million to equip all its vehicles with an automatic vehicle location system, enabling dispatchers to trace each vehicle's location. This system is based both on the number of turns made by a front wheel and on signals emitted from signs beside the street every three to five kilometres.[9] With systems like this one, transit agencies are able to provide customers with precise and up-to-date information by phone. With touch-tone technology, information such as when to expect the next two buses at a particular stop can be given automatically by a computerized voice, rather than requiring a staff member.

In light of the apparently stable market base and chronic financial losses, public transportation would appear to be an unlikely growth industry. On the other hand, increasing public concern with pollution and congestion may encourage more people to use public transport. There are also significant opportunities to improve existing systems.

Managers who can work effectively with labor, provide a good working climate and use inventive methods to provide the proper level of service will continue to be in great demand.

12

FINANCIAL SERVICES

Financial services are among the largest, most complex and most heavily regulated of the service industries. This is not surprising, of course, considering that the very survival of economies can be threatened by financial collapse. Because the scope of this book cannot include all financial services, we have chosen to focus on retail financial services, especially retail banking.

The regulation of retail banks, at one time quite extensive, has been somewhat relaxed in recent years. The current structures of the Canadian and United States banking systems largely reflect their respective histories. Canadian banking is overwhelmingly dominated by the extensive nation-wide branch networks of the five major Canadian chartered banks. In contrast, most United States banks are much smaller, and consequently, there are many more of them. Only recently have these environments begun to change.

The Changing Environment

12.1   Turbulent times

One significant change has been the increased internationalization of banking, particularly in commercial banking, but at the retail level as well. Financial centres are now permanently linked electronically, and foreign bank branches are becoming more common in Canada as legislation is relaxed to allow their entry. Over the past few years, Japanese banks have come to dominate the list of the world's largest banks. And within the United States, great changes are under way. American banking was once dominated by institutions headquartered in New York but recent changes in legislation, aggressive expansion and avoidance of inferior loans have made it possible for about 20 super-regional banks to threaten the once secure status of the money centre banks.[283] Canadian banks are also moving into the United States, although it remains to be seen whether they can succeed against the emerging super-regionals and other foreign banks, notably the Japanese.[309] In Canada, foreign banks are gaining a foothold, as are banking activities by other institutions.

It is common to think of our financial institutions as being particularly stable. Indeed, most large banks are stable. However, banks, by their very nature, are extremely vulnerable to lack of depositor confidence because they typically borrow short and lend long. This means that borrowers treat loans as long-term, fixed assets that they will not have to re-pay for a long time. Indeed, loans are often invested in very personal and non-liquid assets such as houses and automobiles, and borrowers expect the bank to honor loan terms. In contrast, depositors treat deposits as cash that they expect to be able to retrieve at very short notice.

As if this time imbalance were not enough, banks also lend several times as much money as they have on deposit. The whole system is built on mutual trust: customers trust the bank to keep their deposits safe, follow the rules and not call loans before the stated term; banks trust customers to leave most of their deposits in the bank. Naturally, when a bank gets into financial difficulty and trust is lost, this system cannot be maintained; customers try to withdraw their deposits, rapidly causing the bank to collapse. On a global scale, many banks are faced with large potential losses because of loans to third world countries, many of which either cannot repay the loan(s) or refuse to do so. Assessing risk is obviously a key skill for a banker.

During the 1980s, several small Canadian and United States banks failed, as well as some small trust companies and many savings and loan organizations. The result, beyond the obvious loss to shareholders and depositors, has been a marked decrease in confidence in the whole industry. In the collapse of the Principal Group in Alberta, for example, many individuals lost their retirement savings because the British Columbia Teachers Federation had heavily invested its pension fund in the company. And in the United States, the collapse of hundreds of savings and loan organizations, whose deposits are guaranteed by the federal government, has left the government with a liability of several billion, perhaps over a trillion dollars, a truly mind-boggling figure.[267] Some effects of the widespread savings and loan bankruptcies have been tighter government controls of a number of federally guaranteed financial assistance programs, including savings and loans,[298] and increased difficulty in obtaining funding for the building industry.[304] For example, forecasts of housing starts for 1990 have been reduced by 10% according to one source, and by up to 18% according to others.[304] The industry characteristics described above are one cause of the financial problems; however, thousands of charges of outright fraud have also been made.

Another major change within the financial services industry has been the entry of new players. One example is the diversification of Canadian banks into brokerage activities, either through internal growth or acquisition. This move is not without its critics. In at least one bank's experience, the securities business is significantly different from banking in that it involves both quite different relationships and much more sophisticated roles.[206] Bankers must understand their new positions to become successful. In particular, the new task involves bankers dealing as strategic advisers to presidents rather than working with treasurers. Some observers believe that mixing banking and securities will tend to erode the entrepreneurial spirit and creativity of the service that clients now receive from separate securities houses.

The corresponding trend is the diversification of brokerage houses and other financial organizations, such as Merrill Lynch and American Express, into banking. These moves, as well as international competition, businesses widening their geographical scope when seeking financial services and automated teller machine (ATM) technology which has changed the nature of retail banking, have combined to make it harder for banks to be profitable. Credit card companies, including many banks, are also facing competition from outsiders, notably American Telephone and Telegraph (AT&T), which threatens profitability.[236]

12.2   Changing approaches for a changing mentality

In an article on how different types of organizations try to improve the quality of their services, a Citibank vice-president was quoted as saying: "People tell us: don't be polite — be effective, fast and knowledgeable." Such a statement reflects a change in the way people perceive the relative importance of different criteria used to evaluate banking services. However, no one can deny the importance of personalized service. The president of Stillwater Bank & Trust (of Stillwater, Oklahoma), a bank with an excellent record, moved his desk to the bank's main floor and makes a point of greeting customers and making them feel at ease.[237] The apparent conflict between the views of Citibank and Stillwater executives may reflect cultural differences between big cities and smaller communities or simply changes over time.

Unfortunately, banking has become so entrenched in controls and procedures that many banks have lost touch with what their customers really want. Because managers are much more exposed in cases of fraud or negligence than in cases of poor customer service, they tend to focus on security. Until the early 1970s, defense against fraud was relatively simple, but the advent of extensive computerization has made it possible to commit fraud from thousands of miles away virtually instantaneously. Consequently, controls have become much more important. But do extensive and tight controls automatically mean poor service? Or do people simply complain when they are in fact reasonably satisfied?

One paper reports that from 1971 to 1987, between 71 and 86% of Canadians viewed banks favorably, stressing security, stability, wide range of services, fair lending policies and interest rates on deposits as reasons.[177] Although 84% thought that banks offered courteous, polite and friendly service, almost as many (78%) felt that these institutions were trying to provide fast and efficient service, and 73% felt that banks were committed to providing personalized and individual service. This result is somewhat surprising; speed and efficiency are often seen as the antithesis of personalized service. The positive view is not universal, of course; the 10-12% in this survey who looked unfavorably on banks felt that service was inefficient and impersonal. One thing to keep in mind when interpreting such statistics is that up to half the customers of many banks never go into them anymore; most of them probably don't phone, either.[155]

One study, performed by the U.S. Federal Reserve, concluded that bank (labor) productivity remained unchanged over the 30-year period from 1950 to 1979.[204] But during that period, standards have been introduced, both for back-office operations and for customer contact personnel, including tellers. Why, then, has productivity not improved? Is it because the costs of performing transactions have offset productivity increases?

For a long time, banks have operated with two cornerstones of their service delivery strategy: bricks and paper. Both these foundations are changing. After years of living with a reputation for conservatism, banks are now focusing more and more on improving customer service. Electronic data, only recently collected in unified bank-wide data bases, is the new cornerstone. The number of bank branches is decreasing and those that remain are shrinking and becoming more specialized as ATMs allow customers to do much of their routine banking without direct access to the branch. And branches themselves are getting 'face-lifts' to make customers more comfortable. One branch has been re-designed to look like a shopping mall and is apparently very successful.[228]

The use of electronic data has also reduced paper flow in banks, although the number of cheques per household has continued to rise. Banking has always been labor intensive; this is unlikely to change overnight despite improved technology. However, bank jobs are changing. Increasingly, employees enter and retrieve information directly. Efficiency is not the only result; service is much faster and based on much better information. The speed of electronic processing is, of course, a mixed blessing. Slow procedures benefit those whose cheques take a few days to process. Paper processing is important to internal and external auditors and others who need physical evidence of transactions. And the old adage — garbage in equals garbage out — is relevant. A bank executive tells about a clerk who erased a day's worth of the bank's transactions by manually overriding six computer warnings. Needless to say, the bank executive was not amused as it took several people a few days to reconstruct the records.

As is true of most products retailers, a retail bank's service level is greatly influenced by the ratio of staff to customers in any given period. Computer programs are now available to forecast expected work load based on previous activity by the time of day, the day of the week, the day of the month and the month. The variable work load implies that many part-time tellers or many cross-trained staff members are required.

In summary, banks are adapting to a changing environment and giving better customer service by simplifying procedures and paperwork, providing new types of services, delivering the services in different ways, improving the interpersonal skills of customer-contact staff and using advanced technology.

12.3   Increased focus on customers

The location of any given bank branch was most likely chosen to be an advantage — perhaps it was near traffic flows, where it would be visually prominent, or near where customers live, work or shop. Over the years, however, cities develop, customers become more sophisticated and customer behavior changes. People are shopping around more for rates and services, using ATMs and even doing their banking using home computers. What was once a good site may now be a poor one.

Computers enable banks to proliferate the number of products they offer to meet the needs of small market segments — niche marketing. However, niches come and go. How banks will react to niche marketing is an interesting question. A high proportion (70-85%) of costs are allocated shared costs, necessary for a variety of services or market segments, that will not vanish when a service is discontinued.[30] One recent response is to unbundle services by charging customers fees for specific services. The idea behind this thinking is that the fee should reasonably reflect the cost of the service provided and that only those who use a service should have to pay for it. Ideally, average service charges should decline.

Computer data bases make tracking information easy. However, the procedure may well be fundamentally flawed because the cost allocation is far from perfect. Also, customers may feel that the numerous small charges constitute harassment. They are certainly more noticeable than incremental savings in other charges. Banks must carefully consider the impact on customers.

> There is no longer a need for each bank to offer every possible product in the name of building customer relationships... Increasingly, both corporations and individuals are looking for preferred product/price combinations regardless of the source.[280, p. 47]

If these authors are correct, market focus and niche strategies might well become the name of the game as they have in many retail services. A strategy of focusing on a particular specialty is very different from trying to offer a full product line: customers have every right to expect you to be particularly proficient at your specialty, whereas if you are a full-time operation, customers are more interested in breadth.

Another team of writers, while approaching the solution differently, nevertheless agree on the message: banks must be responsive to customers. In their words:

> ... each individual will be provided with those services that he requires, based on his resources, his sophistication, and his ability to pay, rather than services being provided at the convenience of the institution... Services today are...structured more to make it easier for the institution to provide the services than they are structured to provide the specific service that an individual may require.[181, p. 23]

These authors insist that organizational flexibility is the way to serve the different needs of customers. Consequently, an organization may have to offer a wide range of services. How can the apparently conflicting views of offering a very narrow specialized service versus offering a wide range be resolved? As has been pointed out, the concept of factory focus does not necessarily mean a narrow product mix; rather it means task homogeneity, repetition and experience in the production task.[123] Organizations that focus on choice as their competitive strength obtain that focus by offering a broad product range.[300] So, there may well be room for both 'boutique' and 'department store' approaches.

No matter how customer service is provided, there is ample evidence that banks are now focusing on providing it.[10, 205, 207, 228, 282] Reported innovations include installing chairs for people waiting for service, working with customers to help structure loans, actively visiting commercial customers' premises, bundling bank products in new ways and simply talking to customers. The fact that this last is even considered an innovation says a lot about banking's image. The current thinking is that it takes more than new products to satisfy customers.[205] The new focus is not on what is sold but on how it is sold. And the banks are not changing their attitude because of some new altruism. They firmly believe that good (personal) customer service will lead to increased profits.[220] There is evidence to support this idea: companies known for customer satisfaction often out-perform their competitors. American Express, for example, showed growth in sales from 1987 to 1989 of 14.4% compared to 13.3% for the financial services industry in general. American Express' return on equity over the same period was 18.3% compared to an industry average of 15.6%.[233]

One way that banks are trying to improve customer service is by generating new relationships with their employees — motivating them by appealing to their need for special recognition. The idea is that good service by an empolyee is impossible if the employee does not feel good about him- or herself. To this end, organizations like American Express have taken to rewarding those special employees who go that extra mile to serve customers.[213] In 1989, the company made 49 such awards (out of 48,000 employees), each of which cost American Express perhaps $10,000. The rewards to the company far exceed that, of course.

12.4   The technology flood

One of the more notable changes in banking over the past 20 years has been the growth of banking through ATMs. This approach is a natural extension of the self-service found in many retail services. There are now about 125,000 ATMs in the United States and an additional 7,500 in Canada. Particular efforts are now being made to serve customers who have difficulty using ATMs, for example, when a machine 'eats' a card. Such incidents are rare, but naturally are very disturbing to the customer who may be significantly inconvenienced and may well perceive his or her financial security to be at risk. Many ATM locations are equipped with telephones to enable customers to contact a customer service representative when a problem arises. This approach helps to reduce complaints.

Approximately 50% of bank clients have ATM cards but only 35% use them regularly.[95] This level of activity is not sufficient to offset the annual ATM operating costs ($50,000) including depreciation of the cost of an ATM ($50,000-100,000). However, the variable cost of a transaction is lower for ATMs ($0.10) than for human tellers ($0.58). Furthermore, an ATM can perform at three times the rate of a human teller and offers bank customers much greater accessibility to their accounts, both in time and geographically. Large ATM networks make 24-hour per day access possible nation-wide, even in large countries like Canada and the United States. One early study of ATMs in Canadian banks found that over a three-month period, one network recorded significant activity in the evening and on weekends outside normal banking hours and, more interestingly, that there was no half-hour period during the week with no ATM activity.[111] Not surprisingly, banks are keen to increase ATM use.

But ATMs, like any other technology, should be an integral part of an overall strategic business plan that ensures such ventures are evaluated strategically as well as economically. Technology, although indispensable, is not as much of an edge as one might think. As one bank information systems expert said, "... it is pointless for an institution to try to keep its technology proprietary... It has become relatively simple to copy technology." Furthermore, every technology has a lifespan; many become obsolete after only five to seven years.

In 1986 alone, United States banks invested nearly $10 billion in information systems;[280] this investment was reported to have increased to about $20 billion by 1989.[228] These seem like huge sums to invest annually (about $40-80 per person, possibly more, per bank customer) and probably lead in many cases to excess capacity. Many managers are beleaguered by problems in managing the new systems. Managing the implementation of new technology always poses problems, of course, but this case has some added features that make it particularly troublesome. As Steiner and Teixeira said,

> Investing in technology itself, across the board, is not a strategy at all... What used to be a financial business in which capital and credit skills were the means of production is moving steadily toward a record-keeping and accounting business in which processing skills and systems are the means of production...[280, p. 44]

This technology, introduced to increase the work done by the back-office infrastructure, has fundamentally changed the nature of bank work. It is small wonder that bankers with the traditionally-valued skills might have difficulty in this new environment. Fixed costs have increased while variable costs have decreased, forcing managers to manage portfolios more wisely and to change their thinking in major ways. The large investments involved may preclude small banks from competing successfully.

Needless to say, banking is extremely important to computer companies — so important that many have specialized departments dealing solely with banks. More than one computer company manager has lost his or her job because of losing an account with a bank. Often, a bank's top MIS managers are sold on the latest technology and then left to find out for themselves how to use all the computing power they have obtained. Computer vendors could provide better service to their bank customers by working closely with them to decide what changes are required for increased operational efficiency and effectiveness, and then by trying to find the best way to achieve those objectives. New equipment, or even software, may not be the only possible approach. Figure 12-1 pictures the convergence of technological and service factors to satisfy customers.

FIGURE 12-1   Banking technology as a means to two ends

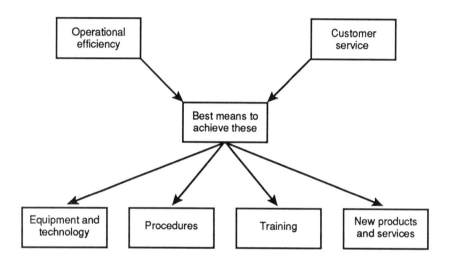

What, then, is the best strategy for banks? One study concludes that...

> ... the geographic competitors with the best results are those that have a higher share of channel locations and the right type of channels (for example, branch, ATM and so on) in the right place.[30, p. 68]

Not only is it important to locate facilities properly (hardly surprising), but it is also important to tailor channels to meet individual markets. This fine-tuning is useful and necessary to reach an appropriate balance. Experiments are now being made regarding the location of ATMs (in grocery and variety stores, for example), the features they have available (some are merely cash dispensers, others can perform dozens of services) and in electronic funds transfer directly from the buyer's account to the seller's.

Banking through home computers has not been as successful as ATM use.[228] The penetration of computers, and at least as importantly, computer expertise into homes is not yet high, the systems are reputedly difficult to use and no home computer can give what many people want from a bank transaction — cash.

Trends

12.5   New service avenues

Quite a few new financial service developments are on the horizon or have just arrived on the scene. Debit cards have long been discussed as a foundation of the cashless society. Debit cards are presented at the time of purchase and the amount of the transaction is electronically transferred from the buyer's account to the seller's. This approach is similar to direct deposit of salaries or benefits. It has a couple of real advantages for merchants: they receive the funds immediately and less cash on hand reduces the possibility of robbery. However, customers may react negatively; some prefer to pay cash, others depend on time delays between purchase and receipt of a credit card bill and still others rely on credit cards as a loan vehicle. Debit cards require significant investments in equipment and security systems. They also require acceptance by both merchants and customers. Historically, customers have been rather conservative when confronted by new technology involving their money. Direct deposit of salaries, ATMs (particularly when used for deposits) and electronic scanning in grocery stores have all taken considerable time and educational effort to become widespread. Debit cards are likely to be received similarly — with curiosity but suspicion.

An alternative to the debit card is a credit card, sold by the merchant, with a specific dollar amount registered on a microchip encased in the card. Each time a purchase is made, the amount is deducted from the balance. This sort of device is already used for student photocopying at one university. The advantage of this kind of system to the merchant is that the funds are pre-paid, but, of course, this is a disadvantage to customers, particularly infrequent ones or ones who wish to leave town with an unclaimed balance. Presumably, systems can be devised to credit such cards with interest and to refund unspent balances.

Credit card operations were originally set up on the premise that customers would use them for credit. However, many customers pay the entire balance within the allowed grace period. This is not surprising considering the high interest rates charged on unpaid balances, but it is a source of some disappointment to manaagers of credit card companies. Many are considering changing their present policies by charging higher fees, either per transaction or per time period, or cancelling the free payment period and charging interest from the date of purchase.[242] Such a move transfers the benefit of delays from the customer to the credit card company and may well make debit cards more attractive.

One possible explanation for the evolution of retail banking delivery systems is a service delivery system design life cycle.[134] According to this idea, service delivery systems in retail banking follow a predictable pattern of development. Such a life cycle would explain why so many modes of account enquiry and transactions exist in the banking system. A close examination of the historic pattern of evolution in delivering a service may help in forecasting when a particular mode will become the generally accepted standard. This life cycle could also help an institution to leapfrog its competitors in a systematic and well analyzed manner.

Increased internationalization will certainly play an important role in modifying the delivery modes and the spectrum of services being offered. Traditional financial considerations such as interest and exchange rates will still be important, of course. But even for individuals, banking will increasingly mean more than having an account at a local branch.

Some of the easiest changes a bank manager can make are often right under his or her nose. One study demonstrated that employee perceptions of service quality are often closely related to customer perceptions.[269] Customers evaluated service on criteria such as teller courtesy and competence, employee turnover, adequacy of staffing levels and branch administration. Is it possible that the low-tech solution of simply giving customers good service is more effective and efficient than innovative, fancy and probably expensive solutions? Only the future will tell.

CHAPTER **13**

PROFESSIONAL SERVICES

Professionalism and Professional Associations

13.1   Is everyone a professional ?

There is something magic about the word 'professional' and associated
words like 'profession' and 'professionalism.' They seem to convey competence and confer status on those performing a job. At one time, only
divinity, medicine and law were recognized as professions but now many
more occupations are classified in this group: engineering, architecture,
advertising, mediation, dentistry, accounting, consulting, nursing,
teaching, etc. And many more groups call themselves professionals or
advertise their work as being professional.

In fact, the word is used by so many people in so many ways that it
can mean almost anything — and therefore nothing. The word is used in
at least three different senses. 'Professional' is used in contrast to 'amateur': a professional athlete, for example, earns an income from the
application of athletic skills and talents; in contrast, an amateur pursues
athletic activities simply for enjoyment. The term is also used to describe particular expertise in carrying out a specific task, as in 'she did a
really professional job.' Samrén defines professionalism as 'doing the
right things and doing the right things in the right way.'[263] If this were
the case, everyone working effectively and efficiently could be considered
to be a professional. The final sense of the word, and the one we will use
in this book, refers to members of the most highly respected occupations, those most commonly known as professions.

The differences are more than purely semantic. As Figure 13-1 illustrates, there is an increasing tendency to use the word 'professional' across our society to reduce the perceived gap between 'elite' professionals and mere mortals. Managers sometimes call themselves 'professionals' in an attempt to raise their stature in the eyes of the professionals they manage. (Because of some interesting general characteristics, professionals can be difficult to manage).

FIGURE 13-1   The closing gap between professionals and other groups

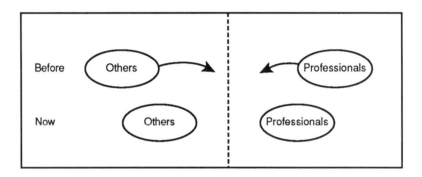

Firms commonly characterized as providers of professional services include an incredibly wide range of technical specialties. From a managerial viewpoint, however, they are remarkably similar. Common characteristics found across the spectrum of the professions make them very different from most other types of organization.[192] Among them are:

- a fund of specialized knowledge
- the creation and maintenance of a body of knowledge, skills and procedures
- a highly intellectually trained membership, usually having undergone many years of formal education and training
- workers who exercise considerable individual judgment and autonomy in their work
- independence of employee-employer relationships
- work that intimately affects the affairs of others
- a self-policing professional association
- a code of ethics
- a spirit of altruism
- personnel independent of suppliers of other services or goods
- service that is advisory and problem-oriented

- service as an assignment given by the buyer to the seller for a fee
- self motivation
- sense of belonging to the profession (possibly at the expense of an employer).[102, 137, 154, 196]

It is important to note that although virtually no profession has all of these characteristics, every profession has several of them. For example, nurses certainly intimately affect the affairs of others, have a self-policing professional association, have a code of ethics, etc., but they also work directly for an employer and thus have less autonomy and independence than other professionals. This line of argument leads naturally to the idea that some professions are more professional than others because they encompass a greater number of the characteristics listed above or because they exhibit some of the characteristics to a greater degree.[103, 117, 276] Indeed, it has been argued that many occupations not normally identified by intellectuals as professions have some of the characteristics of professions.[117] For example, the comedian who tailors his material to fit a specific audience, the restaurant manager who must deal with an irate customer and the football quarterback who must call a play based on his judgment of the defensive lineup all represent degrees of individual judgment and job autonomy. Conversely, members of most professions routinely perform many tasks that do not require the acknowledged features of professionalism.

A noted feature of many professions is the existence of one or more professional associations. These perform a number of roles. Most are concerned with developing and promoting the body of knowledge the profession is based on. To this end, they may keep a library, abstract articles for members, publish periodicals or books, fund research, arrange educational programs and sponsor conferences. The association usually tries to ensure that only individuals with the necessary level of knowledge and skill become members of the profession. This may involve critical evaluation of presented credentials and/or some sort of testing and licensing procedure; many professions are self-regulating to the extent that the professional association has the exclusive right to issue the mandatory license enabling the professional to practise.

Professional associations are often responsible for ensuring that members perform work according to accepted technical and ethical standards. This involves developing and publicizing standards as well as dealing with complaints of malpractice, perhaps through hearings and discipline. Particularly when dealing with acts involving judgment on technical matters, only members of the profession have the knowledge to evaluate another member's actions.

The professional association may become involved in establishing guidelines for setting professional fees. One area of some contention is the attempt by many professions to severely restrict advertising by members. Finally, the professional association may lobby on behalf of its members.

Although professional associations sometimes protect members who have transgressed the limits of acceptable behavior, it is clearly not in the best interests of the profession to do so repeatedly. The privileges of professionalism demand responsible action.

13.2   Building a professional image

Professional fees can be very high, so most people do not use professional services unless they have to. Often, though, there is no choice. Only a practising professional accountant can conduct an acceptable audit of a public company. Only a practising physician can write a prescription and only a licensed pharmacist can fill it. Creditors often give more credence to statements audited by a major accounting firm; consequently, clients will hire one rather than a smaller competitor, often at some financial penalty. Not all professional service firms are equal (or perceived to be equal).

As noted above, professionals are often severely restricted in their ability to advertise, although the limitations are being relaxed. The extent of the restriction depends on the jurisdiction. In Ontario, for example, a doctor establishing a new practice is allowed only three discreet announcements in a local newspaper and a sign outside the premises. The profession controls such variables as the size, location, orientation and working of signs. Lists of available services and prices are forbidden. Given such constraints, how does a professional market his or her services? Professional services are often best sold by the professional. Because of advertising restrictions, the very intangible nature of professional work and the frequently high stakes involved, it is not surprising that referrals by satisfied clients and other professionals are a major source of new clients. Therefore, it is of the utmost importance that professionals provide excellent services to existing clients as a means of developing a larger client base. This does not mean that the professional can get by without good marketing skills; technical competence is not sufficient in a buyer's market.

Image is extremely important in professional services. Of the large number of factors that affect image, two stand out. One is the firm's philosophy, reflecting the personalities of its founder and senior professionals. The second is the firm's distinctive competencies, based on the special expertise and abilities of its personnel. It is no surprise that senior professionals join clubs, serve as volunteers, write articles and go on the lecture circuit. Other important image-forming characteristics include the procedures, fees, location, decor and geographic scope of a firm. Figure 13-2 represents the influence of these factors on the professional service firm's image. The relative importance of the factors will vary from profession to profession, by the type of jobs a firm does, over time and from place to place, but each of the factors will affect all professional service firms, large and small.

FIGURE 13-2   Building an image in a professional service firm

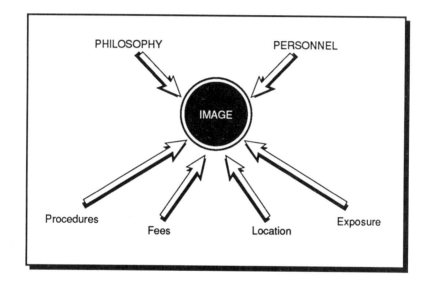

The source of a firm's image is different for a potential client than for an experienced one. The potential client has to rely on visual clues and what he or she has heard. In short, the decision is risky. An experienced client will be much less influenced by such things as how the professional is dressed or the condition of the office. More important things, such as the satisfied client's confidence in the professional's technical competence, supersede the more obvious but less value-adding criteria used by potential clients. One author distinguishes between the initial and permanent image:

> Whereas the permanent image factors have the most influence when the time comes for the definition of the evoked set of suppliers (in the tender offer, for example), the interaction factors of atmosphere will prevail when the contact is established.[90, p. 296]

Why is this so? The important service characteristic of intangibility is one reason. Even successful past work by a professional for other clients is not sufficient proof that he or she can achieve the same results again. In the words of one author,

> Professionals are paid not so much for what they do as for what they know: the knowledge, expertise, judgment, skill, training, experience and creativity brought to bear on their work, rather than the volume of measurable output.[55, p. 201]

As mentioned in earlier chapters, there will always be room for excellent service as long as the purchaser perceives value. Even when he or she does not perceive value, there might be no reasonable alternative to using the provider. And when there is an alternative, it often consists of going to another provider who charges a similar fee but is perceived to provide more value for it. The pattern is the same for professional services.

Professional Service Firms (PSFs)

13.3 Organizational structure: the example of accounting firms

Many professionals work in private practice in organizations generically called professional service firms. The structure of a PSF is fairly consistent from one profession to another, but quite different from more traditional organizations. We have chosen to focus on accounting firms which are good examples of PSFs, but the same general principles apply to law firms, consultancies, consulting engineering firms, etc.

In contrast to the usual rigid hierarchical structure, the professionals in accounting firms are organized in a relatively loose triangular arrangement of three distinct levels as shown in Figure 13-3.[192] The firm's non-professionals are organized more traditionally. The top, and smallest, level of the triangle is composed of the firm's most senior members, typically called partners, who in effect own the firm. The second level is composed of managers and supervisors. The largest, and bottom level, is composed of students in accounts, often divided into juniors and seniors.

Although the fluid 'pool' structure is common in PSFs, an alternative 'team' approach (discussed in more detail in Section 13.5) can also be found. In the pool system, each professional staff member is expected to perform a number of tasks within the firm, but the prime responsibility for each task lies with one of the three levels. The principal task of the numerous juniors and seniors is to carry out the auditing and other

FIGURE 13-3   Professional service firm structure

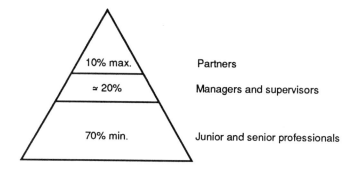

accounting work. The main task of the managers and supervisors is to manage the audit project. The task of managing client relations and the accounting firm falls to the partners, involves evaluation of other staff members for promotion decisions. These concentractions lead to the vernacular description of the three tiers of professionals as 'grinders,' 'minders' and 'finders' respectively.

The fluid structure suggested by Figure 13-3 implies that no staff member has a permanent 'boss.' The structure is appropriate because of the nature of the work and the management needs of the firm. Accounting work consists largely of series of projects for different clients. Naturally, each project will be of different duration and may pose quite different problems. Also, partners tend to specialize in the types of clients they work with. It is in the best interests of both the staff and the firm to move staff from partner to partner to help in staff development. Evaluating the performance of a staff member requires considerable judgment, and partners must have direct supervisory line exposure to him or her to make intelligent decisions. Only in very small firms can every partner have direct experience working with each staff member, but even in large firms a range of opinion can be obtained. It is also in the interests of the firm to move staff around to facilitate staff evaluation.

The ratio of staff members in the three staff levels shown in Figure 13-3 is a critical managerial variable. Accounting firms may typically have 10% partners, 20% managers and supervisors, and 70% juniors and seniors. These ratios represent the firm's balance. Two important variables affect the balance: the types of projects undertaken and the economics of the business. PSFs can undertake different kinds of projects, known as brains, grey hair or procedures projects (in which the firm is focusing on expertise, experience or efficiency, respectively.)[192] Firms specializing in brains projects require relatively more of the most prestigious senior professionals because their expertise creates the firm's main added value. In contrast, firms concentrating on procedures projects create their principal value through well established processes and thus require a greater percentage of junior staff members. Auditing is a relatively straightforward task so accounting firms tend to have relatively broad, flat triangles. Consulting, which many accounting firms perform, takes much more of a grey hair or brains approach, so it calls for a narrower, steeper triangle. Many feel that an accounting firm performing both consulting and auditing services for the same client may undermine the independence of its auditors. It is no accident that the consulting branches of accounting firms are organizationally separate from the auditing and tax functions.

Partners typically share annual profits rather than working for a salary. Staff members, on the other hand, earn salaries. Project time for each staff level is billed to clients at the established rate for that level. A project will usually require the full-time effort of several juniors and seniors, about half the time of one or two managers and supervisors, and about one tenth of the time of a partner. The driving force behind the economics of the PSF is its ability to charge clients a much higher fee for the services of a junior or senior than it actually pays those staff members. Conversely, the partners' hourly profit (their pay) is much more than their clients are charged.

So, under the circumstances, why do juniors and seniors stay with the PSF? Part of the answer lies in the other name for these staff members — students in accounts. In effect, they are in educational (apprentice) programs and their reduced pay is their tuition fee for the training and opportunity to become full-fledged members of the profession in due course. Another reason is that they have few options. On their own, juniors and seniors have little credibility and would have difficulty charging the going rate for their services without the backing of an established firm.

The firm, on the other hand, has to retain its staff, but it also has to ensure turnover to maintain the balance of its triangular structure and the resulting economic relationship. Although most professional staff members aspire to achieve partnership at some point, because many firms operate on an up-or-out basis, non-promotion means leaving the firm. Consequently, although at times firms may have to lay off employees, at other times they may have to provide incentives to encourage them to stay. North American universities provide a clear example of organizations out of balance. Many departments have very few or no junior faculty with consequential financial problems and a shortage of fresh ideas.

One problem faced by professional service firms is expansion. As noted above, professionals are very autonomous and it is difficult to hold large groups of them together. Accounting firms are an exception — they are among the larger service firms in the world. As their clients expanded through multi-site operations, many accounting firms followed suit to be able to serve clients better and avoid losing them to competitors.

A study of large British accounting firm concluded that new offices were opened for four reasons:

1. to increase market share by being represented in more cities
2. to take advantage of business opportunities arising in areas of industrial expansion
3. to obtain more small-firm clients
4. to expand because of public-sector offices expanding geographically.[59]

Larger accounting firms are able to hire more specialists to expand both the depth and breadth of their most valuable marketing commodity — their collective expertise. Expansion is an attractive, albeit difficult, route to follow.

For these reasons, there was a notable increase in the concentration of accounting capacity in the late 1980s, largely because of mergers, some between members of the internationally known majors and many more between majors and smaller firms. The larger firms' gain is often at the expense of medium-sized firms, which have to pay similar or higher salaries but charge their clients lower fees. The familiar name (along with the reputation) has a value, both in the market and for staff. Medium-sized firms are in a difficult position: their smaller competitors can offer lower rates and more personal service; larger firms have prestige and offer a wider range of specialized services and expertise.[85] They have four options: merge with other firms, grow internally, split to become a number of smaller firms, which face less competition from large firms, or remain an aggressive medium-sized firm, ready to add new small clients and lose larger ones.

Most firms have chosen the merger option, although some have chosen one of the other strategies. In the future, large firms can be expected to exhibit more internal growth — fewer medium-sized firms remain as potential merger partners.

Internal growth is not necessarily easy. It is important to grow slowly enough to keep the firm's staff balance, that is to maintain the triangular shape of the organization. This means resisting the temptation or pressure to promote staff prematurely and controlling the types of projects done for clients. Increasing the number of partners without a proportionate increase in fee income reduces the income of all partners. Retrenchment is not easy either. Reduced fee income will result in economic pressure to reduce staff.

13.4   The importance of PSF staff

Despite all efforts to create loyalty between a client and the PSF, the real allegiance may be between members of each firm. Not only that, but there are often strong working relationships between lower level staff members in the two organizations. After all, they spend a lot more time together than the top people do, and clients may well reason, perhaps with some merit, that a key staff member is more crucial to a project's success than an absent partner. After all, knowledge and expertise are more likely to reside with individuals than with organizations. Figure 13-4 shows this reasoning.

FIGURE 13-4   Professional services: relative importance to the client of the consultant and the professional firm

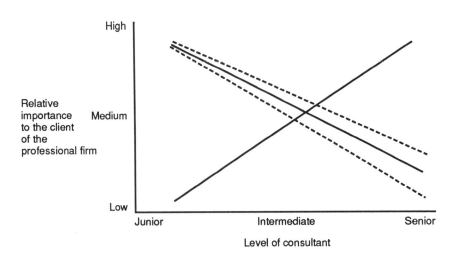

Because of the importance of these individual relationships, it is not uncommon for a dissatisfied staff member, often at the managerial level but occasionally at the partnership or lower level, to leave the firm and take a number of clients with him or her. The advertising agency, Lord Geller Federico Einstein, was essentially destroyed by such a desertion when six senior executives walked out, along with several staff members and numerous clients, and established a new agency which quickly became larger than the remains of the one they had left.[251] Firms sometimes require that employees sign an agreement agaitns this practice, at least without making some compensation, but enforcing such agreements can be difficult, time-consuming and expensive. Still, they may become more common; professional staff turnover in consulting firm is reported to be 16%, and there is no evidence that it is lower in other types of PSFs.[13] Indeed, it may well be considerably higher in firms specializing in grey hair and procedures projects. Even in the consulting field, higher numbers are known. The figure for Booz Allen and Hamilton is reported to be 25%. This figure is very high considering the value to clients of personnel continuity and the usual association of a firm with a few familiar faces, even friends. Many clients have several consulting jobs and many options when purchasing consulting services. High turnover may be enough to tip the scales to one of these options.

Keeping professional staff satisfied is not easy, especially in good economic times when there are many attractive alternatives — working for a competitor, leaving the industry (perhaps to work for a client) or establishing a new firm.

13.5   The problem of job assignment

A critically important function in a PSF is deciding which staff members will work on which jobs. There are four general factors to consider in making such decisions: satisfying the client, satisfying the staff, developing the staff and controlling costs.[193] Clients may want the best staff available or even specific staff members. The staff members may also have preferences regarding the types of industry or task they want to work on. The long-term interests of the firm are served by developing appropriate levels of breadth and depth in staff. A related consideration is ensuring that different staff members work together for the purposes of evaluation. Finally, the economic consequences of a project depend on how many hours staff members at each level spend on the project.

There are two basic approaches to making job assignments: the pool system, described in Section 13.3, and the team system. The pool approach consists of having everyone in a large pool from which project teams are formed as needed. This method allows staff members to work with a wider variety of co-workers, ensures development of staff depth and is more efficient from the point of view of resource usage. In the team technique, staff members are assigned to a team that is responsible for a group of clients. When they are not busy, team members may be lent to another team for a short period. This method works well in businesses like auditing, where continuity from year to year is economically important. It is also common when dealing at the leading edge of technological development in brains projects in which specialized skills are needed. For example, many hospitals have organ transplant teams and critical care units staffed by specialists.

Scheduling staff for professional services like auditing can be done well in advance; many firms have schedules, albeit not entirely fixed ones, a year in advance. The annual and predictable nature of auditing makes this possible. In contrast, consulting is much less predictable — often jobs are of an emergency nature with relatively short lead times, so it is difficult to schedule staff more than six weeks ahead with any confidence. One Canadian consulting firm, however, specializes in long-term organizational development work where the consultant works in the client company for up to a year. They have a much easier scheduling job. In any PSF, staff members have to be flexible, and both willing and able to work long hours on some jobs; clients expect this in return for the high hourly fees charged.

As implied above, the scheduler must make numerous trade-offs in virtually every assignment decision. Should preference be given to putting a staff member on a job led by a partner with whom he or she has had no direct contact? Should the staff member concentrate on developing depth or breadth? Should a person be assigned to out-of-town jobs? How heavily should the staff member's preferences be weighted? What about the feelings of potential co-workers? How much should the firm be involved in an individual's development and what should be left up to the individual staff member? No matter what the decisions are, some employees and partners will be more pleased than others. The trick as a scheduler is to keep the goals of the scheduling system in mind and optimize decisions over a reasonably long time frame.

13.6   Developments in providing professional services

Some important moves have recently occurred in many professional services, especially the trend toward de-professionalization. This can take many forms — fewer professional staff members, automation, different forms of organization. Each of these developments will be discussed.

One interesting development has been the increased use of paraprofessionals to work in conjunction with, and in some cases instead of, professionals. These people do not have a professional designation but do have the necessary education and training to do the technical work that does not have to be performed by a costly professional. Often they do an excellent job at considerable cost savings. In this regard, they are like junior professionals. The ultimate responsibility for their work lies with the partner but the risk can be very low and the rewards well worth it, particularly in the lower fees charged to clients.

Another significant development in the area of professional services has been office automation. Putting in place new hardware and software has helped many professionals to be more organized. In many services, the core professional service is being automated as well as the support functions. This helps not only those PSFs, like accounting firms, that are able to do much of their work by direct computer links, but also groups like architects and consulting engineers, that can use computer aided design systems to test hypotheses much more quickly and with more confidence than ever before. One travel agency has developed software that matches corporate travel policies with available airline, hotel and car rental prices.[292] The agency's corporate clients can interact with this software by means of a personal computer and a modem. Whether automation of professional services threatens the very existence of the professional remains an open question.[116]

In medicine and dentistry, the number of individual practitioners is falling as more professionals join partnerships, some to offer the same services but with shared costs, some to add services and some to become integrated multi-service firms like those in accounting. Clients may well choose a professional service provider based on the provider's characteristics, environmental features and the expected impact on the client.[122] For example, a client selecting an individual practitioner may prefer the personal contact, whereas one who patronizes a partnership may be attracted by more convenient hours, and one who seeks a multi-service firm may want the perceived technical excellence. Figure 13-5 shows the various available options. The practitioner's selection of the service production and delivery process, and the organizational structure will affect not only the client; they will directly influence the practitioner's independence, working hours, word-of-mouth publicity and overhead as well.

FIGURE 13-5   Ways to provide a professional service

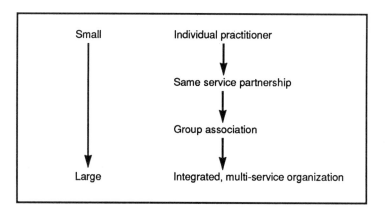

Whatever approach a professional selects, the fee he or she sets is important in an interesting way. Unlike the many services where low price is an attractive feature, in professional services clients often equate low fees with low quality. Naturally, this is particularly so when clients have difficulty assessing quality. Few clients, if any, boast that they have just done business with the cheapest professional in town!

Franchising, a business structure normally associated with non-professional services, is also beginning to appear in professional services. Tridont was reported in 1988 to have 350 dentists in 108 franchise and franchise-like partnerships across Canada.[253] The Tridont concept includes easy access for patients needing routine dental work. It is significant that Tridont tries to make the patient loyal to the Tridont system rather than to an individual dentist. Tridont dentists can concentrate on technical work; Tridont handles the administrative functions — site selection, site development, training of support staff, bookkeeping and marketing. Similar PSF franchises are also making an appearance in law, accounting, pharmacy and medicine. Unfortunately, a sound idea is no guarantee of success: the Tridont organization has been in severe financial trouble because...

> as leaders of a fledgling public company, they were pressured by analysts to spend, to expand, to do deals — anything to move the stock price up... [The principals] thought they could market other health-care services just as successfully as they had dentistry. They went on a hiring binge and got into businesses they knew little about. In short, as one former executive says, "They were greedy."[262, p. 75]

Earlier in this chapter, we referred to control of professionals by professional associations. This control is beginning to erode in some professions. The legal profession in the United Kingdom is a case in point. Cloaked in ancient restrictive practices, its membership is rigidly divided into barristers and solicitors, each group with its own exclusive rights.[79] The British government is proposing to remove some of the profession's privileges. Similar moves in North America have led to more freedom for professionals to advertise and, as has already been discussed, for certain non-professionals to perform work previously restricted to professionals. One report cites increased control of lawyers by corporate clients seeking more accountability, particularly in the areas of justifying fees and productivity.[127]

PSFs have been classified based on the degree to which power rests with the professional, the client or management.[109] According to this model, the way some key operating decisions, such as allocation of senior professionals, design of the interface between professionals and short-term capacity management, are made depends on the power balance. This power balance depends on a number of internal and external forces. Examples include: the markets for clients and professionals, how the professionals get paid, the required investment in facilities, the importance of infrastructure, the consequences of the professional service and the extent to which value lies in the individual professional.

Power can shift as the factors change over time, as we have already discussed.

Finally, many professions are dominated by one or a few firms that stand out because of the way they are managed. It seems likely that the power balance favors management in these firms. In Maister's view, the excellent firms in many professions share a common managerial approach that he calls the one-firm firm.[195] In one-firm firms, management emphasizes loyalty to the firm and co-operation between groups within the firm. Although these characteristics seem to fly in the face of traditional professional autonomy, one-firm firms have been unusually successful. It might well be time to apply the skills of what some identify as an emerging profession — management — to the problems faced by other professions.

CHAPTER 14

HOSPITALITY SERVICES

Hospitality Services

Hospitality services affect almost everyone; they account for a large part of the service economy; and they have been the subject of numerous books and periodicals. Many schools have been established to study hospitality services. Because the existing material is extensive, and because of the diversity of the hospitality industry, we have chosen to present only a brief overview of this important sector.

14.1 The lodging industry

The American hotel industry expanded faster than demand did during the early 1980s.[296] Consequently, average occupancy dropped from 73% in 1979 to 65% in 1985. The industry was responding to expectations that opportunities would arise from better identification of the level of quality, higher demand and targeting properties at specific market segments. However, when many players increase capacity simultaneously, especially in a recessionary period, there is bound to be costly excess capacity.

Although there is a range of types of hotels and motels, there are three basic ones: budget, business and deluxe. They correspond to economy, business and first class seats on an airline. Although their revenue per bed-night is relatively low, budget hotels may be the most profitable because, even in tough times, there is always a market for them. Customers are not looking for frills, but simply for a comfortable bed, clean facilities, a television set that works and perhaps a coffee shop. Budget lodging is usually made possible by lower overhead and labor costs. Labor costs may account for 20% of revenues instead of the 30-35% that is standard in luxury hotels. Occupancy rates and location are critical variables. Budget facilities are often found along highways that have year-round traffic so as to be easily accessible to motorists. They are less likely to be found in cities catering to destination travellers. Budgetel is one of many budget motel chains. It tries to provide high quality at a low price and accomplishes this by emphasizing training (using tapes for housekeeping and front desk personnel) and inspection (using data from guest comment cards, silent shoppers, company inspectors and district directors).[281]

Business hotels attract people looking for comfort and extra services at a reasonable price. They are usually located in urban areas or near airports. Many are part of chains and have facilities such as health clubs, frequent traveller plans, executive floors, non-smoking rooms, room service, nightly entertainment, restaurants, conference rooms, and possibly FAX machines, computers and photocopy machines to cater to business travellers. These amenities push up costs, but may be unavoidable. As one senior financial executive of a hotel chain said: "Whether we like them or not, they're a fact of our lives."[94, p. 47] Like any service industry with lots of extras, no operator in this segment wants to be the first to cut back on services.

Most deluxe hotels are located near city centres and may or may not be part of a chain. Many of the world's top hotels are independent units or members of small chains. The Waldorf in New York, the Royal York in Toronto, the Ritz Carlton in Montreal and Raffles in Singapore have all passed the test of time. Other, newer hotels are also trying to join the club by offering or trying to offer superior service, including amenities such as restaurants with elaborate menus. The clientele of deluxe hotels is very demanding — after all, they pay a lot of money. One study of the deluxe hotels in Montreal determined that guests look for quality of service first and then for a varied and refined menu.[246] The key to success, therefore, is selecting personnel that is not only competent and oriented to serving the customer, but also able to add that little something extra. Deluxe hotels depend on their staffs to add value; in contrast, budget properties depend more on their 'systems.'

The position of the top hotels is not necessarily unassailable. They have built their reputations with their traditional decor and the ambience of a by-gone age that it represents. Of course, facilities gradually deteriorate. It is a major challenge to strike the right balance between maintaining the old image and renovating to provide modern services. Getting it wrong will result in a shift in, or possibly a gradual loss of, clientele.

During the 1970s and 1980s, manufacturing in North America was revolutionized by fundamentally different practices that originated in Asia, particularly in Japan. The airline and hospitality industries are facing a similar upheaval. Some of the world's best hotels are located in Thailand, Korea, Taiwan, Hong Kong, Singapore and Japan.[12] For instance, in 1989, the readers of Institutional Investor Magazine voted the Mandarin Oriental in Bangkok the world's best hotel for the ninth consecutive year.[307] Other hotels in the Mandarin Oriental chain were also highly rated. And here is one example why: most Hong Kong chickens are fed on fish meal. In response to complaints by guests that its (purchased) eggs had a fishy taste, the Hong Kong unit reportedly started its own grain-fed poultry flock.[307] Needless to say, this unusual sideline for a hotel demonstrates its attention to customer satisfaction. In the words of one satisfied guest writing a travel column:

> The Mandarin's approach to hospitality can best be described as intimate. Instead of trying to overwhelm you with size, the Mandarin bowls you over with attention to details and service. It has a huge staff for a hotel of its size, including two people whose sole job seems to be to polish the brass... Service is instinctive and unobtrusive yet merely raising an eyebrow will summon a waiter. This is perhaps the only place on the planet where waiters don't seem to magically have something very important to do just when you want their attention.[135, p. A14]

The Regent Hong Kong reportedly excels in luxurious rooms and has the largest wine cellar in Asia (8,000 bottles).[136] However, it does not come cheap.

One analysis of what makes Asian hotels successful lead its authors to propose a hybrid between the Asian and American approaches to customer service in order to improve overall quality of service. They call it total customer service (TCS) or Theory S. The cornerstones are employee training and developing operating procedures. A critical component of the program is eliminating any rule or policy that impedes customer satisfaction. Employees are trained to anticipate and respond to all the needs of the guests. After comparing hotels in the United States and Asia, the authors concluded that they used about the same number of staff per room and paid them about the same relative to alternative jobs. In their view, the quality of performance is the key difference. The authors cite the example of the Tawaraya Inn in Kyoto, Japan, selected by *Esquire* as the best hotel in the world. The Tawaraya Inn is surrounded by well-kept gardens so the city's hustle and bustle are left behind. The inn goes out of its way to remove the usual discomforts of checking in. Guests are greeted by an employee who takes their shoes and has an uncanny ability to anticipate when guests will need them back. Guests are also greeted by the general manager who escorts them through the gardens to their rooms. The inn unpacks guests' clothes, provides

colorful cotton kimonos, hosts a private tea ceremony and makes available a luxurious bath. In the authors' words:

> For the new guest, one of the most striking aspects of the inn is that the
> service dimension becomes invisible. Every guest soon feels at home
> and forgets his or her normal environment.[12, p. 95]

The proposed TCS program to transfer this level of service to the
United States has ten steps:

1. establish the potential for customer service
2. establish a customer service department
3. create standard customer service procedures
4. incorporate evaluation of an employee's orientation to customer
   service into employee selection
5. initiate employee-participation and incentive programs
6. deliver total customer service
7. motivate employees for total customer service
8. implement a TCS control program
9. create rites, rituals and ceremonies
10. establish long-term TCS program strategies.

It seems that North American hoteliers should pay attention to
developments in Asia. Hotel services cannot be exported in the same
way as manufactured goods so hoteliers might avoid the fate of North
American manufacturers, many of whom have suffered severely because
of competition from Asian imports. However, services can be 'exported'
by establishing outlets abroad and repatriating funds. Asian hotel chains
are expanding into North American markets. As international travel
becomes more commonplace, North Americans are more likely to be
exposed to a superior level of service. It may be possible for hotels to
survive without responding to the competition, but there are definite
advantages to remaining at or near the top in quality. It would appear
that some North American hotels will have to change just to keep up.

One trend in accommodation is the development of packages of
services. The all-inclusive Club Med resort pioneered by Club Méditerranée has proven to be very successful in many of the world's vacation
destinations. The Hyatt Regency Waikoloa in Hawaii was the most
expensive resort ever built ($360 million) in 1989 when it opened but in
the view of one guest, it will change the way people think about resorts
— and the way the 'superluxe' hotels do business.[96] The 1,241-room
resort sits on 25 hectares and is packed with attractions designed to
ensure that every guest takes home a memorable experience. The staff
spent time developing a menu of activities to fit the Fantasy Resort
theme. Although the activities are 'fantastically' pricey, capacity cannot
always keep up with demand. The basic room rate in 1989 was US$265
per night and a single activity — renting a helicopter, riding for a day

with local cowboys, hunting wild pigs, goats or pheasants, or a luxury banquet — can cost several hundred dollars. The company had plans to develop 25 properties in a similar vein by 1994.

14.2   The restaurant industry

Food and beverage services make up the other half of the hospitality industry. Like the hotel industry, food and beverage operations fall into a number of types, ranging from haute cuisine to fast food.

Over the past quarter century, the fast food industry has really revolutionized the concept of eating out. It started out with drive-in restaurants that had 'table' service at the customer's car window. Those evolved into sit-down units located along a 'strip,' and then into malls and downtown locations that used to be occupied by traditional restaurants. Car service has returned, but this time it is with drive-through windows. McDonald's is considered to be the pioneer in bringing the discipline and approach of the manufacturing sector to food service.[173] Others, such as Burger King, Wendy's, Kentucky Fried Chicken and Domino's have contributed both to the dynamic growth of this sector and to the development of improved operating methods. Although individual outlets are usually modest, the success of fast food restaurants have made them the largest restaurant companies in the world; many operate in several countries. McDonald's had sales of $6.1 billion in 1989, ranking 18th among retailers and about 48th overall in the Fortune Service 500 listings (excluding savings organizations and commercial banks).[294] These figures would rank the company 76th in the Industrial 500.[290]

Despite the growth of the fast food sector, some observers believe it is reaching its saturation point and will do well to maintain its market share within the restaurant industry in the future.[36] McDonald's alone controls about 30% of the market.

Of fast food restaurants, those specializing in hamburgers have the lowest food costs and, consequently, the highest pre-tax earnings. Others have studied the pizza market and conclude that it is booming and will continue to attract new operators because the profit margin is about 20% for small operators and up to 50% for large ones.[47, 60]

The pizza industry is very competitive. Innovations can pay for themselves very quickly. Pizza Pizza introduced the use of one catchy phone number for the whole Toronto area, (the number is now a registered trade mark), a computerized ordering system, delivery within 30 minutes or a free pizza, and two-for-the-price-of-one offers. Pizza Pizza was the clear leader in Metropolitan Toronto in 1988, with a reported market share of 65%. In 1989 and 1990, it was expanding into other

Canadian cities but looking over its shoulder nervously as the large United States chain, Domino's, began moving into their market. Pizza Pizza's computer system records information from first-time callers and checks it during repeat calls. The system records data such as preferred toppings for faster order processing and more personal service. Pizza Pizza is considering completely automating the ordering process; instead of speaking to a person, the caller will place an order directly to the closest kitchen using touch-tone codes.

Godfather's Pizza is another example of fruitful innovation. It has also been quite successful, owing to its pizza hot-line number and selling pizza by the slice. Owner, Pillsbury, is similarily reexamining all operational aspects of all the types of restaurants it owns. Selling slices of pizza seems so incredibly simple that it is surprising no commercial pizza restaurant thought of it before. Pizza Hut comes close with its small pizzas, but they are a sit-down restaurant with no delivery.

The restaurant industry continues to generate new concepts. Mr. Shoes Pizza in Rochester, NY challenged Domino's head on with a product that weighed twice as much and an upbeat marketing campaign.[235] One feature was to offer a $2 discount for every Domino's advertisement torn from the Yellow Pages. In Chicago, an entrepreneur combined a restaurant with a micro-brewery.[107] Several organizations have tried build-your-own gourmet hamburger concepts, and in London, Ontario, one of the most popular places in town is an establishment called Joe Kool's that goes out of its way to downplay its service and to insult customers.

Innovation is not restricted to newly established organizations. Pillsbury analyzed Burger King, one of its better known subsidiaries, to answer questions such as: should packaged salads have one tomato or two?[234] The question may appear mundane and trivial, but in the context of the whole chain, it could mean a difference of over $100,000 annually. The important variable is whether or not customers feel that fewer tomatoes make a difference to the salad's perceived value. This sort of analysis is the principle underlying the renowned uniformity and phenomenal success of McDonald's.

Innovations can result from internal operational problems as well as from market opportunities. Because low wages and a production strategy of chasing demand (see Chapter 4) through the extensive use of part-time labor are extremely important determinants of profit margin, it is not surprising that fewer and fewer people are interested in working in fast food restaurants. This is especially true when the economy is healthy and there are other employment opportunities. This labor shortage and the increasing acceptability of customers serving themselves in other types of organizations have prompted managers to consider having customers dispense their own soft drinks, enter their orders into a computer and warm their meals in microwave ovens. This may not increase the speed of service, but it does keep costs (and prices) down. It is conceivable that some organizations may have to take the word 'fast' out of fast food restaurant.

The image is that fast food restaurants standardize virtually everything, with the possible exception of location. This is not true for all operators, though. Au Bon Pain has left development up to its unit managers under its partner-manager program; the company now operates several outlets which are apparently different but are uniformly clean and offer good service.[187] And there is an Arby's outlet in Maine that has added to the chain's standard menu and attracts a different kind of customer.[126] This sort of move many threaten franchising as a form of business organization if it continues.

Other types of restaurants have come up with new ideas, too. For example, an increasing number of restaurants use computerized work stations or hand-held electronic devices that send orders directly to a terminal in the kitchen.[289] This practice may well be acceptable, even expected, in fast food or middle-of-the-road establishments, but may not be acceptable at the upper end because it gives the service an image of being less personal.

Pizza Pizza's use of computers to personalize and speed up service and computerized transmission of orders to the kitchen are not the only ways that electronics can be used. One novel approach to advertising has restaurants using a low-power FM transmitter to attract passing drivers.[198] And a computer can control customers who make reservations and don't show up. 'No-shows' are costly because they tie up seats without generating sales. The manager of Mijanou, a posh 30-seat French restaurant in London, England estimated that no-shows cost the restaurant $8,850 per year. Some British restaurants charge no-shows a fee through a data base of repeat offenders compiled by the 500-member Restaurateurs Association of Great Britain.[140] This approach to the problem is an alternative to the deliberate overbooking used by airlines.

Not all capacity management systems are as sophisticated. The Hourglass Tavern in New York has an hourglass above each table. The rules are simple: when the hourglass runs out, the customer must leave.[221] And at Hibachi-style Japanese restaurants like Benihana of Tokyo, where the chef prepares the meal in front of the customer on a specially-designed grill that's part of the table, the production process is designed to give the restaurant control over the customer's movements. The goal of capacity management systems is to serve more people per day, using the same fixed assets and keeping cost-of-sales (and prices) competitive.

Quality is another very significant concern in restaurants. In most restaurants, the overall quality of the service is probably as closely associated with the attributes of individual employees as with the quality of the food itself, but many other factors also play a role.[263] Restaurant managers must pay close attention to the personality of staff when they are hired and trained. Many restaurants rely on tips to compensate for very low wages. The logic is that customers will reward good service so tips are a direct incentive to satisfy customers. Relying on tips may give staff the message that management doesn't care enough about them to pay a higher wage. It is also unfair in that neither management nor the server has complete control over tipping. Factors completely beyond the control of either may affect the result, either positively or negatively. It would be interesting to see if there is a correlation between tips and quality of service but accurate measures of both are needed.

Having the right manager, either in the hotel or the restaurant business, (and probably in allied fields such as airlines and hospitals) is very important to success in the hospitality industry. It is a notoriously tough business. The skills required are specific to each segment of the industry. It is rare that a manager can successfully move from a fast food operation to a four-star restaurant. However, there are exceptions. As one author indicated, some people have the golden touch.[165] One is Richard Melman of Lettuce Entertain You, who has opened 27 successful restaurants, each one different from the others. Visitors flock to Chicago to visit the restaurants and pick up ideas. In the words of one former partner:

> The guy just has the ability to know what's right about a restaurant. He knows how it's supposed to feel.[165, p. 77]

And in those of a competitor:

> He's got this uncanny ability to know what you'll want to eat six months from now, even though *you* may not know.[165, p. 75]

These quotes show that properly managing a restaurant, hotel or most other types of service business is still very much an art (as well as a science). However, as this chapter has illustrated, there are important aspects to delivering service that exceeds customer expectations: provide the types of services that the targeted customer really wants in all details, package the services if it seems reasonable to do so, and remain innovative. Despite their apparent differences, services also have similarities which allow transfer of knowledge from one sector to another. These features also make services difficult, but interesting, to operate. We have tried to illustrate this closing of the loop throughout this book.

CONCLUSION _____

Some of the characteristics of services make them easier to manage than other industries; others have the opposite effect. However, all industries need good managers and not everyone can manage service firms successfully. Grönroos suggested that organizations should develop service know-how and a service culture.[100] He suggests five rules to achieve these goals. They can serve any service organization:

1. The general approach: employees should act like consultants.
2. Demand analysis: the contact person has to do his or her own analysis of the customer's needs and wants.
3. Service quality: self-control when the service is produced.
4. Marketing: the server is the marketer.
5. Organizational support: the structure, technology and management should support and motivate the producer.

We feel that only with such an all-encompassing philosophy that involves everyone acting in concert toward well-defined, focused goals can organizations produce consistently high quality service, along with satisfied customers, employees and managers.

There have been many research developments in services management, many of which have both theoretical and direct practical applications. In addition, many opportunities remain in what some believe to be the fledgling academic field of services management. Although services are less tangible than goods, everyone is familiar with them. Thus, as is appropriate in an emerging field, there are as yet few complex theoretical models with little practical application. It is likely that researchers will continue to develop a common core of knowledge but most articles and developments will retain an identity with one area only, despite possibilities for generalization. Astute scholars and managers will try to transfer knowledge between areas of the service sector.

Although service organizations have too often been identified with poor management, many of the examples in this book illustrate that it is possible to manage service organizations well. We hope that this overview of service management will be useful to practitioners who have to achieve results daily, to students who may work in a service industry, and to those who have to deal frequently with service organizations.

REFERENCES _____

1. ALEXANDER, Judith W., and RANDOLF, W. Alan, "The Fit Between Technology and Structure as a Predictor of Performance in Nursing Subunits," *Academy of Management Journal*, Vol. 28, No. 4, December 1985, pp. 844-859.

2. ALTER, Jonathan, FINEMAN, Howard, and CLIFT, Eleanor, "The World of Congress," *Newsweek*, Vol. 113, No. 17, April 24, 1989, pp. 28-34.

3. AMENT, Jon M., "Change a Queue System from Passive to Active," *Industrial Engineering*, Vol. 12, No. 4, April 1980, pp. 40-44.

4. ANDREASEN, Alan R., "Nonprofits: Check Your Attention to Customer," *Harvard Business Review*, Vol. 60, No. 3, May-June 1982, pp. 105-110.

5. ANGIOLILLO, Paul Jr., PAYNE, Seth, ICHNIOWSKI, Tom, and HAMILTON, Joan O'C., "Boston to Pilot: Buzz Off," *Business Week*, March 7, 1988, p. 34.

6. ANTLE, David W. and REID, Richard A., "Managing Service Capacity in an Ambulatory Care Clinic," *Hospital & Health Services Administration*, Vol. 33, No. 2, Summer 1988, pp. 201-211.

7. ARMISTEAD, Colin, JOHNSTON, Robert, and SLACK, Nigel, "The Strategic Determinants of Service Productivity," *International Journal of Operations and Production Management*, Vol. 8, No. 3, 1988, pp. 95-108.

8. "Auditing the IRS," *Business Week*, April 16, 1984, pp. 84-92.

9. "Automatic Vehicle Location Comes to Toronto," *Metro Magazine*, May-June 1987, pp. 20-24.

10. "Bankers Learn a Smile on Their Face Puts a Buck in Their Pocket," *The Economist*, Vol. 312, No. 7611, July 15, pp. 73-74.

11. BARRAS, Richard, "Towards a Theory of Innovation in Services," *Research Policy*, Vol. 15, No. 4, August 1986, pp. 161-173.

12. BARSKY, Jonathan D. and DITTMANN, Susan, "Theory S: Total Customer Service," *Cornell Hotel and Restaurant Administration Quarterly*, Vol. 31, No. 1, May 1990, pp. 88-95.

13. BAUM, Laurie, "Is Booz Allen Having a Mid-life Crisis?" *Business Week*, March 9, 1987, pp. 76 and 80.

14. BEDNARZIK, Robert W., "The Quality of US Jobs," *The Service Industries Journal*, Vol. 8, No. 2, April 1988, pp. 127-135.

15. BERGER, Joan, "Productivity: Why It's the No. 1 Underachiever," *Business Week*, April 20, 1987, pp. 54-55.

16. BERGLIND, Bradford L. and SCALES, Charles D., "White-Collar Productivity: Seeing Through the Camouflage," *Management Review*, Vol. 76, June 1987, pp. 41-46.

17. BERRY, Leonard L., "Services Marketing Is Different" in: Lovelock, Christopher H., *Services Marketing*, Prentice Hall, Englewood Cliffs, New Jersey, 1984, pp. 29-37.

18. BERRY, Leonard L., LEFKOWITH, Edwin F., and CLARK, Terry, "In Services, What's in a Name?" *Harvard Business Review*, Vol. 66, No. 5, September-October 1988, pp. 28-30.

19. BERTHIAUME, Christiane, "Libéraliser les airs, une opération parfois douloureuse," *Le Devoir économique*, March 1988, pp. 7-9.

20. BLACK, Larry, "Hamburger Diplomacy," *Report on Business Magazine*, Vol. 5, No. 2, August 1988, pp. 30-36.

21. BLOIS, Keith J., "The Structure of Service Firms and Their Marketing Policies," *Strategic Management Journal*, Vol. 4, No. 3, 1983, pp. 251-261.

22. BLY, P.H., "Managing Public Transport: Commercial Profitability and Social Service," *Transportation Research*, Vol. 21A, No. 2, March 1987, pp. 109-125.

23. BOOMS, Bernard H. and BITNER, Mary J., "Marketing Strategies and Organization Structures for Service Firms" in : *Marketing of Services*, Donnelly James H. and George, William R., Eds., American Marketing Association, Chicago, Il, 1981, pp. 47-51.

24. BOYETT, Joseph H., CONN, Henry P., "Developing White-Collar Performance Measures," *National Productiviy Review*, Vol. 7, No. 3, Summer 1988, pp. 209-218.

25. *British Columbia Financial and Economic Review*, 47th ed., Province of British Columbia, Ministry of Finance and Corporate Relations, Victoria, B.C., September 1987.

26. BROWN, Mark G. and SVENSON, Raynold, A., "Measuring R & D Productivity," *Research-Technology Management*, Vol. 31, No. 4, July-August 1988, pp. 11-15.

27. BROWN, Paul B., "Piggyback," *Inc.*, Vol. 10, No. 8, August 1988, pp. 92-93.

28. BROWN, Richard E. and PYERS, James B., "Putting Teeth into the Efficiency and Effectiveness of Public Services," *Public Administration Review*, Vol. 48, No. 3, May-June 1988, pp. 735-742.

29. BRUGGEMAN, W., BARTHOLOMEEUSEN L., and HEENE, A., "How Management Control Systems Can Affect the Performance of Service Operations," *International Journal of Operations and Production Management*, Vol. 8, No. 3, 1988, pp. 76-85.

30. BRYAN, Lowell and ALLEN, Paul, "Geographic Strategies for the 1990s," *The McKinsey Quarterly*, Winter 1988, pp. 52-71.

31. BURGER, Alvin L., "Breaking Away," *Inc.*, Vol. 9, No. 4, April 1987, pp. 124-125.

32. BYLINSKY, Gene, "Invasion of the Service Robots," *Fortune*, Vol. 116, No. 6, September 14, 1987, pp. 81-88.

33. CANTON, Irving D., "How Manufacturers Can Move into the Service Business," *The Journal of Business Strategy*, Vol. 9, No. 4, July-August 1988, pp. 40-44.

34. CARLZON, Jan, "Putting the Customer First: The Key to Service Strategy," *The McKinsey Quarterly*, Summer 1987, pp. 38-51.

35. CARLZON, Jan, *Moments of Truth*, Ballinger Publishing Co., Cambridge, MA, 1987.

36. CARON, Jean-Paul, "Profits to Go," *Canadian Banker*, Vol. 95, No. 2, March-April 1988, pp. 10-23.

37. CAVES, Douglas W. and CHRISTENSEN, Laurits R., "The Importance of Economies of Scale, Capacity Utilization, and Density in Explaining Interindustry Differences in Productivity Growth," *The Logistics and Transportation Review*, Vol. 24, No. 2, March 1988, pp. 3-32.

38. CHARON, Kenneth A. and SCHLUMPF, James D., "How to Measure Productivity of the Indirect Workforce," *Management Review*, August 1981, pp. 8-14.

39. CHASE, Richard B., "Where Does the Customer Fit in a Service Operation?" *Harvard Business Review*, Vol. 56, No. 6, November-December 1978, pp. 137-142.

40. CHASE, Richard B., "The Customer Contact Approach to Services: Theoretical Bases and Practical Extensions," *Operations Research*, Vol. 29, No. 4, July-August 1981, pp. 698-706.

41. CHASE, Richard B. and ERIKSON, Warren J., "The Service Factory," *The Academy of Management Executive*, Vol. 11, No. 3, 1988, pp. 191-196.

42. CHASE, Richard B. and GARVIN, David A., "The Service Factory," *Harvard Business Review*, Vol. 67, No. 4, July-August 1989, pp. 61-69.

43. CHASE, Richard B., NORTHCRAFT, Gregory B., and WOLF, Gerrit, "Designing High-Contact Service Systems: Application to Branches of a Savings and Loan," *Decision Sciences*, Vol. 15, No. 4, Fall 1984, pp. 542-556.

44. CHASE, Richard B. and TANKIK, David A., "The Customer Contact Model for Organization Design," *Management Science*, Vol. 29, No. 7, September 1983, pp. 1037-1050.

45. CHAUMEL, Jean-Louis, "L'implantation d'une technologie nouvelle: Leçons de l'expérience de la mécanisation du tri postal," *Gestion*, Vol. 8, No. 4, November 1983, pp. 4-8.

46. CHELST, Kenneth, "A Public Safety Merger in Grosse Point Park, Michigan — A Short and Sweet Study," *Interfaces*, Vol. 18, No. 4, July-August 1988, pp. 1-11.

47. CHISHOLM, Patricia, "Chasing Pizza Profits," *Maclean's*, Vol. 101, No. 33, August 8, 1988, pp. 24-25.

48. CHRISTOPHER, Martin, "The Strategy of Customer Service," *The Service Industries Journal*, Vol. 4, No. 3, 1984, pp. 205-213.

49. COHEN, James K., "Capital Investment and the Decline of Mass Transit in New York City, 1945-1981," *Urban Affairs Quarterly*, Vol. 23, No. 3, March 1988, pp. 369-388.

50. COLL, Steve, "India's Terminal Frustrations," *Manchester Guardian Weekly*, Vol. 142, No. 8, February 25, 1990, p. 17.

51. COLLIER, David A., "The Service Sector Revolution: The Automation of Services," *Long Range Planning*, Vol. 16, No. 6, December 1983, pp. 10-20.

52. COLLIER, David A., "Managing a Service Firm: A Different Management Game," *National Productivity Review*, Vol. 3, No. 1, Winter 1983-84, pp. 36-45.

53. CONYBEARE, John A. C., "Air Wars: Regulation and Deregulation in the International Air Passenger Market," *Policy Studies Review*, Vol. 6, No. 3, February 1987, pp. 425-438.

54. COOK, Dan, "Wendy's Tries Warming Up the Basic Burger," *Business Week*, May 18, 1987, p. 51.

55. COWPERTHWAITE, Gordon H., "Measuring Professional Performance," *The Accountant*, Vol. 178, No. 5378, February 16, 1978, pp. 201-202.

56. CRANDALL, Robert L., "Solving the Crisis in the Skies," *Fortune*, Vol. 116, No. 7, September 28, 1987, pp. 203-204.

57. CROSS, James C. and WALKER, Bruce J., "Service Marketing and Franchising: A Practical Business Marriage," *Business Horizons*, Vol. 30, No. 6, November-December 1987, pp. 50-58.

58. DAILEY, Robert C., "Productivity Monitoring Systems in Hospitals: A Work Group Focus," *Hospital & Health Services Administration*, Vol. 33, No. 1, Spring 1988, pp. 75-88.

59. DANIELS, P.W., LEYSHON, A., and THRIFT, N.J., "Large Accountancy Firms in the UK: Operational Adaptation and Spatial Development," *The Service Industries Journal*, Vol. 8, No. 3, July 1988, pp. 317-346.

60. DAVIES, Pat, "A Pizza the Action," *Report on Business Magazine*, Vol. 4, No. 11, May, 1988, pp. 103-105.

61. DAVIS, Jo Ellen and ENGARDIO, Pete, "What It's Like to Work for Frank Lorenzo," *Business Week*, May 18, 1987, pp. 76-78.

62. DE COINTET, E., "L'hôpital public peut-il se comporter comme une entreprise ? *Administration hospitalière et sociale*, Vol. 33, No. 6, November-December 1987, pp. 28-33.

63. DIIULIO, John J. Jr., "What's Wrong with Private Prisons," *The Public Interest*, No. 92, Summer 1988, pp. 66-83.

64. DOYLE, Peter and CORSTJENS, Marcel, "Optimal Growth Strategies for Service Organizations," *The Journal of Business*, Vol. 56, No. 3, 1983, pp. 389-405.

65. DROR, Moshe, TRUDEAU, Pierre, and LADANY, Shaul P., "Network Models for Seat Allocation on Flights," *Transportation Research*, Vol. 22B, No. 4, August 1988, pp. 239-250.

66. DRUCKER, Peter, F., *People and Performance*, Heinemann, London, 1977, Ch. 16.

67. DRUCKER, Peter F., "Sell the Mailroom," *The Wall Street Journal*, July 25, 1989, p. A18.

68. DUDIK, Evan, "Profiting from the Turmoil in Service Industries," *The Journal of Business Strategy*, Vol. 9, No. 5, September-October 1988, pp. 32-36.

69. DUMAINE, Brian, "Japan's Next Push in US Markets," *Fortune*, Vol. 118, September 26, 1988, pp. 135-142.

70. DUNKIN, Amy, ONEAL, Michael, and PHILLIPS, Stephen, "Power Retailers," *Business Week*, December 21, 1987, pp. 86-92.

71. DURANT, Michel, "Le prêt-à-coiffer de 6 millions $," *Productividées*, February 1986, pp. 5-8.

72. DYGERT, Paul K., "Imaginative Fare Structures Can Increase Ridership," *Management Focus*, Vol. 26, No. 5, September-October 1979, pp. 39-43.

73. EDVARDSSON, Bo, "Service Quality in Customer Relationships: A Study of Critical Incidents in Mechanical Engineering Companies," *The Service Industries Journal*, Vol. 8, No. 4, October 1988, pp. 427-445.

74. EGDAHL, Richard H., "Should We Shrink the Health Care System?" *Harvard Business Review*, Vol. 62, No. 1, January-February 1984, pp. 125-132.

75. EIGLIER, Pierre and LANGEARD, Eric, "Une approche nouvelle du marketing des services," *Revue française de gestion*, November 1975, pp. 97-114.

76. EIGLIER, Pierre and LANGEARD, Eric, "La qualité de l'offre des services," *Harvard-L'Expansion*, No. 46, Fall 1987, pp. 48-58.

77. "Eliminating 'Surprises'," *Inc.*, Vol. 9, No. 9, August 1987, p. 81.

78. ENGLADE, Kenneth F., "The Bottom Line on Kinder-Care," *Across the Board*, April 1988, pp. 44-53.

79. "English Lawyers: Waking Them Up," *The Economist*, Vol. 307, No. 7549, May 7, 1988, pp. 17-20.

80. ETIENNE, Eisenhower C., "La gestion de la production dans les entreprises de service," *Gestion*, February 1981, pp. 50-62.

81. EVANS, Warren, "Service Excellence," *CGA Magazine*, June 1987, pp. 36-37.

82. EWING, Blair G., BURSTEIN, Carolyn, and WICKMAN, Colette, "Meeting the Productivity Challenge in the Federal Government," *National Productivity Review*, Vol. 5, No. 3, Summer 1986, pp. 252-261.

83. "Facing the Unavoidable Evil," *The Economist*, Vol. 308, No. 7560, July 23, 1988, p. 57.

84. FENNELL, Tom, "Turbulence in the Air," *Maclean's*, Vol. 101, No. 19, May 2, 1988, pp. 30-31.

85. FERGUSON, Peter, WATT, Callum, and LEMBOYE, O., "The Strategy Problem of the Medium-sized Accounting Firm," *The Service Industries Journal*, Vol. 8, No. 3, July 1988, pp. 347-357.

86. FITZGERALD, Lin, "Management Performance Measurement in Service Industries," *International Journal of Operations and Production Management*, Vol. 8, No. 3, 1988, pp. 109-116.

87. FITZSIMMONS, James A., "Consumer Participation and Productivity in Service Operations," *Interfaces*, Vol. 15, No. 3, May-June 1985, pp. 60-67.

88. FITZSIMMONS, James A. and SRIKAR, Bellur N., "Emergency Ambulance Location Using the Contiguous Zone Search Routine," *Journal of Operations Management* McGraw-Hill, New York, 1982.

89. FITZSIMMONS, James A. and SULLIVAN, Robert S., *Service Operations Management* McGraw-Hill, New York, 1982.

90. FLIPO, Jean-Paul, "On the Intangibility of Services," *The Service Industries Journal*, Vol. 8, No. 3, July 1988, pp. 286-298.

91. FRISET, Chantal and NOLLET, Jean, "Le système de classification des lits: leur impact sur le niveau d'occupation à l'intérieur de l'hôpital," *Administration hospitalière et sociale*, September-October 1986, pp. 10-17.

92. "From a Budgeting Standpoint the Fair Fared Pretty Well," *The Financial Post*, December 29, 1986, p. 3.

93. FRY, Joseph N. and KILLING, J. Peter, *Strategic Analysis and Action*, 2nd ed., Prentice-Hall Canada, Scarborough, ONT., 1989.

94. GATES, Bruce, "Little Extras Go Long Way to Lure Traveller's Dollar," *The Financial Post*, September 21, 1987, p. 47.

95. GENDRON, Louise, "Banque à la carte," *Revue Commerce*, September 1988, pp. 11-12.

96. GIBBS, Nancy, "Wait'll We Tell the Folks Back Home," *Time*, Vol. 133, No. 9, February 27, 1989, pp. 67-68.

97. GOLDSMITH, Jeff, "A Radical Prescription for Hospitals," *Harvard Business Review*, Vol. 67, No. 3, May-June 1989, pp. 104-111.

98. GORDON, Judith R., CORSINI, Louis S., and FETTERS, Michael L., "Restructuring Accounting Firms for Better Client Service," *Sloan Management Review*, Vol. 26, No. 3, Spring 1985, pp. 43-55.

99. GRANT, Rebecca A., HIGGINS, Christopher A., and IRVING, Richard H., "Computerized Performance Monitors: Are They Costing You Customers?" *Sloan Management Review*, Vol. 29, No. 3, Spring 1988, pp. 39-45.

100 GRÖNROOS, C., "New Competition in the Service Economy: The Five Rules of Service," *International Journal of Operations and Production Management*, Vol. 8, No. 3, 1988, pp. 9-19.

101 GROVER, Ronald, VAMOS, Mark N., and MASON, Todd, "Disney's Magic," *Business Week*, March 9, 1987, pp. 62-69.

102 GUMMESSON, Evert, "Toward a Theory of Professional Service Marketing," *Industrial Marketing Management*, Vol. 7, No. 2, 1978, pp. 89-95.

103. HALL, Richard H., "Professionalization and Bureaucratization," *American Sociological Review*, Vol. 33, No. 1, 1968, pp. 92-104.

104. HART, Christopher, W.L., "The Power of Unconditional Service Guarantees," *Harvard Business Review*, Vol. 66, No. 4, July-August 1988, pp. 54-62.

105. HARTMAN, Curtis, "A Night at the Movies," *Inc.*, Vol. 8, No. 10, October 1986, pp. 100-106.

106. HARTMAN, Curtis, "Fear of Franchising," *Inc.*, Vol. 9, No. 7, June 1987, pp. 104-122.

107. HARTMAN, Curtis, "New Brew," *Inc.*, Vol. 10, No. 4, April 1988, pp. 86-93.

108. HARVEY, Jean, "Measuring Productivity in Professional Services," *Public Productivity Review*, Winter 1987, pp. 29-38.

109. HARVEY, Jean, "Operations Management in Professional Service Organizations: A Typology," *International Journal of Operations and Production Management*, Vol. 10, No. 4, 1990, pp. 5-15.

110 HAWKEN, Paul, "Truth or Consequences," *Inc.*, Vol. 9, No. 9, August 1987, pp. 48-52.

111. HAYWOOD-FARMER, John, "The Effect of Service Automation on Bank Service," *Business Quarterly*, Vol. 49, No. 1, Spring 1984, pp. 55-59.

112. HAYWOOD-FARMER, John, "A Conceptual Model of Service Quality," *International Journal of Operations and Production Management*, Vol. 8, No. 6, 1988, pp. 19-29.

113. HAYWOOD-FARMER, John and NOLLET, Jean, "Productivity in Professional Services," *The Service Industries Journal*, Vol. 5, No. 2, July 1985, pp. 169-180.

114. HAYWOOD-FARMER, John, SHARMAN, Todd, and WEINBRECHT, Markus S., "Using Simple Simulation Models to Manage Sports Services," *Journal of Sport Management*, Vol. 2, No. 2, July 1988, pp. 118-128.

115. HAYWOOD-FARMER, J. and STUART, F.I., "Measuring the Quality of Professional Services" in: *The Management of Service Operations*, Johnston, Robert, Ed. IFS Publications, London, 1988, pp. 207-220.

116. HAYWOOD-FARMER, John and HILL, Neil F., "The Impact of CAD on Consulting Engineering Firms: A Survey of CAD Users and Non-users," *The Service Industries Journal*, Vol. 9, No. 4, October 1989, pp. 71-89.

117. HAYWOOD-FARMER, John and STUART, F. Ian, "An Instrument to Measure the 'Degree of Professionalism' in a Professional Service," *The Service Industries Journal*, Vol. 10, No. 2, April 1990, pp. 336-347.

118. HENSHER, David A., "Productive Efficiency and Ownership of Urban Bus Services," *Transportation*, Vol. 14, No. 3, 1987, pp. 209-225.

119. HESKETT, James L., *Managing in the Service Economy*, Harvard Business School Press, Boston, MA, 1986.

120. HESKETT, James L., *Shouldice Hospital Limited*, Case No. 9-683-068 and Teaching Note No. 5-686-120, Harvard College, 1983, 1986.

121. HESKETT, James L., "Lessons in the Service Sector," *Harvard Business Review*, Vol. 65, No. 2, March-April 1987, pp. 118-126.

122. HILL, C. Jeanne and FANNIN, William R., "Professional Service Marketing Strategies in the 80s," *Journal of Professional Services Marketing*, Vol. 2, Nos. 1 and 2, Fall-Winter 1986, pp. 11-23.

123. HILL, Terry, *Manufacturing Strategy: Text and Cases* Richard D. Irwin, Homewood, IL, 1989.

124. HIRSCHHORN, Larry, "The Post-Industrial Economy: Labor Skills and the New Mode of Production," *The Service Industries Journal*, Vol. 8, No. 1, January 1988, pp. 19-38.

125. HOCKIN, Thomas A. and DOWNE, Bret, *The A.D.M. and the Trade Marks Office*, Case No. 9-83-H029, The University of Western Ontario, School of Business Administration, 1983.

126. HOPKINS, Michael, "Franchise Plus," *Inc.*, Vol. 9, No. 5, May 1987, p. 11.

127. HOPKINS, Thomas, "The Case against Lawyers," *Report on Business Magazine*, Vol. 2, No. 9, April 1986, pp. 84-90.

128. HOROVITZ, Jacques, "La non-qualité tue," *Harvard-L'Expansion*, Summer 1986, pp. 53-61.

129. HORTON, Raymond D., "Expenditures, Services, and Public Management," *Public Administration Review*, Vol. 47, No. 5, September-October 1987, pp. 378-384.

130. HOUSTON, Christopher and HAYWOOD-FARMER, John, *University Hospital: The In-Vitro Fertilization Program (A)*, Case No. 9-87-D009, The University of Western Ontario, School of Business Administration, 1987.

131. HOWARD, John L., "Mixed Service Delivery: A Private Sector Perspective," *Canadian Public Administration*, Vol. 29, No. 4, Winter 1986, pp. 553-555.

132. HU, Michael Y., TOH, Rex S., and STRAND, Stephen, "Frequent Flier Programs: Problems and Pitfalls," *Business Horizons*, Vol. 31, No. 4, July-August 1988, pp. 52-57.

133. HUDSON, James A., "First Differentiate Service — Then Reshape Logistics," *Business Quarterly*, Vol. 53, No. 1, Summer 1988, pp. 66-71.

134. HUETE, Luis M. and ROTH, Aleda V., "The Industrialization and Span of Retail Banks' Delivery Systems," *International Journal of Operations and Production Management*, Vol. 8, No. 3, 1988, pp. 46-66.

135. IMMEN, Wallace, "High Living in Hong Kong," *The Globe and Mail*, February 18, 1989, pp. A14-15.

136. IMMEN, Wallace, "At the Regent Hong Kong There Are No Half Measures," *The Globe and Mail*, February 18, 1989, p. A17.

137. IMSE, Thomas P., *The Professionalization of Business Management*, Vantage Press, New York, 1962.

138. "In Which We Serve," *The Economist*, Vol. 307, No. 7556, June 25, 1988, p. 74.

139. IRONS, Ken, "How to Manage Services," *Management Today*, November 1983, pp. 90-93, 168.

140. JACKSON, Maggie, "Court Will Fine Diners Who Reserve, Don't Show," *The Globe and Mail*, June 25, 1988, p. B3.

141. JACOBY, Tamar, "An End to Judicial Roulette," *Newsweek*, Vol. 113, January 30, 1989, p. 76.

142. JEANNIOT, Pierre-J., "L'entreprise face à la révolution microélectronique," *Gestion*, September 1983, pp. 22-26.

143. JOHNSTON, Robert, "Service Industries — Improving Competitive Performance," *The Service Industries Journal*, Vol. 8, No. 2, April 1988, pp. 202-211.

144. JOHNSTON, Robert and MORRIS, Barbara, "Monitoring and Control in Service Operations," *International Journal of Operations and Production Management*, Vol. 5, No. 1, 1985, pp. 32-38.

145. KAHN, Joseph P., "Life After Success," *Inc.*, Vol. 8, No. 2, February 1986, pp. 61-65.

146. KEARNEY Richard C. and SINHA, Chandan, "Professionalism and Bureaucratic Responsiveness: Conflict or Compatibility?" *Public Administration Review*, Vol. 48, No. 1, January-February 1988, pp. 571-579.

147. KENTRIDGE, Catherine, "Companies at Work and Play," *The Financial Post*, September 21, 1987, pp. 56.

148. KIEPPER, Alan F. and BAKER, Randolf, "Houston Metro's Turnaround," *Management Review*, Vol. 74, December 1985, pp. 33-35.

149. KILLEYA, John C. and ARMISTEAD, Colin G., "The Transfer of Concepts and Techniques Between Manufacturing and Service Systems," *International Journal of Operations and Production Management*, Vol. 3, No. 3, 1983, pp. 22-28.

150. KINKEAD, Gwen, "Humana's Hard-Sell Hospitals," *Fortune*, Vol. 102, November 17, 1980, pp. 68-81.

151. KIRKLAND, Richard I. Jr., "The IRS Is Getting Tougher," *Fortune*, Vol. 109, April 2, 1984, pp. 82-88.

152. KIRKLAND, Richard I. Jr., "Are Services Jobs Good Jobs?" *Fortune*, Vol. 111, June 10, 1985, pp. 38-43.

153. KIRKLAND, Richard I. Jr., "The Bright Future of Service Exports," *Fortune*, Vol. 115, June 8, 1987, pp. 32-38.

154. KLEINGARTNER, Archie, *Professionalism and Salaried Worker Organization*, Industrial Relations Research Institute, University of Wisconsin, Madison, WI, 1967.

155. KOEPP, Stephen, "Why Is Service So Bad?" *Time*, Vol. 129, No. 5, February 2, 1987, pp. 45-53.

156. KOTLER, Philip, *Marketing Management: Analysis, Planning, and Control*, 2nd ed., Prentice-Hall, Englewood Cliffs, NJ, 1972.

157. KUHN, Patricia and HOEY, Thomas P., "Improving Police 911 Operations in Washington D.C.," *National Productivity Review*, Vol. 6, No. 2, Spring 1987, pp. 125-133.

158. LABICH, Kenneth, "How to Cure Those #@*&! Airline Delays," *Fortune*, Vol. 110, October 1, 1984, pp. 34-38.

159. LABICH, Kenneth, "Winners in the Air Wars," *Fortune*, Vol. 115, May 11, 1987, pp. 68-79.

160. LABICH, Kenneth, "Boeing Battles to Stay on Top," *Fortune*, Vol. 116, September 28, 1987, pp. 64-72.

161. LACERTE, Pierre, "Duel en plein ciel," *Affaires +*, March 1988, pp. 91-101.

162. LAMBERT, Douglas M. and LEWIS, Christine M., "Managing Customer Service to Build Market Share and Increase Profit," *Business Quarterly*, Vol. 48, No. 3, Fall 1983, pp. 50-58.

163. LANGBEIN, Laura I. and KERWIN, Cornelius M., "An Analysis of Case Processing Complexity in Public Bureaus," *Policy Studies Review*, Autumn 1987, pp. 28-42.

164. LANGEARD, Eric, "Le comportement du consommateur de services," *Institut d'Administration des entreprises*, Working Paper #176, January 1980.

165. LARSON, Erik, "The Man with the Golden Touch," *Inc.*, Vol. 10, No. 10, October, 1988, pp. 66-77.

166. LARSON, Richard C., "Perspectives on Queues: Social Justice and the Psychology of Queuing," *Operations Research*, Vol. 35, No. 6, November-December, 1987, pp. 895-905.

167. LARSON, Richard C., "There's More to a Line than Its Wait," *Technology Review*, Vol. 91, No. 5, July 1988, pp. 60-67.

168. LEENDERS, Michiel R. and NOLLET, Jean, "The Gray Zone in Make or Buy," *Journal of Purchasing and Materials Management*, Vol. 20, No. 3, Fall, 1984, pp. 10-15.

169. LEENDERS, Michiel R., FEARON, Harold E., and ENGLAND, Wilbur B., *Purchasing and Materials Management*, 9th ed., Richard D. Irwin, Homewood, IL, 1989.

170. LEES, J. and DALE, B.G., "Quality Circles in Service Industries: A Study of Their Use," *The Service Industries Journal*, Vol. 8, No. 2, April 1988, pp. 143-154.

171. LEONARD, Stew, "Love That Customer! " *Management Review*, Vol. 76, October 1987, pp. 36-39.

172. LEVINE, Joanne, "Frequent-Flyer Plans," *Incentive Marketing*, March 1988, pp. 18-23.

173. LEVITT, Theodore, "Production-line Approach to Service," *Harvard Business Review*, Vol. 50, No. 5, September-October, 1972, pp. 41-52.

174. LEVITT, Theodore, "The Industrialization of Service," *Harvard Business Review*, Vol. 54, No. 5, September-October 1976, pp. 63-74.

175. LEVITT, Theodore, "Marketing Intangible Products and Product Intangibles," *Harvard Business Review*, Vol. 59, No. 3, May-June 1981, pp. 94-102.

176. LEWIS, Barbara R., "Customer Care in Service Organizations," *International Journal of Operations and Production Management*, Vol. 8, No. 3, 1988, pp. 76-75.

177. LIGHTSTONE, Ian, "Canadians Positive about Banks," *Canadian Banker*, Vol. 95, No. 5, September-October 1988, pp. 6-9.

178. LINDER, Carl and HANCOCK, Walton M., "Computerized Work Measurements Can Help Hospitals Identity Cost Reduction Possibilities," *Industrial Engineering*, Vol. 18, No. 3, March 1985, pp. 70-77.

179. LITUCKY, T., "The Socialization of Customers as Partial Employees: Generic Skills, and When They Are Learned," Presented at the Academy of Management National Meeting, August 1988, Anaheim, CA.

180. LOCKYER, Keith, "Service — A Polemic and Proposal," *International Journal of Operations and Production Management*, Vol. 6, No. 3, 1986, pp. 5-9.

181. LONG, Donald, G. and NADLER, Paul S., "Technology vs. Tradition," *The Bankers Magazine*, May-June 1982, pp. 22-28.

182. LONG-BECKER, Linda and LANDAUER, Edwin G., "Service Assessment Matrix: A Measurement Technique for Service Group Evaluation," *Industrial Management*, September-October 1987, pp. 10-16.

183. LOVE, Myron, "Blizzard Forces Review of Winnipeg's Snow Clearing Operations," *Civic Public Works*, February 1988, pp. 9 and 26.

184. LOVELOCK, Christopher H., "Strategies for Managing Demand in Capacity-Constrained Service Organizations," *The Service Industries Journal*, Vol. 4, No. 4, November 1984, pp. 12-30.

185. LOVELOCK, Christopher H., "Classifying Services to Gain Strategic Marketing Insights," *Journal of Marketing*, Vol. 47, No. 3, Summer 1983, pp. 9-20.

186. LOVELOCK, Christopher H. and YOUNG, Robert F., "Look to Consumers to Increase Productivity," *Harvard Business Review*, Vol. 57,, No. 3, May-June 1979, pp. 168-178.

187. LYTLE, Lucy N. and SASSER, W. Earl, *Au Bon Pain: The Partner/Manager Program*, Case No. 9-687-063, Harvard College, 1987.

188. MAGRATH, A.J., "When Marketing Services, 4 Ps Are Not Enough," *Business Horizons*, Vol. 29, No. 3, May-June 1986, pp. 44-50.

189. MAIN, Jeremy, "Toward Service Without a Snarl," *Fortune*, Vol. 103, March 23, 1981, pp. 58.66.

190. MAIN, Jeremy, "Why Government Works Dumb," *Fortune*, Vol. 104, August 10, 1981, pp. 146-158.

191 MAIN, Jeremy, "The Worsening Air Travel Mess," *Fortune*, Vol. 114, July 7, 1986, pp. 50-55.

192. MAISTER, David H., "Balancing the Professional Service Firm," *Sloan Management Review*, Vol. 24, No. 1, Fall 1982, pp. 15-29.

193. MAISTER, David H., "Job Assignments Set the Pace in Professional Service Firms," *Journal of Management Consulting*, Vol. 1, No. 1, 1982, pp. 32-37.

194. MAISTER, David H., "The Psychology of Waiting Lines" in: *The Service Encounter: Managing Employee/Customer Interaction in Service Businesses*, Czepiel, John A., Solomon, Michael R., and Surprenant, Carol F., Eds., Lexington Books, Lexington, MA, 1985, pp. 113-123.

195. MAISTER, David H., "The One-Firm Firm: What Makes It Successful," *Sloan Management Review*, Vol. 27, No. 1, Fall 1985, pp. 3-13.

196. MAISTER, David, "Partnership Politics," *The American Lawyer*, October 1988, pp. 6-8.

197. "Making Service a Potent Marketing Tool," *Business Week*, June 11, 1984, pp. 164-170.

198. MANGELSDORF, Martha E., "Tune in, Turn on, and Drive by," *Inc.*, Vol. 10, No. 6, June 1988, p. 13.

199. MAREMONT, Mark and ROSSANT, John, "Europe Heads Toward an Air Safety Crisis of Its Own," *Business Week*, September 21, 1987, pp. 44-45.

200. MASLOW, Abraham H., *Motivation and Personnality*, 2nd ed., Harper & Row, New York, 1970.

201. MCCONKEY, Dale, "Are You an Administrator, a Manager, or a Leader?" *Business Horizons*, Vol. 32, No. 5, September-October, 1989, pp. 15-21.

202. MCDAVID, James C., "Part-time Fire Fighters in Canadian Municipalities: Cost and Effectiveness Comparisons," *Canadian Public Administration*, Vol. 29, No. 3, Fall 1986, pp. 377-387.

203. MCDAVID, James C. and SCHICK, Gregory K., "Privitization Versus Union-Management Cooperation: The Effect of Competition on Service Efficiency in Municipalities," *Canadian Public Administration*, Vol. 30, No. 3, Fall 1987, pp. 472-488.

204. MCDONELL, Edwin D. and KLIPSCH, Arthur W., "Controlling Teller Costs," *The Bankers Magazine*, May-June 1988, pp. 20-24.

205. MCNISH, Jacquie, "Friendlier Banks Count on Happy Returns," *The Globe and Mail*, September 11, 1989, pp. C1, C4.

206. MCNISH, Jacquie, "Dick Thompson's Born-Again Bankers," *Report on Business Magazine*, Vol. 6, No. 4, October 1989, pp. 51-60.

207. MCNISH, Jacquie, "Bank of Montreal Seeking Its Customer Roots," *The Globe and Mail*, March 19, 1990, pp. B1, B4.

208. MERLINE, John W., "What's Causing Airline Delays," *Consumers' Research Magazine*, Vol. 71, No. 5, May 1988, pp. 11-15.

209. MILLS, Peter K., CHASE, Richard B., and MARGULIES, Newton, "Motivating the Client/Employee System as a Service Production Strategy," *Academy of Management Review*, Vol. 8, No. 2, April 1983, pp. 301-310.

210. MILLS, Peter K. and MARGULIES, Newton, "Toward a Core Typology of Service Organizations," *Academy of Management Review*, Vol. 5, No. 2, April 1980, pp. 255-265.

211. MILLS, Peter K. and MOBERG, Dennis J., "Perspectives on the Technology of Service Operations," *Academy of Management Review*, Vol. 7, No. 3, July 1982, pp. 467-478.

212. MILLS, Peter K. and MORRIS, James H., "Clients as 'Partial' Employees of Service Organizations: Role Development in Client Participation," *Academy of Management Review*, Vol. 11, No. 4, October 1986, pp. 726-735.

213. MITTELSTAEDT, Martin, "American Express's 'Great Performers' Win Honors," *The Globe and Mail*, March 7, 1990, p. B7.

214. MOORE, Thomas, "Would You Buy a Car from This Man? " *Fortune*, Vol. 117, April 11, 1988, pp. 72-74.

215. MORGAN, Ivor P., "Preserving the Multi-service Concept in the Change from Entrepreneurial to Professional Management," *International Journal of Operations and Production Management*, Vol. 8, No. 3, 1988, pp. 20-30.

216. MORRIS, Barbara, "Accommodating Multiple Objectives in the Design of Customer Treatment Operations," *International Journal of Operations and Production Management*, Vol. 8, No, 3, 1988, pp. 86-94.

217. MORRIS, Barbara and JOHNSTON, Robert, "Dealing with Inherent Variability: The Difference Between Manufacturing and Service? " *International Journal of Operations and Production Management*, Vol. 7, No. 4, 1987, pp. 13-22.

218. MOSER, Penny, "The McDonald's Mystique," *Fortune*, Vol. 118, July 4, 1988, pp. 112-116.

219. MUHLEMANN, Ap, "A Simulation Study of the Operations of a Telephone Bureau," *Omega*, Vol. 9, No. 6, 1981, pp. 633-637.

220. NEWPORT, John Paul Jr., "American Express: Service that Sells," *Fortune*, Vol. 120, November 20, 1989, pp. 80-94.

221. ROTHMAN, Andrea, "'Nice to See You, How Are Things? Pass the Salt, No Dessert, Goodbye'," *The Wall Street Journal*, January 25, 1988, p. 33

222. NOLLET, Jean, KELADA, Joseph, and DIORIO, Mattio O., *Production/ Operations Management: A Systemic Approach*, G. Morin Publisher Ltd., Boucherville, Qc, 1990.

223. NORMANN, Richard, *Service Management: Strategy and Leadership in Service Businesses*, John Wiley & Sons, Chichester, 1984.

224. NORTHCRAFT, Gregory B. and CHASE, Richard B., "Managing Service Demand at the Point of Delivery," *Academy of Management Review*, Vol. 10, No. 1, 1985, pp. 66-75.

225. NULTY, Peter, "America's Toughest Bosses," *Fortune*, Vol. 119, February 27, 1989, pp. 40-54.

226. NYMAN, Judy, "Revenue Canada Flubs 40% of Tax Questions in Star Test," *Toronto Star*, March 28, 1984, pp. A1 and A8.

227. NYQUIST, Jody D., BITNER, Mary J., and BOOMS, Bernard H., "Identifying Communication Difficulties in the Service Encounter: A Critical Incident Approach" in: *The Service Encounter: Managing Employee/Customer Interaction in Service Businesses*, Czepiel, John A., Solomon, Michael R., and Surprenant, Carol F., Eds., Lexington Books, Lexington, MA, 1985, pp. 195-212.

228. PARÉ, Terence P., "Banks Discover the Consumer," *Fortune*, Vol. 121, February 12, 1990, pp. 96-104.

229. PERRY, James L. and BABITSKY, Timlynn T., "Comparative Performance in Urban Bus Transit: Assessing Privatization Strategies," *Public Administration Review*, Vol. 46, No. 1, January-February 1986, pp. 57-66.

230. PETERS, Thomas J. and WATERMAN, Robert H., *In Search of Excellence: Lessons from America's Best-Run Companies*, Warner Books Inc., New York, 1982.

231. PETERS, Thomas J. and WATERMAN, Robert H., *In Search of Excellence* (film), John Nathan and Sam Tyler, producers, Nathan/Tyler Productions, Waltham MA, 1985.

232. PHALON, Richard, "That Convenient Bottleneck at Narita," *Forbes*, August 8, 1988, pp. 84-85.

233. PHILLIPS, Stephen, DUNKIN, Amy, TREECE, James B., and HAMMONDS, Keith H., "King Customer," *Business Week*, March 12, 1990, pp. 88-90.

234. PITZER, Mary J., "The Fast Food Industry Is Slowing Down," *Business Week*, May 18, 1987, pp. 50-51.

235. "Pizza Fight Mushrooms into Guerrilla War," *Inc.*, Vol. 8, No. 12, December 1986, p. 12.

236. "Playing for High Stakes," *The Economist*, Vol. 315, No. 7659, June 16, 1990, pp. 86, 91.

237. POSNER, Bruce G., "Smart Money," *Inc.*, Vol. 8, No. 1, January 1986, pp. 58-68.

238. POTTER, Chris, "Airlines: No Revenue until the Plane Is in the Air," *CGA Magazine*, Vol. 20, No. 6, June 1986, pp. 20-25.

239. POTTS, George A., "Exploit Your Product's Service Life Cycle," *Harvard Business Review*, Vol. 66, No. 5, September-October 1988, pp. 32-36.

240. QUINN, James B., BARUCH, Jordan J., and PAQUETTE, Penny C., "Exploiting the Manufacturing-Services Interface," *Sloan Management Review*, Vol. 29, No. 4, Summer 1988, pp. 45-56.

241. QUINN, James Brian and GAGNON, Christopher E., "Will Services Follow Manufacturing into Decline?" *Harvard Business Review*, Vol. 64, No. 6, November-December 1986, pp. 95-103.

242. QUINN, Jane Bryant, "Credit-Card Dropouts," *Newsweek*, Vol. 112, October 24, 1988, p. 58.

243. RAAB, Steven S. and MATUSKY, Gregory, *The Blueprint for Franchising a Business*, John Wiley & Sons, New York, 1987.

244. RATHI, Ajay K., "A Control Scheme for High Traffic Density Sectors," *Transportation Research*, Vol. 22B, No. 2, April 1988, pp. 81-101.

245. REED, Grace B., "Public-Sector Productivity: A Success Story," *National Productivity Review*, Vol. 3, No. 2, Spring 1984, pp. 155-162.

246. RÉGINSTER, Hélène, "Le charme discret des grands hôtels," *Revue Commerce*, January 1989, pp. 34-41.

247. REICHEL, Arie, "Strategic Management: How to Apply It to Firms in the Hospitality Industry," *The Service Industries Journal*, Vol. 3, No. 3, 1883, pp. 329-343.

248. RESENER, Madlyn, DEBES, Cheryl, LLOYD, Graham, and TURNER, Rik, "From Singapore to Sao Paulo, A Network of True Believers," *Business Week*, October 13, 1986, pp. 80-81.

249. "Return to Sender," *The Economist*, Vol. 308, No. 7561, July 30, 1988, pp. 64, 66.

250. RHODES, Lucien, "Triple A Rating," *Inc.*, Vol. 8, No. 9, September 1986, pp. 31-32.

251. RICE, Faye, "Madison Avenue's Bloodiest Brawl," *Fortune*, Vol. 118, September 26, 1988, pp. 106-112.

252. RIDDLE, Dorothy I., *Service-Led Growth: The Role of the Service Sector in World Development*, Praeger, New York, 1986.

253. RITTS, Morton, "Professional Moves on the World of Franchises," *En Route*, October 1988, pp. 56.66.

254. ROMZEK, Barbara S. and DUBNICK, Melvin, J., "Accountability in the Public Sector: Lessons from the Challenger Tragedy," *Public Administration Review*, Vol. 47, No. 3, May-June 1987, pp. 227-238.

255. ROSS, Bernard H., "Public and Private Sectors: The Underlying Differences," *Management Review*, Vol. 77, No. 5, May 1988, pp. 28-33.

256. ROSS, Jerry and STAW, Barry M., "Expo 86: An Escalation Prototype," *Administrative Science Quarterly*, Vol. 31, No. 2, June 1986, pp. 274-297.

257. ROTHKOPF, Michael H. and RECH, Paul, "Perspectives on Queues: Combining Queues Is Not Always Beneficial," *Operations Research*, Vol. 35, No. 6, November-December 1987, pp. 906-909.

258. ROWE, David L., "How Westinghouse Measures White Collar Productivity," *Management Review*, Vol. 70, No. 11, November 1981, pp. 42-47.

259. RUIMY, Joel, "Result of Star's Tax Test Has Bussieres Concerned," *Toronto Star*, March 29, 1984, p. A2.

260. RUNDLE, Rhonda L., "Hospitals Cite Mortality Statistics in Ads to Attract Heart Patients," *The Wall Street Journal*, July 28, 1987, p. 35.

261. RUPPENTHAL, Karl M., "U.S. Airline Deregulation — Winners and Losers," *The Logistics and Transportation Review*, Vol. 23, No. 1, March 1987, pp. 65-82.

262. SALTER, Michael, "How to Wreck a Great Idea," *Report on Business Magazine*, Vol. 5, No. 10, April 1989, pp. 74-81.

263. SAMRÉEN, Ivar, "Service Strategies in Practice," *European Research*, Vol. 16, No. 1, February 1988, pp. 27-33.

264. SANSFAÇON, Jean-Robert, "Frits: L'art de couler une franchise," *Commerce*, April 1988, pp. 90-99.

265. SASSER, W. Earl, "Match Supply and Demand in Service Industries," *Harvard Business Review*, Vol. 54, No. 6, November-December 1976, pp. 133-140.

266. SASSER, W. Earl, OLSEN, R. Paul, and WYCKOFF, D. Daryl, *Management of Service Operations*, Allyn and Bacon, Boston MA, 1978.

267. SAUNDERS, John, "Numbers Explode in Thrift Debacle," *The Globe and Mail*, August 2, 1990, pp. B1-2.

268. SCHMENNER, Roger W., "How Can Service Businesses Survive and Prosper? " *Sloan Management Review*, Vol. 27, No. 3, Spring 1986, pp. 21-32.

269. SCHNEIDER, Benjamin, PARKINGTON, John J., and BUXTON, Virginia M., "Employee and Customer Perceptions of Service in Banks," *Administrative Sciences Quarterly*, Vol. 25, No. 2, June 1980, pp. 252-267.

270. SHAY, David, "Peat Marwick's Secrets of Increased White-Collar Productivity," *Boardroom Reports*, August 15, 1988, pp. 5-6.

271. SHERDEN, William A., "Gaining the Service Quality Advantage," *Journal of Business Strategy*, Vol. 9, No. 2, March-April, 1988, pp. 45-48.

272. SHOSTACK, G. Lynn, "Designing Services That Deliver," *Harvard Business Review*, Vol. 62, No. 1, January-February 1984, pp. 133-139.

273. SHUKLA, Ramesh K. and O'HALLARON, Richard D., "AM Admissions/PM Discharges Can Reduce Length of Stay," *Hospital & Health Services Administration*, Vol. 31, No. 4, July-August 1986, pp. 74-81.

274. KINNER, Wickham, "The Focused Factory," *Harvard Business Review*, Vol. 52, No. 3, May-June, 1974, pp. 113-121.

275. SMITH, Frederick W., "Federal Express Spreads Its Wings," *The Journal of Business Strategy*, Vol. 9, No. 4, July-August 1988, pp. 15-20.

276. SNIZEK, William E., "Hall's Professionalism Scale: An Empirical Reassessment," *American Sociological Review*, Vol. 37, No. 1, 1972, pp. 109-114.

277. SNYDER, Charles A., COX, James F., and JESSE, Richard R. Jr., "A Dependent Demand Approach to Service Organization Planning and Control," *Academy of Management Review*, Vol. 7, No. 3, 1982, pp. 455-466.

278. SOLOMON, Stephen D., "Head of the Class," *Inc.*, Vol. 12, No. 3, March 1990, pp. 76-83.

279. "Space Junk," *Aviation Week & Space Technology*, Vol. 129, No. 3, July 18, 1988, p. 15.

280. STEINER, Thomas D. and TEIXEIRA, Diogo, "Technology Is More than Just a Strategy," *The McKinsey Quarterly*, Winter 1988, pp. 39-51.

281. STRATTON, Brad, "The Low Cost of Quality Lodging," *Quality Progress*, Vol. 21, No. 6, June 1988, pp. 49-53.

282. STRAUSS, Marina, "Banks Trying to Get to Know You," *The Globe and Mail*, June 29, 1990, p. B6.

283. "Super-Regionals Lead in the National Banking Race," *The Economist*, Vol. 314, No. 7646, March 17, 1990, pp. 73-76.

284. SURPRENANT, Carol F. and SOLOMON, Michael R., "Predictability and Personalization in the Service Encounter," *Journal of Marketing*, Vol. 51, No. 2, April 1987, pp. 86-96.

285. TANSIK, David A. and CHASE, Richard B., "The Effects of Customer Induced Uncertainty on the Design of Service Systems" Presented at the Academy of Management National Meeting, August 1988, Anaheim, CA.

286. TAYLOR, James D., JOHNSON, Robert L., and IVERSON, Gene B., "Wall Drug Store" in: Thompson, Arthur A. and Strickland, A.J., *Strategy and Policy: Concepts and Cases*, Business Publications Inc., Dallas TX, 1978, pp. 303-321.

287. TEBOUL, James, "De-Industrialize Service for Quality," *International Journal of Operations and Production Management*, Vol. 8, No. 3, 1988, pp. 39-45.

288. " 'Test Drive' a Haircut," *The Globe and Mail*, December 1, 1988, p. B32.

289. "The Automated Check," *Inc.*, Vol. 10, No. 10, October, 1988, p. 24.

290. "The Fortune 500," *Fortune*, Vol. 121, No. 9, April 23, 1990, pp. 337-396.

291. "The Inc. 100," *Inc.*, Vol. 11, No. 5, May 1989, pp. 92-102.

292. "The In-House Travel Agent," *Inc.*, Vol. 9, No. 10, September 1987, p. 110.

293. "The Right Approach to Bank Technology," *The Bankers Magazine*, July-August 1988, pp. 5-8.

294. "The Service 500," *Fortune*, Vol. 121, No. 13, June 4, 1990, pp. 297-335.

295. THOMAS, Dan R.E., "Strategy Is Different in Service Businesses," *Harvard Business Review*, Vol. 58, No. 4, July-August 1978, pp. 158-165.

296. TOY, Stewart, ELLIS, James E., and DOBRZYNSKI, Judith H., "Vacancy Signs Are Lit, but More New Hotels Are on the Way," *Business Week*, March 17, 1986, pp. 78-79.

297. ULVILA, Jacob W., "Postal Automation (ZIP + 4) Technology: A Decision Analysis," *Interfaces*, Vol. 17, No. 2, March-April 1987, pp. 1-12.

298. "Uncle Sam Sends Them Next Door," *The Economist*, Vol. 315, No. 7655, May 19, 1990, pp. 92-94.

299. UTTAL, Bro, "Companies That Serve You Best," *Fortune*, Vol. 116, December 7, 1987, pp. 98-116.

300. VAN DIERDONCK, R. and BRANDT, G., "The Focused Factory in Service Industry," *International Journal of Operations and Production Management*, Vol. 8, No. 2, 1988, pp. 31-38.

301. VENTRONE, James M., ZANOTTI, Marie, and MORAVA, Myra, "Dressing for Success: Measuring Productivity Can Ensure Continuing Success," *Health Care Financial Management*, August 1988, pp. 31-40.

302. VOSS, C.A., "The Service Despatcher/Receptionist Role," *International Journal of Operations and Production Management*, Vol. 3, No. 3, 1983, pp. 35-39.

303. WICKENS, Barbara, "Clearing the Air," *Maclean's*, Vol. 101, No. 53, December 26, 1988, pp. 55-57.

304. "Who'll Bid for Dallas? " *The Economist*, Vol. 315, No. 7657, June 2, 1990, pp. 23-24.

305. WOOD, Albert R. and ELGIE, Richard J., "Problems in Early Versus Later Adoption of Manufacturing Innovations," *Proceedings of the Academy of Management National 35th Annual Meeting*, August 1975, New Orleans, LA, pp. 92-94.

306. WOOD, Charles T., "Relate Hospital Charges to Use of Services," *Harvard Business Review*, Vol. 60, No. 2, March-April 1982, pp. 123-130.

307 "World's Best in Bangkok," *London Free Press*, February 10, 1990, p. G6.

308. WOSKA, William J., "Pay for Time Not Worked: A Public-Sector Budget Dilemma," *Public Administration Review*, Vol. 48, No. 1, January-February 1988, pp. 551-556.

309. "Wrong Again," *The Economist*, Vol. 314, No. 7648, March 31, 1990, pp. 76-77.

310. YOUNG, David W. and SALTMAN, Richard B., "Preventive Medicine for Hospital Costs," *Harvard Business Review*, Vol. 61, No. 1, January-February 1983, pp. 126-133.

311. ZEITHAML, Valarie A., BERRY, Leonard L., and PARASURAMAN, A., "Communication and Control Processes in the Delivery of Service Quality," *Journal of Marketing*, Vol. 52, No. 2, 1988, pp. 35-48.

312. ZEITHAML, Valarie A., PARASURAMAN, A., and BERRY, Leonard L., *Delivering Service Quality: Balancing Customer Perceptions and Expectations*, The Free Press, New York, 1990.

313. ZVEGINTZOV, S., "Services: Towards a Unified View," *International Journal of Operations and Production Management*, Vol. 3, No. 3, 1983, pp. 29-34.

BIBLIOGRAPHY _____

ADAM, Everett, E. Jr., "Operations Change Interactions in a Service Environment: Attitudes, Behaviors, and Profitability," *Journal of Operations Management*, Vol. 2, No. 1, October 1981, pp. 63-76.

AKEHURST, Gary, "The Economics of Services: An Introduction," *The Service Industries Journal*, Vol. 7, No. 4, October 1987, pp. 1-11.

AMEND, Patricia, C., BAER-SINNOTT, Sara, FENN, Donna, POSNER, Bruce G., and SOLOMON, Stephen, D., "Capital: The Small-Bank Advantage," *Inc.*, Vol. 9, No. 6, June 1987, p. 136.

ANNETT, Bill, "The Banks: Succeeding in Spite of Affluence," *CGA Magazine*, Vol. 18, No. 2, February 1983, pp. 15-20.

ARMSTRONG, Larry, "Disneyland Abroad: Today Tokyo, Tomorrow the World," *Business Week*, March 9, 1987, pp. 68-69.

BANQUE NATIONALE DU CANADA, "La déréglementation du transport au Canada," *Revue économique*, Vol. 6, No. 3, 3rd Trimester, 1985.

BARKOW, Ben, "Tellers that Whirr and Go Beep," *The Canadian Banker & ICB Review*, Vol. 89, No. 3 June 1982, pp. 16-19.

BARRETT, Derm and OMAN, Keith, "Micro-Based Performance and Productivity for Managers and Professionals," *Business Quarterly*, Vol. 48, No. 1, Spring 1983, pp. 61-69.

BECK, Melinda, HAGER, Mary, BRADBURN, Elizabeth, and DREW, Lisa, "Costs vs. Quality of Care: Tracking the Side Effects," *Newsweek*, Vol. 113, January 30, 1989, pp. 48-49.

BEERWORTH, Richard, "Tomorrow Is Here," *The Canadian Banker & ICB Review*, Vol. 88, No. 3, June 1981, pp. 34-39.

BEHN, Robert D., "Management by Groping Along," *Journal of Policy Analysis and Management*, Vol. 7, No. 4, 1988, pp. 643-663.

BERNSTEIN, Peter W., "Profit Pressures on the Bid Law Firms," *Fortune*, Vol. 105, April 19, 1982, pp. 84-100.

BLOIS, Keith J., "Productivity and Effectiveness in Service Firms," *The Service Industries Journal*, Vol. 4, No. 4, November 1984, pp. 49-60.

BLOOM, Paul N., "Effective Marketing for Professional Services," *Harvard Business Review*, Vol. 62, No. 5, September-October 1984, pp. 102-110.

BOYCE, David E., "Route Guidance Systems for Improving Urban Travel and Location Choices," *Transportation Research*, Vol. 22A, No. 4, July 1988, pp. 275-281.

BROKAW, Leslie, "New Businesses," *Inc.*, Vol. 10, No. 10, October 1988, p. 24.

BROKAW, Leslie, HYATT, Joshua, and LAMMERS, Teri, "Letters of Credit," *Inc.*, Vol. 10, October 1988, p. 113.

BROWN, Mark B., "Defining Quality in Service Businesses," *Quality*, January 1988, pp. 56-58.

BROWN, Paul B., "Batting One for Nine," *Inc.*, Vol. 8, No. 12, December 1986, pp. 19-20.

BURSTEIN, Carolyn and SEDLAK, Kathleen, "The Federal Productivity Improvement Effort: Current Status and Future Agenda," *National Productivity Review*, Vol. 7, No. 2, Spring 1988, pp. 122-133.

BUTLER, Richard J., "User Satisfaction with a Service: An Approach from Power and Task Characteristics," *The Journal of Management Studies*, Vol. 17, No. 1, February 1980, pp. 1-18.

BYRNE, John A., "Nuts-and-Bolts Bosses," *Forbes*, Vol. 132, No. 7, September 26, 1983, pp. 128-130.

"Call Me Usmail," *The Economist*, Vol. 308, No. 7564, August 20, 1988, p. 59.

CANTON, Irving D., "Learning to Love the Service Economy," *Harvard Business Review*, Vol. 62, No. 3, May-June 1984, pp. 89-97.

CARMAN, James M. and LANGEARD, Eric, "Growth Strategies for Service Firms," *Strategic Management Journal*, Vol. 1, No. 1, 1980, pp. 7-22.

CASE, John, "The 1988 Inc. 500 America's Fastest Growing Private Companies," *Inc.*, Vol. 10, No. 12, December 1988, pp. 62-67.

CHASE, Richard B., "The 10 Commandments of Service System Management," *Interfaces*, Vol. 15, No. 3, May-June 1985, pp. 68-72.

CHIPPINDALE, Warren, "Solving the Case of the Enigmatic Third 'E' " *CA Magazine*, Vol. 121, No. 1, January-February 1988, pp. 38-45.

COHEN, Bernard R., "Taking the Customer Out of the Branch," *The Bankers Magazine*, May-June 1987, pp. 57-59.

CONNELL, Bertrum C., ADAM, Everett E. Jr., and MOORE, Aimee N., "Aggregate Planning in Health Care Foodservice Systems with Varying Technologies," *Journal of Operations Management*, Vol. 5, No. 1, November 1984, pp. 41-55.

CORBY, Michael E., "How Will the British Post Office Cope with Technological Change? " *Long Range Planning*, Vol. 15, No. 6, December 1982, pp. 58-66.

COSMETATOS, George P., "Increasing Productivity in Exponential Queues by Server-sharing," *Omega*, Vol. 11, No. 2, 1983, pp. 187-193.

CRANE, Dwight B. and HAYES, Samuel L. III, "The New Competition in World Banking," *Harvard Business Review*, Vol. 60, No. 4, July-August 1982, pp. 88-94.

CZEPIEL, John A., SOLOMON, Michael R., and SURPRENANT, Carol F. *The Service Encounter: Managing Employee/Customer Interaction in Service Businesses*, Lexington Books, Lexington MA, 1985.

DAVIS, Jo Ellen, ELLIS, James E., and HAWKINS, Chuck, "Continental: Full Planes May not Mean Full Coffers," *Business Week*, March 16, 1987, p. 37.

DAVIS, Samuel G. and REUTZEL, Edward T., "Manual versus Automated Check Encoding in Commercial Banks," *Journal of Operations Management*, Vol. 3, No. 3, May 1983, pp. 105-112.

DAVIS, Stanley M. *Future Perfect*, Addison-Wesley, Reading, MA, 1987.

DELVIN, Eric, "Les derniers pharmaciens," *Revue Commerce*, July 1988, pp. 72-77.

DESCHAMPS, Pierre, "Bientôt nous pourrons parler en l'air," *Le Devoir économique*, Vol. 4, No. 2, March 1988, pp. 20-21.

DEVENY, Kathleen, PLUENNEKE, John E., YANG, Dori Jones, MAREMONT, Mark, and BLACK, Robert, "McWorld? " *Business Week*, October 13, 1986, pp. 78-86.

DUBIN, Reggi Ann, "Growing Pains at People Express," *Business Week*, January 28, 1985, pp. 90-91.

DUNCAN, Keith and ASTON, David, "Service Charges in Perspective," *Canadian Banker*, Vol. 95, No. 4, July-August 1988, pp. 6-8.

EARLE, Dennis M., "Technological Investment: Why More Is Not Necessarily Better," *The Bankers Magazine*, July-August 1988, pp. 16-20.

"The FAA's Bid to Keep Control over Schedules," *Business Week*, February 6, 1984, pp. 25-26.

FALVEY, Jack, "Customer Service: Who Delivers? " in: Lovelock, Christopher H. *Managing Services — Marketing, Operations, and Human Resources*, Prentice Hall, Englewood Cliffs, New Jersey, 1988, pp. 277-279.

"The Fast Food War: Big Mac Under Attack," *Business Week*, January 30, 1984, pp. 44-46.

FENN, Donna, LAMMERS, Teri, POSNER, Bruce G., and SOLOMON, Stephen D., "Customer Relations: Covering the Bases," *Inc.*, Vol. 9, No. 11, October 1987, p. 140.

FERDERBER, Charles J., "Measuring Quality and Productivity in a Service Environment," *Industrial Engineering*, Vol. 13, No. 7, July 1981, pp. 38-47, p. 84.

FILLEY, Richard D., "Putting the 'Fast' in Fast Foods: Burger King," *Industrial Engineering*, Vol. 15, No. 1, January 1983, pp. 44-47.

"Cost-Effective Patient Care: Harper-Grace Hospitals," *Industrial Engineering*, Vol. 15, No. 1, January 1983, pp. 48-52.

FORAND, Claude, "Le grand ménage des banques," *Affaires +*, November 1987, pp. 40-45.

FRIEDMAN, Margaret L. and CHURCHILL, Gilbert A. Jr., "Using Consumer Perceptions and a Contingency Approach to Improve Health Care Delivery," *Journal of Consumer Research*, Vol. 13, No. 4, March 1987, pp. 492-510.

GELBY, Betsy D., SMITH, Samuel V., and GELB, Gabriel M., "Service Marketing Lessons from the Professionals," *Business Horizons*, Vol. 31, No. 5, September-October 1988, pp. 29-34.

GLISSON, Charles A. and MARTIN, Patricia Y., "Productivity and Efficiency in Human Service Organizations as Related to Structure, Size and Age," *Academy of Management Journal*, Vol. 23, No. 1, March 1980, pp. 21-37.

GOURDE, Sylvie, "Jours comptés pour petits comptables," *Revue Commerce*, October 1988, pp. 118-124.

GREENE, Richard, "My Lawyer, the Nurse," *Forbes*, Vol. 132, September 26, 1983, p. 128.

GRÖNROOS, Christian, "Designing a Long Range Marketing Strategy for Services," *Long Range Planning*, Vol. 13, No. 2, April 1980, pp. 36-42.

GUMMESSON, Evert, "The Marketing of Professional Services — An Organizational Dilemma," *European Journal of Marketing*, Vol. 13, No. 5, 1979, pp. 308-318.

"Marketing Cost Concept in Service Firms," *Industrial Marketing Management*, Vol. 10, No. 3, July 1981, pp. 175-182.

"How Professional Services Are Bought" in: *Marketing Handbook*, 2nd ed., Rines, Michael Ed., Gower Publishing Co., Aldershot 1981, pp. 31-41.

"The Marketing of Professional Services — 25 Propositions" in: *Marketing of Services*, Donnelly, James H. and George, William R., Eds., American Marketing Association, Chicago, IL, 1981, pp. 108-112.

HALL, Randolph W., "Passenger Delay in Rapid Transit Station," *Transportation Science*, Vol. 21, No. 4, November 1987, pp. 279-292.

HAMMER, Joshua, "Improving," *Newsweek*, Vol. 113, February 20, 1989, p. 8.

HARDWICK, Leo P., "Understanding the Debit Card," *The Bankers Magazine*, May-June 1982, pp. 41-47.

HARTMAN, Curtis, "Redesigning America," *Inc.*, Vol. 10, No. 6, June 1988, pp. 58-74.

HARVEY, Jean and NOLLET, Jean, "Étude empirique sur la mesure et l'amélioration de la productivité dans un service professionnel," *Proceedings of the Administrative Sciences Association of Canada 1986 Annual Conference*, Vol. 7, Part 7, Whistler, B.C., 1986, pp. 59-72.

HAWKEN, Paul, "The Employee as Customer," *Inc.*, Vol. 9, No. 11, November 1987, pp. 21-22.

HAYASHI, Paul M. and TRAPANI, John M., "The Impact of Energy Costs on Domestic Airline Passenger Travel," *Journal of Transport Economics and Policy*, Vol. 21, No. 1, January 1987, pp. 73-86.

HAYWOOD-FARMER, John, ALLEYNE, Anthony, DUFFUS, Balteano, and DOWNING, Mark, "Controlling Service Quality," *Business Quarterly*, Vol. 50, No. 4, Winter 1985, pp. 62-67.

HENDERSON, John C., KRAJEWSKI, Lee J., and SHOWALTER, Michael J., "An Integrated Approach for Manpower Planning in the Service Sector," *Omega*, Vol. 10, No. 1, 1982, pp. 61-73.

"How Academia Is Taking a Lesson From Business," *Business Week*, August 27, 1984, pp. 58-60.

HUTTON, Cynthia, "America's Most Admired Corporations," *Fortune*, Vol. 113, January 6, 1986, pp. 16-27.

"Hyatt Hotels: Putting Out the Welcome Mat for a Broader Clientele," *Business Week*, October 31, 1983, pp. 68-70.

INMAN, Virginia, "Hold the Onions, Pickles and Services," *Inc.*, Vol. 8, No. 3, March 1986, pp. 17-18.

JOHNSTON, John, "Public Servants and Private Contractors: Managing the Mixed Service Delivery System," *Canadian Public Administration*, Vol. 29, No. 4, Winter 1986, pp. 549-552.

KATCHER, Brian S., "Our Overmedicated Elderly," *American Druggist*, July 1988, pp. 38-40.

KIECHEL, Walter, III, "Explosion in the Bank-Card Cafeteria," *Fortune*, Vol. 102, September 8, 1980, pp. 76-82.

KOLESAR, Peter, "Stalking the Endangered CAT: A Queuing Analysis of Congestion at Automated Teller Machines," *Interfaces*, Vol. 14, No. 6, November-December, 1984, pp. 16-27.

KRAAR, Louis, "Putting Pan Am Together Again," *Fortune*, Vol. 104, December 28, 1981, pp. 42-47.

LABICH, Kenneth, "Fare Wars: Have the Big Airlines Learned to Win? " *Fortune*, Vol. 110, October 29, 1984, pp. 24-28.

"Why Air Traffic Is a Mess," *Fortune*, Vol. 116, August 17, 1987, pp. 54-58.

LALAND, Suzanne, "Pour les routiers, l'ordinateur ou la vie," *Le Devoir économique*, September 1987, pp. 25-37.

LANDEL, Robert D. and DIXON, J. Robb, "Assessing the Potential for Office-Productivity Improvement," *Operations Management Review*, Fall 1983, pp. 3-8.

LEVITT, Theodore, "La productivité dans le tertiaire," *Harvard-L'Expansion*, Winter 1976-77, pp. 86-95.

LEWIS, Geoff, "Japan Is Getting a Truly Smart Credit Card," *Business Week*, October 12, 1987, p. 166C.

LOCKYER, Keith G. and OAKLAND, John S., "An Operations Manager's Audit," *Service Industries Journal*, Vol. 7, No. 1, January 1987, pp. 5-13.

LOISEAU, James, "Les cercles de qualité dans un centre hospitalier : est-ce possible ? " *Administration hospitalière et sociale*, October 1985, pp. 12-20.

LOOMIS, Carol. J., "Citicorp's Rocky Affair with the Consumer," *Fortune*, Vol. 101, March 24, 1980, pp. 66-82.

LOUIS, Arthur M., "Visa Stirs up the Big Banks — Again," *Fortune*, Vol. 108, October 3, 1983, pp. 196-203.

LOVELOCK, Christopher H. *Managing Services — Marketing, Operations, and Human Resources*, Prentice Hall, Englewood Cliffs, New Jersey, 1988.

LUSH, Patricia, "Old Customers Beat New Ones, Marketing Specialist Says," *The Globe and Mail*, August 2, 1988, p. B3.

MABERT, Vincent A., "Service Operations Management: Research and Application," *Journal of Operations Management*, Vol. 2, No. 4, August 1982, pp. 203-209.

MACSTRAVIC, Scott, "The Patient as Partner: A Competitive Strategy in Health Care Marketing," *Hospital & Health Services Administration*, Vol. 33, No. 1, Spring 1988, pp. 15-24.

MAGNET, Myron, "Here Comes McDentists," *Fortune*, Vol. 107, February 21, 1983, pp. 135-139.

MAMIS, Robert A., "Servicing the Bottom Line," *Inc.*, Vol. 9, No. 8, August 1987, pp. 96-99.

"Meat and Potatoes," *Inc.*, Vol. 8, No. 8, July 1986, pp. 53-63.

MANGELSDORF, Martha E., "Hotline," *Inc.*, Vol. 10, No. 8, August 1988, p. 15.

MARKLAND, Robert E. and NAUSS, Robert M., "Improving Transit Check Clearing Operations at Maryland National Bank," *Interfaces*, Vol. 13, No. 1, February 1983, pp. 1-9.

MEADOWS, Edward, "How Three Companies Increased Their Productivity," *Fortune*, Vol. 101, March 10, 1980, pp. 92-101.

MERCER, James L., "Growing Opportunities in Public Service Contracting," *Harvard Business Review*, Vol. 61, No. 2, March-April 1983, pp. 178-188.

METZGER, Robert O., "Barriers to Bank Productivity Improvement," *The Bankers Magazine*, January-February 1982, pp. 58-63.

MILLER, Luther S., "LRRT Confounds the Skeptics," *Railway Age*, May 1988, pp. 35-36.

MILLS, Peter K., *Managing Service Industries*, Ballinger Publishing Company, Cambridge, MA, 1986.

MILLS, Peter K., HALL, James L., LEIDECKER, Joel K., and MARGULIES, Newton, "Flexiform: A Model for Professional Service Organizations," *Academy of Management Review*, Vol. 8, No. 1, January 1983, pp. 118-131.

MILLWARD, Robert, "The UK Services Sector, Productivity Change and the Recession in Long-Term Prospective," *The Service Industries Journal*, Vol. 8, No. 3, July 1988, pp. 263-276.

MOE, Ronald C., "Exploring the Limits of Privatization," *Public Administration Review*, Vol. 47, No. 6, November-December 1987, pp. 453-460.

MOK, D.W., "Information as a Strategic Weapon," *CMA Magazine*, Vol. 60, No. 2, March-April 1986, pp. 14-19.

MORAZAIN, Jeanne, "Dorval et Mirabel: sur le chemin de l'autonomie," *Revue Commerce*, January 1989, pp. 14-15.

NATIONAL BANK OF CANADA, "The Service Sector," *Economic Review*, Vol. 8, No. 2, 2nd quarter, 1987.

NULTY, Peter, "Friendly Skies for Little Airlines," *Fortune*, Vol. 103, February 9, 1981, pp. 45-53.

"A Champ of Cheap Airlines," *Fortune*, Vol. 105, March 22, 1982, pp. 127-134.

"Emery Returns Federal Express's Fire," *Fortune*, Vol. 105, May 17, 1982, pp. 119-121.

PARASURAMAN, A., BERRY, Leonard L., and ZEITHAML, Valarie A., "Service Firms Need Marketing Skills," *Business Horizons*, Vol. 26, No. 6, November-December 1983, pp. 28-31.

PICHERACK, J. Richard, "Service Delivery and Client Satisfaction in the Public Sector," *Canadian Public Administration*, Vol. 30, No. 2, Summer 1987, pp. 243-254.

POWELL, Warren B., SHEFFI, Yosef, NICKERSON, Kenneth S., BUTTERBAUGH, Kevin, and ATHERTON, Susan, "Maximizing Profits for North American Van Lines' Truckload Division: A New Framework for Pricing and Operations," *Interfaces*, Vol. 18, No. 1, January-February 1988, pp. 21-41.

QUINN, James Brian, BARUCH, Jordan J., and PAQUETTE, Penny C., "Technology in Services," *Scientific American*, Vol. 257, No. 6, December 1987, pp. 50-58.

RHEA, James T., "Long-term Improvement in Cost and Quality within Hospitals," *Hospital & Health Services Administration*, Vol. 31, No. 4, July-August 1986, pp. 64-73.

ROSENBERG, Richard E., and DAVIDSON, Robert C., "A Technological Approach to Retail Banking," *The Bankers Magazine*, September-October 1988, pp. 30-33.

ROUSSEL, Robert, "Guérilla dans le ciel," *Revue Commerce*, July 1988, pp. 14-15.

"Russell Hogg (Master Card) and Charles Russell (Visa) Discuss Bank Cards," *The Bankers Magazine*, May-June 1981, pp. 59-63.

SALADIN, Brooke A., "Goal Programming Applied to Police Patrol Allocation," *Journal of Operations Management*, Vol. 2, No. 4, August 1982, pp. 239-249.

SCHAINBLATT, Alfred H., "How Companies Measure the Productivity of Engineers and Scientists," *Research Management*, Vol. 25, No. 3, May 1982, pp. 10-18.

SCIAMBI, Lonnie L., and NYSTROM, Wayne K., "Fundamentals of ATM Program Success," *The Bankers Magazine*, March-April 1980, pp. 33-39.

"Services That Satisfy: A Fortune Portfolio," *Fortune*, Vol. 103, March 23, 1981, pp. 69-75.

SHERMAN, Stratford P., "An Airline Rebel Takes off Again," *Fortune*, Vol. 112, No. 12, November 25, 1985, pp. 129-136.

SHIFFLER, Ronald E. and COYE, Ray W., "Monitoring Employee Performance in Service Operations," *International Journal of Operationos and Production Management*, Vol. 8, No. 2, 1988, pp. 5-13.

SMITH, Lee, "Burger King Puts Down Its Dukes," *Fortune*, Vol. 101, June 16, 1980, pp. 90-98.

SOLOMON, Stephen, "How One Hospital Broke Its Inflation Fever," *Fortune*, Vol. 99, June 18, 1979, pp. 148-154.

STOFFMAN, Daniel, "New Antidote for Health-care Hemorrhage," *Canadian Business*, Vol. 56, No. 9, September 1983, pp. 52-59.

STUART, Alexander, "Braniff's Dizzying Takeoff into Deregulated Skies," *Fortune*, Vol. 99, March 26, 1979, pp. 52-58.

"The Airlines Are Flying in a Fog," *Fortune*, Vol. 102, October 20, 1980, pp. 50-56.

SULLIVAN, Harold J., "Privitization of Public Services: A Growing Threat to Constitutional Rights," *Public Administration Review*, Vol. 47, No. 6, November-December 1987, pp. 461-467.

SULLIVAN, Robert S., "The Service Sector: Challenges and Imperatives for Research in Operations Management," *Journal of Operations Management*, Vol. 2, No. 4, August 1982, pp. 211-214.

SWART, William and DONNO, Luca, "Simulation Modeling Improves Operations, Planning, and Productivity of Fast Food Restaurants," *Interfaces*, Vol. 11, No. 6, December 1981, pp. 35-47.

TALUKDAR, Rahim B. and MCLAUGHLIN, Curtis P., "Monitoring and Improving the Productivity of Semi-autonomous Human Service Units," *Journal of Operations Management*, Vol. 5, No. 4, August 1985, pp. 375-393.

TANSIK, David A., "Balance in Service Systems Design," *Journal of Business Research*, Vol. 20, No. 1, January 1990, pp. 55-61.

TARPEY, John P., "Federal Express Tries to Put More Zip in Zapmail," *Business Week*, December 17, 1984, pp. 110-111.

THOMPSON, Phillip, DESOUZA, Glenn, and GALE, Bradley, T., "The Strategic Management of Service Quality," *The Pimsletter on Business Strategy*, No. 33, 1985, pp. 1-12.

"TIPS Turns Commuters On," *Railway Age*, August 1988, pp. 56, 69.

TURNER, Arthur N., "Consulting Is More Than Giving Advice," *Harvard Business Review*, Vol. 60, No. 5, September-October 1982, pp. 120-129.

TUTTLE, Thomas C. and ROMANOWSKI, John J., "Assessing Performance and Productivity in White-Collar Organizations," *National Productivity Review*, Vol. 4, No. 3, Summer 1985, pp. 211-224.

VAN DEN HAAG, Ernest, "How to Make Hospitals Hospitable," *Fortune*, Vol. 105, May 17, 1982, pp. 123-129.

WELCH, Norma and GUSSOW, James, "Expansion of Canadian National Railway's Line Capacity," *Interfaces*, Vol. 16, No. 1, January-February 1986, pp. 51-64.

WELTER, Therese R., "New-Collar Workers," *Industry Week*, Vol. 237, No. 4, August 15, 1988, pp. 36-39.

WENK, Jonathan, "State-Owned Air Canada: Learning to Fly on Its Own," *Business Week*, October 1, 1984, p. 91.

WERNER, Manuel, "The Deregulated Canadian Airline Industry," *Canadian Banker*, Vol. 95, No. 3, May-June 1988, pp. 10-15.

WHITE, P.R. and TURNER, R.P., "Development of Intensive Urban Minibus Services in Britain," *The Logistics and Transportation Review*, Vol. 23, No. 4, December 1987, pp. 385-400.

WILLIAMS, Monci Jo, "McDonald's Refuses to Plateau," *Fortune*, Vol. 110, November 12, 1984, pp. 34-40.

WINTHROP, Grant F., "'Agony Airlines' Becomes a High Flyer," *Fortune*, Vol. 101, June 30, 1980, pp. 104-108.

Printed in Canada